CLASS DISMISSED

Class Dismissed

WHEN COLLEGES IGNORE
INEQUALITY AND STUDENTS
PAY THE PRICE

ANTHONY ABRAHAM JACK

PRINCETON UNIVERSITY PRESS

PRINCETON & OXFORD

Published by Princeton University Press
41 William Street, Princeton, New Jersey 08540
99 Banbury Road, Oxford OX2 6JX

press.princeton.edu

Library of Congress Cataloging-in-Publication Data

Names: Jack, Anthony Abraham, author.
Title: Class dismissed : when colleges ignore inequality and
    students pay the price / Anthony Abraham Jack.
Description: Princeton ; Oxford : Princeton University Press, [2024] |
    Includes bibliographical references and index.
Identifiers: LCCN 2024001869 (print) | LCCN 2024001870 (ebook) | ISBN
    9780691237466 (hardback) | ISBN 9780691237473 (e-book)
Subjects: LCSH: Minorities—Education (Higher)—United States. | Minority
    college students—United States—Social conditions. | Universities and
    colleges—United States—Evaluation. | Educational equalization—United
    States.
Classification: LCC LC3727 .J334 2024 (print) | LCC LC3727 (ebook) | DDC
    378.1/980973—dc23/eng/20240403
LC record available at https://lccn.loc.gov/2024001869
LC ebook record available at https://lccn.loc.gov/2024001870

British Library Cataloging-in-Publication Data is available

Editorial: Meagan Levinson, Eric Crahan, Rebecca Binnie
Jacket: Heather Hansen
Production: Erin Suydam
Publicity: Maria Whelan (US), Kathryn Stevens (UK)

This book has been composed in Arno Pro

Printed in the United States of America

10 9 8 7 6 5 4 3 2 1

To those we lost
To those learning to smile again

To Aleshia, Shakia, Makayla, Amari, and Tareem Jr.
for helping me with the latter

Come celebrate with me
that everyday something has tried to kill me
and has failed.

—LUCILLE CLIFTON, *BOOK OF LIGHT*

CONTENTS

CLASS DISMISSED

Introduction

UNPRECEDENTED CLASSES
IN UNPRECEDENTED TIMES

"WE ARE NOT who we once were." That is what elite colleges across the United States want you to believe about them. It's true. They aren't. Universities are touting unprecedented diversity numbers with respect to race and class. According to Princeton University, the class of 2021 was its most diverse "in the modern era," including more first-generation college students than ever before. Many other colleges are also making similar headlines—particularly notable are the rapidly growing number of schools that have admitted their first majority-minority classes, meaning there are more students of color than White students. In 2017, Cornell University recorded its third consecutive year in which prospective students set a new record for the number of applicants who self-identify as an underrepresented racial minority. The glee is palpable: according to the university, these remarkable numbers signal that Cornell is "well on our way toward our goals to broaden and diversify the incoming class."[1]

Harvard University is no different. In 2017, after 380 years of existence, Harvard admitted its first majority-minority class with respect to race: 50.8 percent of admits were not White. Economic diversity is another issue; that same class remains mostly rich and wealthy. Still, as one spokesperson for the university noted, the class of 2021 testifies to the fact that "Harvard remains committed to enrolling diverse classes of students."

Keeping its well-publicized word, the university delivered parallel performances in the years that followed.[2]

Like proud parents sharing pictures of their newborn baby, colleges broadcast these "wins" everywhere they can: purported testament to the fact that they value diversity. From staged pictures in glossy viewbooks handed out at high school open houses to (slightly) more organic "Student Takeover" days on Instagram, universities don't let you miss the fact that they look different. These carefully curated displays of color serve as blatant marketing, and as a shield from criticism—both from prospective students critical of long-standing patterns of exclusion and from critics who say universities are raising tuition and hoarding resources. Everywhere you look, you are sure to find a smiling Black or Brown face, along with a White student with a "First Gen" shirt, highlighted for all to see—what sociologists Karly Ford and Megan Holland call "cosmetic diversity."[3]

These achievements, to be clear, are no small feat. They are a profound shift in campus demographics, in just a few decades. And they are certainly not cheap. Universities are investing millions of dollars in financial aid to support such initiatives. Amherst College, which in 1999 replaced loans with scholarships and grants for students who come from lower-income families, announced that it would dedicate $71 million to financial aid annually starting in 2021. In 2022 Smith College became the most recent college to go "no loan," in what has become something of an arms race among elite colleges to pledge that all lower-income students—and increasingly even middle-class students—will graduate without debt. Stanford University has the most robust no-loan policy and expanded it even further in 2023: the university now offers full tuition for families that make less than $150,000, up from $125,000. Princeton and Harvard doubled down on their no-loan policies and increased the income cutoff to $100,000 and $85,000, respectively. What's more, Harvard and Princeton extend their no-loan policy to all students, regardless of immigration status, bringing the number of colleges in the country that do so to six.[4]

Changing admissions' priorities and expanding financial aid don't just make college more affordable for individual students; they also pave a smoother path toward upward mobility. To be clear, elite colleges are not the biggest drivers of social mobility for marginalized students. Economist Raj Chetty and his collaborators point out that certain mid-tier public universities, such as the City University of New York and California's web of state colleges, are actually the most effective at bottom-to-top quintile mobility, meaning moving people from the lowest 20 percent of the country's income distribution to the top 20 percent. Yet Chetty offers a sobering fact about mobility in America: for those same students it is elite universities, both private and public (like Amherst and Harvard, and the University of Michigan and the University of California, Berkeley), that offer the surest shot at "making it."[5]

The more selective the college, the higher the odds of graduation. And this is especially true for students from underrepresented groups. But that's just the start. Attending an elite college increases a student's chances for entering elite occupations upon graduation, regardless of background (and often without the oppressive weight of loans). Sociologist Lauren Rivera documents how alumni of elite colleges are overrepresented in high-status positions—consulting, investment banking, venture capital, and other particularly lucrative sectors of the economy. From established Fortune 500 companies to new venture capital firms to the Supreme Court, students at elite colleges are far more likely than anyone else to secure elite jobs.[6]

Yet so much happens in the interim, between matriculation and graduation, between the thrill of getting in and the slog of getting out. There is a lot of life lived in those intervening years. And for so many students it is not easy living. I have found, again and again, that colleges are not paying enough attention to the everyday realities of those they let in. While elite colleges are content with recruiting "the most diverse class," patting themselves on the back for a job well done, it is not enough just to get students to campus. It is not just about financial aid. Colleges remain woefully unprepared to support the students who make it in.[7]

In an almost twisted act of fate, the students admitted in 2017 who make up these unprecedented classes at elite colleges are also those who were on campus in March 2020, when COVID-19 entered our world and shut so much of it down. Like many colleges across the country, members of Harvard's first record-breaking class were juniors, settling into their spring semesters and progressing toward graduation. They were gearing up for the all-important junior summer, when so many companies extend offers for employment after grueling yet revelatory summer internships. The next crop of students, now sophomores, and similarly record-breaking, had just declared their concentrations (Harvard-speak for academic majors), a big day on campus. Another group was gearing up for housing day, the annual celebration when first-years get sorted into their houses, the dorms they will live in for the next three years. The seniors, of course, were mere weeks away from gradu-ation. Each of these groups of students were marching toward mile-stones and taking part in age-old traditions, almost as one. Then campus closed. The closure of campus revealed just how different the paths of these students through college had already been and foreshadowed how much more divergent they would become. And will continue to be. What happened when campus closed begs a crucial question: Do col-leges know how to support a diverse class of students, or do they just know how to foot the bill for one?[8]

———

Buzz. Ding. Buzz. Ding. The morning of March 10 was a cacophony of vibrations and beeps across campus, as the phone of every student brought life-altering news. "Students are asked not to return to campus after Spring Recess and to meet academic requirements remotely until further notice." This message first came from Harvard's then-president Lawrence Bacow. Different deans repeated various versions of the same message throughout the day, as if the whole university were playing a harrowing game of telephone. The news dropped at 8:27 A.M. I read it as soon as it hit my inbox. I was on the faculty at the time. It was a Tues-day. Much of campus was still asleep. That quickly changed. The first burst of notifications spread across campus, followed by a second and third round, as students texted each other with their own screenshots and snippets of the original email. Just over seven thousand students emerged into a new reality. COVID-19 closures had begun.

But as I read the email that morning, and again months later, it reminded me of a very different message I got about spring break a decade and a half prior, during my first year in college. I was a nineteen-year-old freshman at Amherst, a member of a very different kind of cohort—we were celebrated for being unlike anything the college had seen. There was a group of us—we were Black, Latino, and the first in our families to go to college. Amherst was thrilled to have us—it took pride in how unusual we were. We weren't quite paraded around like a traveling circus. But we were definitely asked to smile for the camera more than our White peers. We were highlighted at the first and only assembly that our class would gather for until senior spring. Yet for all the attention on the front end, getting us to campus and sharing the news that we accepted the offer of admission, I realized that the college had no idea what to do with us once we arrived.[9]

The notice that Valentine Dining Hall, our sole cafeteria, would close came just before spring break of my freshman year. Universities just assume that students will leave campus for spring break because, well, nearly all of them do. I was from Miami, and plane tickets to return to the Sunshine State were already too expensive, even when it wasn't vacation time. Then, as more and more college students, both at Amherst and around the country, booked flights for fun in the Miami sun, tickets grew even farther out of reach. I decided to stay on campus. It wouldn't be all bad: I could work at the check-in desk at Alumni Gym and make some extra money. I didn't then realize how lucky I was to be able to pick up those extra hours. Each hour would become a lifeline. Money for me to eat. And also money for my mom, who would ask me to send "anything I could" to help pay the bills. What my nineteen-year-old self hadn't yet reckoned with was that while Amherst had opened its doors to welcome poor students like me, they forgot to keep the doors open for those of us who couldn't afford to leave.

Valentine would be closed for the entirety of break. I was shocked. And then I was angry. Angry at myself for assuming there would be food. Angry at Amherst for making a fool out of me. I remember walking past Valentine Dining Hall en route to town to try and find something to eat. I knew whatever I would find would not be cheap. Nothing is truly cheap when you're broke, not even greasy pizza in a college town. And definitely not when you unexpectedly have to provide for yourself three times a day for ten days. The irony of my route stung for the whole week: before I could even make it across College Street to venture into town, I first walked by the entrance to the dining hall. The lights were out. Only the emergency exit signs blazed red in the darkness. Peering through the large bay window, I could see the chairs stacked on top of the tables as if someone were just vacuuming but had moved out of sight. The towering stack of food trays stood waiting, just behind the gates that now barred me from entry.

Campus truly felt empty. Valley Transporter, the van service to Bradley International Airport, was packed to the gills heading down I-91. So many of my classmates left campus long before Valentine served its last meal for the week. It didn't hurt so much to see them go. What hurt was the college's ignorance of how those of us who remained were faring.

A decade and a half later, I confronted this reality anew as a scholar. In my first book, *The Privileged Poor*, I met students at an elite college who found themselves in the same situation I was in all those years ago. Their college, like Amherst, also closed eateries during break. And they, like me, learned to chart hungry days on their calendars. The students I spoke with stayed on campus because of what they didn't have. For some of them, it was money. For others, it was security. For a fair few, it was safety. Little did I know that exactly a year after *The Privileged Poor* was published, a global pandemic would make all of these issues even more urgent. The blind spots and fault lines of well-meaning college campuses would be exposed like never before, in ways both devastating and very illuminating.[10]

I read and reread President Bacow's email. I fixated on that one line. *Students are asked not to return to campus after Spring Recess.* In my heart of hearts, I knew the president was right. Closing campus was the only safe option. COVID-19 was a killer, and we didn't even know yet how deadly it would be. But each time I read the president's words, a different set of questions surfaced. What about the students who weren't going to leave for break? What are we doing for students who *can't* leave? What are we sending students home to? There wasn't clear messaging, no clear plan forward for those who "need to remain." I discovered over and over, in the days and weeks to come, that students seeking support were met with blank stares, mixed messages, and bureaucratic hurdles. Some students were even chastised for not having an exit strategy at the ready.

Jerome, a bespectacled, soft-spoken junior with South Asian roots, had to reckon with the full gamut of these difficulties. I met him on Zoom as he sat in his dorm room almost a year to the day since campus closed. His blue plaid shirt, buttoned to the very top, complemented his brown-butter complexion. He sat next to an open window in his room, soaking in the early spring sun. Although in his third year at Harvard, he had not made any "real connections" on campus with peers or professors. He felt disconnected from folks at Harvard from the beginning, a feeling that persisted. He tried to involve himself in different ways on campus, but the more he tried, the more "it dawns on me that I am alone in my situation."

Jerome struggled with what to do a year prior, when he read the president's email. He felt unseen and unheard. "Reading that email, from the president of the university, followed by the dean, it had the assumption that students have a place to go back to. . . . That is how I interpreted that email. I was uncertain. People are telling me, 'Oh, that means everyone needs to go.'" Jerome paused for a second, collecting himself. He began again, voice softer yet sharper, "For me, I didn't have plans to go back home for spring break, on the count that I don't have a home to go back to. 2020 has just been a crazy time for my family. My mother and I, it's just the two of us, we lost our place in the beginning of 2020, in January."

For many lower-income students like Jerome, going to college—let alone Harvard—was more than the exhilarating achievement of a lifelong academic dream. Harvard was an escape. The pandemic-related hardships that millions felt in 2020 weren't anything new for Jerome; those global disruptions were a different flavor of the same kinds he had been enduring for years. For half his life, Jerome and his mother bounced around the country, never staying anywhere for long. He characterized his disjointed housing history with a terrible bluntness: "I've lived where I cannot afford." Evictions were all too familiar. During his three years at Harvard, his mother found herself living "in her car, or right now, in a motel" as she "looked for employment opportunities." Jerome helped out whenever he could, picking up odd jobs when his class schedule permitted. His goals were as specific as they were dire: "trying to earn sufficient funds to get a place to stay for my mother that's more stable than a motel and her car." Things were beginning to look up. For the first time in a long while, even his mother was hopeful; she had just applied for her first batch of jobs after years of unemployment. She even made it past the first round of interviews for one of them.

When times were most dire, they sometimes stayed on the couches and floors of family members. But that arrangement never ended well. Jerome's uncles dismissed his mother for having a child while unmarried and rebuked her for struggling to get, let alone keep, a job. But it went deeper than verbal admonitions: "My uncle almost killed my mother." A fist-sized hole in the wall of their old home, Jerome explains, remains as evidence of a deed long done. His mother wasn't his family's only target. They detested Jerome for his effeminate demeanor, forgiving neither the sin nor the son. "Their hate of my mother is also targeted at me," Jerome explained. "I'm the abnormal one. I'm a bastard."

After President Bacow's email, Jerome made the long, anxiety-inducing trek from campus to his uncle's house on the West Coast. Remote learning was a distant thought. He had hoped the previous summer was the last time he would ever step through his uncle's front door. But then campus closed, and his mom was staying with her brother yet again. So Jerome didn't really have a choice. And then, soon after he arrived, he was reminded all over again why he never wanted to come back. One day after running an errand, he entered the front door of his uncle's house, and waiting for him was the barrel of a gun. Holding the grip was someone, his own flesh and blood, who made it clear how much Jerome was despised. "My cousin was aiming a pellet BB gun at me. It looks like a real gun, but it's not. I was screaming; I was really terrified." Jerome didn't know it was a BB gun at the time. But that fact didn't matter. His cousin took simple pleasure in watching Jerome cower in fear. His aunt mocked him. Instead of reprimanding her son for drawing a weapon on him, Jerome's aunt, watching on from the living room, chastised Jerome for screaming "like a girl. Why are you screaming and yelling? Are you gay?" Jerome's constant refrain was how living with his uncle "was a scary, scary time."

Feeling safe—let alone rested—always eluded Jerome when he was away from campus. COVID-19 wasn't his first time dealing with campus closures. Thanksgiving, winter, and spring breaks never gave what they promised to give: a respite. Breaks were the opposite for Jerome: "very much trauma-inducing; still something that gets me sick." Making Jerome and his mother feel unsafe was a family affair. Campus closures, like every break in the calendar, meant not just loss of room and board, as disruptive as that always was, it meant a loss of security. After all, coming to Harvard, even with all of his misgivings, had been a great gift: it was the first time "I have that stability of having a place, like a room with four walls and a roof."[11]

There are costs to being a member of an unprecedentedly diverse class. One of those costs is living in the university's blind spots. Colleges make many, many assumptions: not just about the books that students have already read, and the academic jargon they are already familiar with, but about what students know about living on a campus, about what students can afford, and about the resources—both financial and relational—that students take for granted. No surprise, then, for an institution that for nearly all of its history has served a painfully homogenous group of people—nearly all White and wealthy—we are only just becoming aware of the gaps in the services that a campus offers. Administrators, deans, and therapists I have worked with are consistently dedicated to their work but also largely ignorant of what it means to be a poor student on a rich campus, and ill-equipped to handle the many issues that emerge.[12]

The hurdles that made college so different, and so much more difficult, for students like Jerome existed long before the COVID-19 pandemic and continue to exist now. But the campus closures that started in March 2020 placed these often-invisible inequalities front and center. Our necessary response to COVID-19 exposed the university's ongoing ignorance—about the entrenched problems that haunt our students, and the fact that many of us don't know how we can, or should, support those students. COVID-19 was a stress test on higher education. It challenged all of us, in many different ways. So many universities failed that test.

To be clear, this failure is not just about money, or the lack thereof. Race matters, often amplifying class differences in distinctive ways. As time passed, the daunting weight of the pandemic exposed how having money, and in some instances even a modicum of wealth, was an imperfect shield for students of color. It wasn't just about getting off campus and gearing up for "Zoom school," although this was an ordeal. The uneven toll the pandemic exacted from disenfranchised communities, already marred by segregation, joblessness, and concentrated poverty, rippled through the student body. After all, students from the most recent historically diverse classes call these neighborhoods home. These communities were already grappling with the generations-long struggles that accompanied students to college—the distracting worries, the distressed calls, and all the other debilitating burdens of poverty that make focusing on schoolwork nearly impossible. As campuses closed and the virus spread, Asian, Black, Latino, and Native communities were hit the hardest, both in terms of COVID-19 cases and fatalities. In these communities, the sharp spikes in COVID-19 deaths were accompanied by the persistently high rates of other deaths—due to police brutality, vigilantism, domestic terrorism, and also the many systemic inequalities that define American life. Each of these manifestations of hate and inequity deepened how we all were being burdened, and also showed how this pain was unevenly dispensed. What's more, the ways that members of the university community—especially White peers and administrators—responded to these moments often did more harm than good, adding salt to ever-fresh wounds.[13]

Even after he was able to return to campus months later, Jerome found himself yet again in a no-man's land. This time he grew increasingly fearful just moving about the world. He obsessively tracked the rise in animosity toward communities of color, and especially Asian Americans. As assaults on Asian Americans rose across the nation, he felt himself split in two. Jerome was not Chinese, but he knew that assailants bent on doing harm did not know the difference between Mandarin and Korean, Nepali, or Tagalog. As much as he wanted to not think about the very people who made his life hell, he couldn't help it. "Every time that I see a headline, 'Asian man gets, whatever, beaten or attacked in these communities,' it always increases my heart rate. I want to read the headline. I want to see—is it my relatives who got attacked?" Each news item that crossed his desk or phone sharpened his loneliness and isolation. When he tried to reach out to classmates and other people at Harvard, he so often met silence. "They just don't want to speak or listen to me . . . people don't bother spending the time to hear me out in that."

———

There is a dire need to understand how students actually make it—or don't—from convocation to commencement, and especially how what happens outside the college gates—in their families, in their communities, and in the nation—permeates the campus. As ever more diverse classes are recruited, admitted, and enrolled, this need grows greater. Even during the height of the pandemic, colleges of all ranks and sizes reported new demographic milestones. In 2021, as Yale admitted its class of 2025, the university bragged that it was not only the largest class in its history but also one that "sets records for diversity."[14] The University of Arizona welcomed its largest, most diverse class in 2022. The University of Minnesota and Virginia Tech celebrated similar milestones. As the demographic makeup of campuses becomes more complex, so too does the slate of issues that students bring with them to college, especially since these students are coming to college in the wake of a global pandemic that deepened already deep-rooted inequalities. Colleges need to think less about the photo shoots and the press releases, and more about the even harder work that comes with making these students actual members of the community.[15]

My goal in these pages is to illuminate what living in poverty's long shadow means for students and, in turn, for colleges and universities. Unless we get a handle on how these durable inequalities—from poverty to joblessness to segregation—affect the transition to college, and the experience of college—and adulthood for that matter—universities will fail the students who they spend millions to recruit. This is not a book about the COVID-19 pandemic. This is a book that uses the disruptions of the pandemic to reveal underexamined inequalities that plague our most vulnerable students. COVID-19 closures and the months after present a time to reflect upon the past as we attempt to build a better future. And there is no better guide in our reflecting than the stories of students themselves. As we'll see, they are our blueprint; their disparate experiences deepen our understanding of the reproduction of inequality in college. It is not just about how savvy one is about navigating exams or office hours. The calls from home—whether asking for money to pay bills or offering news of untimely deaths due to neighborhood woes—fundamentally shape how students move toward graduation. There are new responsibilities attached to having students from every walk of life. Admission is but the first step along this mobility journey.[16]

———

To understand the upended world of college students, I went straight to the source. I spent more than a year speaking with undergraduates to understand the ways in which the pandemic and resulting closures exacerbated the inequalities in their lives. Between January 2021 and March 2022, my team and I interviewed 125 undergraduates at Harvard University, either via Zoom or in person. They were Asian and Black, Native and White, and Latino and Mixed (students who identify with two or more racial/ethnic groups). They came from families across the economic spectrum. They all lived in the United States. In the pages that follow, I use race and socioeconomic identifiers in parentheses to help situate students. (See the appendix for a detailed discussion of how I carried out this research and the abbreviations for an explanation of what the identifiers mean.)

Social class can either create a buffer to the world's problems or bring us closer to those problems. In order to elucidate the tremendous impact of class, I spoke with both lower-income as well as middle- and upper-middle-class students. Of the students I spoke with, sixty-eight were upper-income and sixty-seven were lower-income students. We still shy away from talking about social class, especially the privileges more affluent students have at their fingertips compared to those of their lower-income peers. If anything, the pandemic underscored the ease of privilege. And the obliviousness of the privileged. It also placed private choices—where to go, what to buy—into the public view. From Instagram to Snapchat to Zoom, all of our online platforms provided glimpses into these disparate worlds. At the same time, it gave new insights into just how hard it is to be poor, and especially poor at an institution that caters to the privileged.[17]

Similarly, talking openly about race remains taboo. So often universities keep conversations general and superficial. Sometimes this move is done so as not to offend. Other times it is so as not to reveal one's true thoughts. And yet, universities would be better equipped to help students if frank conversations about the college culture and climate could be had, a finger on the true pulse of the university community.

So much of social science research still focuses on Black/White inequities, in schooling, in pay, and in a host of other outcomes related to mobility. Yet this story would be incomplete without the experiences of Latino undergraduates as well as Asian and Native students. Latinos face historic rises in discrimination, family separations, and anti-immigration sentiment and legislation captured in vows to "Build a Wall." Our country also bore witness to increased racial hostility toward Asian Americans during the pandemic amid claims of the "China virus" coming to hurt the United States by then-president Donald Trump and other conservative pundits. But there were also those who faced targeted attacks before the pandemic and increased hostility since, as well as debilitating rates of death due to COVID-19 who received next to no coverage in the news: Native and Indigenous people. Including the voices of Asian, Latino, and Native students, alongside Black and White students, deepens our understanding of how the pandemic exacerbated inequalities in students' lives as well as shines light on those suffering in silence.[18]

My focus on race and class does not negate the importance of gender and sexuality—quite the opposite. I discuss times when students' gender or sexuality played a particular role in how they navigated closures, as in the case of Jerome. But social class and race serve as the primary focuses of this project.

Some may say Harvard is abnormal, an oddity on the higher education landscape. What can we learn from students' experiences there? A lot. Harvard is not the only school playing the diversity game, amping up outreach to recruit more students of color and those who are first in their families to go to college. What these pages hold is as much an examination of Harvard as it is a look at just how unequal America is. Harvard is not divorced from the world; it sits squarely within it. It plays an outsized role in society, from economic to political affairs. It recruits students from all over the nation and around the globe. Yet, like many elite colleges—from Washington University in St. Louis to University of Southern California—Harvard is a barbell campus demographically: most students are either wealthy or low-income, with very few people in between. This inequality is growing on campuses just as it is growing in society. Students enter the gates from neighborhoods marked by concentrated affluence or concentrated poverty, and both profoundly shaped how students moved through campus long before March 2020 and how they experienced the pandemic. Yet, even at the wealthiest university in the world, there was, at times, little to no shielding from the dangers of the pandemic.[19]

Moreover, being a student of color, regardless of class background, at a predominately White university brings with it a host of challenges, challenges that only got harder with the murders of George Floyd, Breonna Taylor, Delaina Ashley Yaun, and the many missing Indigenous people at the hands of police and vigilantes in 2020 and the months that followed. At times, there were additional burdens placed upon students of color because of just how ill-prepared Harvard—like so many schools that aggressively tout diversity—was to help students process and work through the trauma of witnessing such disregard for human life.

There is power in telling your own story. Yet so many students felt silenced. Some were still at home, and some were back on campus. Yet all, in one way or another, were distanced from the community they had built, and so many were in need of someone to talk to. I had the great fortune to sit with students as they shared their stories, open and honest from the moment we began. There were as many smiles and jokes as there were tears and weighty silences. The words that filled the hours-long interviews gave insight into how poverty and inequality influenced the ways each student moves through college. But their words also gave insights into how to address the many entrenched inequities, on our campuses and beyond.

The longer I sat with these students, the more their words forced me to wear two hats, one of the forever first-generation college student and the other of the academic committed to investigating social ills. There is a responsibility that comes with collecting these stories, one that goes beyond sociology's near directive to just be the objective observer who documents the problem and then moves on. I don't have it in me to sit on the sidelines. I want to be part of the solution, not just one who points a finger at what is going wrong. Throughout, I ask a simple question: Now that we know what we know, what are we going do about it? In line with sociologist W. E. B. Du Bois's vision of engaged scholarship and Monica Prasad's call for "problem-solving sociology," I use students' stories to build out actionable steps that can help ameliorate the long-standing inequalities that COVID-19 exposed.[20]

Part I focuses on students' families. Chapter 1 examines students' relationships with the people they share a bloodline with or who invited them into their family trees. In doing so, we see differences not only in resources but in acceptance and support. Chapter 2 focuses on the family students inherit: their community. Some communities protect students from harm. Others seem to invite dangers into their lives. Chapter 3 offers insights to help colleges understand and prepare for when the problems of home, tucked in next to XL twin sheets, come to college too.

Part II turns to finances, specifically how work and labor shape undergraduate life. Chapter 4 focuses on paid labor and chapter 5, unpaid. In chapter 4, I show how campus closures revealed an unacknowledged class-segregated labor market on campus. Lower-income students stopped working and lost pay, while more privileged students, at least those who worked, kept going with the support of faculty, even getting more hours. In chapter 5, I show how privileged students took on unpaid internships during the pandemic, while lower-income students took on additional unpaid paid labor on behalf of their families. Yet for many lower-income students, I show how the work they did often required more work and higher-order skills than their privileged peers, but they discounted it as just helping their families. Chapter 6 puts forth solutions on how to make campus employment work better for students.

Part III focuses on the racial fault lines on campus and across the United States, respectively. Chapter 7 examines how racist acts before campus closures colored students' reception of wellness checks from White friends and solidarity statements by the university as social unrest gripped the nation. Chapter 8 leaves campus to understand the myriad ways, overt and subtle, that racism impacted students' lives when campus closed and how the heartache of those experiences lingers. Chapter 9 pushes universities to adeptly navigate and close the gaps in recognition—of students as full members of the community and not just props for pamphlets—that students uncomfortably find themselves in and come to resent the university for.

———

It is paramount for colleges to come to terms with entrenched social inequalities, particularly in the wake of the Supreme Court's dismantling of affirmative action. Due to the ruling in *Students for Fair Admissions v. Harvard*, handed down in June 2023, universities are now barred from explicitly using the race of an applicant as a key factor in admissions. In response, universities are doubling down on their recruitment of youth from lower-income families, and especially first-generation college students. While first-generation status captures an individual's history, it does so without the larger context of the United States. Yes, there are common experiences among those who are first in their families to go to college, but we cannot paint all first-generation college-goers with one brushstroke. An uncritical use of first-generation college student status as any kind of proxy, without understanding the many and varied predicaments of these students, is a recipe for betrayal and for pain.[21]

In the *Price of the Ticket*, the ever-prescient essayist James Baldwin notes, "It goes without saying, I believe, that if we understood ourselves better, we would damage ourselves less." I agree. To admit a diverse class mandates that colleges support a diverse class. But without understanding the inequities that shape every facet of college life, we will never be able to live up to that directive, not in good times, and definitely not in bad. Diversity devoid of understanding is worse than a broken promise; it is one that was never intended to be kept. Students need us to be better and do better, to work harder to keep that promise. The testimonies of these students serve as both an invitation and a challenge: to learn from missed opportunities, to do less damage.[22]

PART I

Family

1

And Away We Go

ON MARCH 10, 2020, Holly (UI,B) and Alexander (LI,A), like the seven thousand other students on Harvard's campus, woke up to a barrage of emails. Holly's phone buzzed continually, wave after wave of text messages and Snapchat notifications. Her roommate was frantic. A rush of adrenaline cut through the all-nighter-induced fog. Alexander, up unseasonably early, looked on in disbelief from his computer; Gmail was his bearer of bad news. Fear washed over him. The rumors—and students' own speculations—were indeed true. Harvard was closing. Five days. That's all the time the university gave them to leave. Holly and Alexander began wading through the emails, searching for answers to their countless questions. Holly tried to figure out how Harvard would protect the hard work she put into her classes thus far; Alexander tried to figure out who would protect him. Neither was satisfied with what they found, but for very different reasons.

Holly loves history. It is both passion and friend. She spends time in campus archives in the way that her peers spend time in local cafes. She bounces energetically when speaking about her various research projects, both independent ones and those with faculty. The announcement of closures rocked her. She wasn't worried about getting home, however. Thinking of herself and of her brother, who was also at Harvard, she explained, "Our parents were able to afford a plane ticket in that really, really quick turnaround." Holly wasn't worried about keeping up with her studies either. "I'm really grateful to have a good home situation. . . . I had that safety net." A room all her own. Check. An extra room for studying. Check. Parents who let her do her own thing on her own terms. Check. "It wasn't even a question," Holly said, matter-of-factly, "It was a given." What was less certain was how she would carry on with her research. She would miss the unique joy of being the first person in generations to handle handwritten correspondences, turning each page gingerly so as to not damage the fragile documents. Between fretting on campus and unpacking at home, Holly saw two new emails in her inbox, one coming on the heels of the other. The first email made her angry. The second allowed her to vent her spleen.

On March 28, Harvard officially announced that it would use "pass/fail" grades, instead of traditional letter grades, for all spring semester classes. There had been many discussions, public and private, among students and administrators. Similar conversations were going on across higher education. Students at Yale University in Connecticut and Pitzer College in California, for example, launched campaigns ("No One Fails at Yale" and "Nobody Fails @ Pitzer") advocating for such a change. But the move at Harvard enraged students. A particularly vocal, and surprisingly large, group of students pushed back. They created a separate petition independent of Harvard to pressure the university into reversing their decision. Holly signed it. "I was one of these people saying that it should just be a regular grading system." Pulling her box braids into a ponytail, she continued,[1]

> I was hurt. I was bitter. I was angry. I put work in. It was academically one of my stronger semesters. I had gone to office hours. I had taken time to be thorough with my essays. I put in a lot of time academically to succeed. The thought that I wouldn't get those As on my transcript—that it would be mandatory pass/fail—I felt like all my hard work would go to waste, be erased. That's not fair. I put the work in. Why shouldn't I get the A that I deserve?

Holly was confident she was in the majority. "I was like a lot of people," she said with certainty. Indeed, many students signed the petition. But not all. There was pushback to their pushback. Accusations of selfishness and ignorance abounded in group chats and on house list-servs, even spilling over onto social media. "The replies were so nasty. People were like, 'This is the most self-centered, egotistical, privileged Harvard thing I've ever seen. How could you only think about yourself during a global pandemic?' It was getting messy." It didn't help that this petition sat alongside another one advocating that Harvard move senior week (which had been cancelled) to an island that Harvard seniors would transform into a private paradise.

Both petitions were eventually taken down. But not before Alexander saw them. Not before these messages made his situation feel even more dire.

Alexander, with his straight black hair that sometimes fell across his face, knew his classmates had privileges he could not access. Scarcity was the only steady thing at home. He grew up translating for his parents—who only converse in a rare Chinese dialect that "nobody really speaks"—so he was used to being at the mercy of bureaucracies. The welfare office. The Medicaid customer service line. The school counselor's office. It felt like he spent his whole life subject to the whims of others. But his classmates' uncaring disregard to the differences between them left him feeling defeated in a new way. And yet another blow was to come. This time it came in the form of an email from an administrator he didn't know, who worked in an office he hadn't heard of.[2]

A few days after President Bacow's email announcing the closure, the university initiated a petition process for staying on campus. Something about the whole ordeal—the impersonal, online form—bothered Alexander. It was reminiscent of applying to college years prior. Students from lower-income families are so often coached to pimp their trauma for admissions counselors who like "sob stories," or worse, for counselors who use essays to ensure that an applicant is as poor as their financial aid documents say they are. For Alexander, the online form reminded him particularly of his perpetual frustration with charity: the hand that gives is always over the hand that receives. He struggled with all the things that those who receive charity must experience and do to stay in others' good graces. The fear. The doubt. The capitulating. The uncertainty. The waiting.[3]

Harvard's simple request, which he couldn't ignore, was anything but simple. Completing the petition to stay was an ordeal. Even speaking about it, more than eight months later, brought about a change in Alexander. He began his interview, amiable and conversational, sitting comfortably, almost lounging. But then Alexander's jaw set. His face became a mixture of annoyance and anger. He sat straighter. Slapping his hands together, he shared how he felt like he only had one choice: put his poverty on display. "You had to beg and lay out every trauma you've ever had to stay. That was a problem."[4]

As a part of his application to stay, Alexander said, "I drafted an email." He paused, correcting himself. "No, I drafted an *essay*," drawing the last word out as long as the day. "I worded it to hopefully touch some sympathetic part of these humans, to make them feel guilty." In no uncertain terms, he wanted someone, anyone, at Harvard to know that "you send me home, you will be knowingly sending me back to literal sewage dropping on my head. You will be knowingly sending me back into an unstable home environment. You will be knowingly sending me back to literally the least possible safe place I could be." Alexander explained, "my family lives in government housing," and that comes with a host of problems that their building superintendent refused to acknowledge. His family was "living with a severe roach infestation"— proof that "Darwin's evolution is a real thing. We could only kill the slow ones." Making matters worse, Alexander shared, "I have severe allergies. In that environment, my health was just deteriorating." When the roaches and his allergies didn't keep him up, his noisy neighbors, who, at 3:00 A.M., would be "blasting music," did. Although Alexander "didn't really pay attention to all the drug use and substance abuse in the building," the wall-rattling bass was unavoidable.

Soon after submitting the form, his application was rejected.

He was devastated. He was furious. But he had to let his anger go, which made him angrier and sadder still. He learned that he could appeal the rejection, a lifeline, tenuous as it was. He enlisted friends to help him figure out what to do next, which was not easy. Asking friends to read drafts of his appeal permitted them to learn details about his life he had not yet shared. Moreover, his dance was a complicated one. To be too critical of the university for asking him to broadcast his problems might mean not being allowed to stay. To not share enough—enough pain, enough heartbreak, enough turmoil—could doom his Hail Mary plea. All the while, Alexander couldn't help but feel the deepening divide between him and his classmates. They were signing a petition and complaining about their GPAs; he was signing a petition to be allowed to stay in the only place he felt safe.[5]

One petition showcased privilege, outlining taken-for-granted liberties, and the power to air one's grievances without worry of sanctions, at least from the university. The other petition functioned as a litmus test for poverty and trauma. Holly knew all her needs would be taken care of back home; she would be returning to a safe place to complete her studies. Alexander knew the opposite. He couldn't have cared less about his GPA at that point. And there were differential costs for filling either of them out. One petition required only a name and an email address, nothing more than what Change.org requires for you to support whatever cause strikes your fancy—anything from boycotting Big Oil to bringing back the McDonald's Snack Wrap. The other required permitting others to bear witness to families at their most vulnerable, often making private pains public.

Alexander submitted the appeal and waited. Finally, after forty-eight very long hours, he got a terse email granting him permission to stay on campus.

The contrast in petitions, and even experiences completing them, was a harbinger of things to come. Unequal starts lead to unequal returns. In what follows, I dive into students' lives as campus closed in March 2020, and then across the next academic year. This is not an examination of learning loss, but of something more elemental. We'll see how life during campus closures was marked by fundamental differences in destinations, distractions, and dangers.[6]

Destinations: Up in the Airbnb

For some students, the closing of campus seemed to open up a world of possibilities: home was just one of many potential destinations. When privileged students spoke about where they went, it felt like someone narrating adventures from *Time* magazine's "World's Greatest Places."

One student called her lockdown trip to Alaska "one of the highlights of my life." Similar things were said about Hawaii. But leaving the United States altogether was just as common: Luxembourg, Norway, New Zealand, Taiwan, and Mexico. Pandemic passports were all the rage. South Korea, Egypt, and Morocco made the list, as did Italy. One Harvard student took to TikTok, announcing that campus closing was "your sign to rent an Italian castle with 30 friends." Her "virtual invitation" included a barrage of short clips of a cadre of blonde women piling out of a black Mercedes Benz van, sitting on the veranda to take in the bucolic countryside surrounding the castle, and wearing matching propeller hats while lighting up hand-rolled cigarettes. What vacation would be complete without poorly executed twerking on top of thick, wooden tables followed by beer pong and flip cup (which, to be honest, they seemed better suited for)? "Round the world beerlympics don't fuck around," one caption read. To top off one evening's adventure, a tasting menu table with homemade pasta was included. How fitting that the invitation came with a soundtrack, "C'est Beau la Bourgeoisie," by Discobitch.

This is not to say that home was not also accommodating. Quite the opposite. Privileged students returned to homes where they felt safe, even as the world fell to pieces around them. And they could get work done. Limited interruptions, and even fewer familial responsibilities, awaited them. High-speed internet, a spare room or an extra office, perhaps a Herman Miller chair with lumbar support, a desk at the ready— sometimes even a standing one—were all available. These students stepped into a quiet space in the midst of a global storm. Some said they even found peace; pandemic life turned out to be calmer, even easier, than the normal rigamarole of campus. Joking that, although "privacy in an Asian household is not really existent," Johannes (UI,A), bubbly and high spirited, noted, "There's so much space to choose from. I was fine with that. It was actually pretty good to study in these spaces."

Thomas (UI,W), with a more matter-of-fact demeanor, said that, when it came to studying at home, there was "nothing to complain about. I've just been going to class in my room, which is right next to my dad's office. We're all on the same floor, so it's my room, my dad's office, my sister's room where she's been going to class, my mom's office. But it's not super loud." In fact, the only time it got noisy was when his sister took a jewelry-making class, "which was, I have to say, impressive." A rare smile and laugh broke his more stoic façade as he thought about his baby sister welding. He likened being home to being in Widener Library, a retreat from the typical "level of distraction" elsewhere. The rare pings and bangs coming from his sister's room were no more distracting than a classmate opening a Snapchat that played louder than expected. "When I was on campus, when I really needed to work, I'd go to the library because then you're in an environment where there's nothing to distract you. Everyone around you is focused." Home was no different.

Emily (UI,B) has a waning Southern accent that reminds me of my own cousins. Her love for pastels and pearls complements her rich, deep brown skin. She too talked positively of home. Looking off as if recalling a fond memory, she noted, "Obviously, it's where I studied all of high school. So that wasn't bad. It was kind of taking me back a little." She continued, "My ability to work at home was fine. I would say it was great. I had everything I needed. I had my parents to get food. The only thing that was hard was taking exams. I ended up having to tell my family, which they were very respectful about, 'Hey, I'm taking an exam. Please be quiet.' In terms of being able to transition, it wasn't bad."

Interestingly, Emily notes that the only time that she had trouble working from home is when her family began renovating their house in late 2020. The pandemic may have cancelled some get-togethers, but the plan to remodel the kitchen was never in doubt, COVID-19 or no. There was a slight edge to her voice when speaking about it. After a summer of travel where she could "function on my own time, wake up with no distractions," she returned home to "the workers." Her voice got more annoyed just thinking about them, and the noise they brought with them. "Now that I'm back home, we're dealing with workers in and out of our house, it's a lot harder; It's probably even harder than it was last spring, just because there's so much commotion."

But again, home was often just a pit stop, as familiar as it was temporary. So many upper-income students did not spend the bulk of their time at home. Whether taking classes or taking a leave of absence, which roughly a fifth of incoming students and similar rates of current students at Harvard did, they did not let the moss grow under their feet.[7]

When the novelty of home wore off, some, like Hannah (UI,W), went to their second homes or those of their friends. Talking to Hannah, a California native, in February 2021, she shared that she wasn't "planning any huge trips," but then it became clear that her hiatus was because she had already spent so much of the pandemic traveling. She mentioned casually that one of her many destinations came about because "one of my friends has a house in Martha's Vineyard off the East Coast." And, as if one island stay wasn't enough, she noted that "one of my other friends, actually, from high school, has a house on Nantucket, which is a 20-minute boat ride away . . . I spent a good amount of the summer in Nantucket." When she had her fill of the quaint islands, she came back to Boston and rented an apartment on Newbury Street with her parents' blessing and support. "My parents paid for my apartment," she said, without skipping a beat.[8]

Many more used Airbnb and Vrbo. Jack (UI,W), with his thick dark curls and West Coast tan, is the son of a business executive and a stay-at-home parent. He had a good situation at home, "where I probably would have been OK trying for letter grades." Rather than stay home, however, he opted to stretch his legs and see the world. "This is a very privileged thing to say. I feel very lucky that I haven't really had to worry about money in this context, prior to the pandemic." Jack did what came naturally: he invested. "I did the stock market thing," he noted with a smile. He then spent his gains "to finance my trips to the East Coast and back. I've been traveling like crazy; I've been in six or seven states already, just going to new places every week. I was in North Carolina; I was in South Carolina. I was in Boston for a while. I was here at home. I was in Hawaii. I was in Colorado. Now I'm back at home. I'm going to Washington and Philadelphia next week. I'm trying to go places, you know? It's like, what's the difference?" With a contagious belly laugh, he said, "If you have people who will pay rent for you, it can be a pretty good position." Jack had taken to traveling so much that his friends likened him to Carmen San Diego, as he gave that 1990s cartoon character a run for her money. They've even begun "playing 'Where in the World is Jack this Week?'" Jack told me. "It's kind of funny."[9]

Amy (UI,B), who relishes sand between her toes and catching the next wave, liked to take things slower. Although she had a good setup at home, she too ventured out. While her peers like Jack "bopped around," she liked getting to know a place a little better. Her ideal was "six- to eight-week Airbnb chunks." She exclaimed with glee that she and her friends felt like they were in a 2020 remake of *Girlfriends*—four Black women living their best lives. "We all went to Hawaii for the same chunk of time, which was great. It was really, really great. We got an Airbnb in a small town in O'ahu. It was really cool." With a chuckle and a barely disguised snort, she continued, "Yes. Would recommend."

One of the reasons Amy enjoyed O'ahu so much, beyond the beaches and views, was that she and her friends consciously supported the local community. They were adamant about getting everything "from restaurants that were native Hawai'ian because we were there for a long time. Obviously, we were tourists. But we were also living in a home. We weren't in a hotel. We're trying to not be pandemic American tourists." Yes, she admitted to "posing for the Gram," but she did more. She posted pictures of local people and shops to even things out. Her Instagram began to mimic Yelp. Despite public pleas by Native Hawaiians and residents of the island in 2020 and 2021 to slow tourism because of its effects on the environment, and them, Amy saw her time on the island as innocuous, even helpful. Her stay, at least in her mind, was a flex mixed with travel philanthropy.[10]

Like Jack and Amy, Jo (UI,A) also sought experiences that took her away from home. Jo, the daughter of scientists, did a finance internship during the summer of 2020. The company invited her to continue during the year; Jo declined the offer. Her rationale was simple: she did not want to be tied down. "I was very determined not to do that." Not so secretly, Jo wanted to be near water and not at a desk. Making this wish a reality, she and her roommates took a year off to do just that. As she noted, "Harvard Zoom, Harvard online, is a scam. Especially if it's full tuition." Instead of "Zoom school," she and a friend "have been just Airbnb-ing a bunch of places." When we spoke in March 2021, she outlined their next steps: "We're moving cross country. My roommates, aside from me, really hate cold weather." With a smile, she noted how "I started adding in the condition that I wanted to be around a body of water." Travel plans were carefully curated to maximize everyone's wants, especially hers. As she said, with the lightest shrug, "Why not?"

Privileged students had choices. It wasn't a question of *if* they would go home. For some, it was which home. If waiting out the pandemic with parents and siblings became a bore, the choice became about where to, with whom, and for how long. Beyond the destinations, extravagant as many were, what I was continually taken aback by was how familiar it was to have this battery of choices. Even though some nodded to their privilege, for these students a free room to use, or even a whole house to take over, was just par for the course. It was the same for the ability to focus on schoolwork, or not. Here again, they had choices. The decision to stay enrolled or take time off was one that was left up to them. Parental support of time off was almost a given, just like the financial support they would receive should they exercise that option. Their peers from less privileged backgrounds, of course, faced a different reality.

Distractions: Wings Clipped

On campus, of course, full-pay and full-ride students lived side by side. When campus closed, they were no longer neighbors, but they were still following one another. From Instagram posts on white, sandy beaches and TikToks in villas to glimpses of far-off places on Zoom, the escapades of privileged students were nearly impossible to escape. Marianne (LI,L), a die-hard New Yorker with roots reaching back to the Caribbean, admitted that her wealthy peers' gallivanting created "an intense sense of F.O.M.O" (fear of missing out). But her fear of missing out wasn't because of the parties or exotic locales, she insisted. It was "jealousy, extreme jealousy, for them being able to live life as if it was normal, or even better than normal because it's better than my normal life." Going further, Marianne notes she had "definitely feelings of jealousy, disappointment, and lots of anger." As many students dealt with seemingly endless, and sometimes debilitating, distractions at home, they couldn't help but notice the differences in destinations between them and their more affluent classmates. These endless glimpses were relentless reminders of the gaps between those who had choices and those who didn't.

Michelle (LI,L), with glasses sitting high on her round cheeks, looked half-annoyed and half-defeated recalling an invitation she—and the person who extended it—knew she could never accept. A friend's mom offered up a spacious rental home in Hawaii and said she could bring her four roommates along. They just needed to get there. For her suitemates, flocking to Honolulu for six months was an obvious choice; for Michelle, it was just as obvious that she would decline. The flight alone was way too much money; but more importantly, she just couldn't be that far from home. "They were just studying there while COVID was happening. But I have to stay here and take care of my family," she said, sadly. Michelle never knew when she would be needed for yet another emergency. "Whenever something happens in my family," she began, voice heavy, "I have to text my friends, 'Sorry, guys. We've got to cancel that Zoom date; I have to take care of things at home right now.'"[11]

I heard versions of Marianne and Michele's stories over and over again. While their globetrotting peers had what seemed like endless options and endless freedom, lower-income students had just one choice, and it often didn't feel like a choice at all: go home. Questions surrounding travel logistics to far-off places, or even cool cities nearby, were generally absent; instead, nearly all lower-income students became hyperfocused: first, on making it home, and then managing the myriad uncertainties once there. For them, school became a distraction rather than their prime focus—their studies seemed to be something they did, interspersed amid the omnipresent responsibilities and the uncertain tumult of home, both of which grew the longer they stayed.

Uncertainty abounded. For many lower-income students, the pandemic brought on an unwelcome reunion with life's most basic questions: Am I safe? Is there food today? Where will I sleep tonight? What will I eat tomorrow? Coming to Harvard enabled some distance from these questions, at least for the students themselves. Their families still grappled with them. Living on campus and working, as most scholarship students did, meant two things for the student's family: they had one less mouth to feed, and they could probably count on the student to send some money back home. Campus closing reversed both.[12]

Where will I stay? Mia (LI,M) sat in a used office chair, swiveling like she was in the giant strawberry of the Berry Go Round at the fair. Slowing down, she reached out for a small bowl of blackberries that sat on the table, sharing how they were her attempt to eat better. But they lay untouched, save for the single one she rolled delicately between her fingers. Mia left campus in mid-March like everyone else. But when she got back to Dallas, Texas, she didn't go to her parents' house. Because there was no house. There was a backseat. Her parents and her siblings lived in a beat-up Volkswagen, the same one that housed them for nearly all of the past decade. With an uneven cadence that made her voice waver, she noted, "My parents and family were struggling with the pandemic. If you're living out of your car, a lot of the amenities that are public amenities aren't available anymore." Mia tried to keep up with her classes but had to rely on "internet cafes to get any sort of work done" and "gym showers to get clean." Fortunately, Mia finally secured them an efficiency, applying under her name as her parents' credit scores were in the gutter. And timing proved key; they barely escaped living in their car during the deep freeze that hit Texas in February 2021.[13]

How will I eat? Many parents already struggled to make ends meet before the pandemic. Reduced hours and layoffs made it even harder to do so. And sometimes they couldn't. Yasmine (LI,W), witty and riotous, recalled that after her mom lost her job, tensions ran even higher at home, especially over food. They adopted a vegetarian diet because meat became too expensive. Though this change in diet cut costs, it didn't lighten the strain in the house. Her mother would yell, "You guys better slow the fuck down with the way you guys eat." When her brother ate one too many peaches, she berated him again, "What the fuck? You're eating a whole tree." Michael (LI,L), speaking with tired eyes that made him look older than his years, tried to forestall such battles in his house. To take pressure off of his mother, who also lost her job at the beginning of the pandemic, he applied for CalFresh, California's version of the federal Supplemental Nutrition Assistance Program (SNAP). Applying for aid felt more and more important each month. In between assignments, working at Walmart, and classes, he submitted any application he could find to take "advantage of food banks for help. And also taking advantage of the mortgage stuff," which at least alleviated some of the fear of food insecurity and eviction.

Only after grappling with the foundational concerns of food and shelter could lower-income students actually focus on being students. *Will I be able to log in?* Kevin (LI,W), straight-backed and proper, knew from the start it was going to be impossible to work from home—his family didn't have internet access. But the elderly couple next door did. "We would steal Wi-Fi from our neighbors. We just put a tent up in their backyard. Just took their Wi-Fi," he explained. The neighbors were none the wiser. Like millions of young people around the country, access to internet, let alone a Wi-Fi signal strong enough to support Zoom or Microsoft Teams, was a constant struggle.[14]

No Space for Me

Some parents tried to help make the most of a bad situation. For example, Samantha (LI,M) felt her family, which includes three siblings, "a couple of cats, a couple of chinchillas" was "a little more accommodating than usual." They realized that her focus should be on class, and that studying was more important than doing chores or babysitting the little ones. That said, a fundamental problem remained: "One of the biggest obstacles was not having a solitary workspace. Everyone was in the same room at once, conversations going on, distractions."

No matter their intentions, there were limits to what parents could do. They could neither instantly make their homes bigger when students returned nor make money grow on trees. Lack of space, crowded living conditions, and increased expenses often trumped even the most eager efforts to make remote schooling easier. Maria (LI,M) and I met via Zoom. She sat under a woven tapestry from her mother's home city in Mexico. The blue and white triangles formed a stunning flying geese quilt pattern. She was reserved and thoughtful. Though quiet, her voice commanded attention. Maria told me how her parents supported her educational career, even going against their own conservative Catholic instincts and allowing her to go to boarding school on the East Coast. She left home at 15. Their message was clear: no matter how hard things got at home, "her job was to get good grades." That approach continued as she got to Harvard and looked for work: "They want me to get a job for resumes and for experience, not for the fact that I need to contribute to this household." And even when Maria shared with them, over the summer of 2020, that Harvard, like a number of colleges across the country, was offering students $5,000 to stay at home instead of returning to campus in the fall: "Anything that I contributed to this house is because I wanted to." There was no pressure to take the money. But the weight of saying no weighed heavily on her heart. She knew that the money would help fill the gaps brought upon by her father's hours being reduced at work. And so, she took the carrot and stayed, giving her parents the money as soon as it hit her account.[15]

In the same way they supported her growing up, they were adamant about helping her thrive during this time of uncertainty. When she flew back home in mid-March, her father told her that she should "make a nest here." Over breakfast the next morning, he reiterated his message: "This is your house. You are not a visitor in this house. You are a member of this house." A lighthearted smile crossed her face and she said, "I've been incredibly fortunate that my parents have that mindset." Despite her parents' valiant efforts, however, Maria said that she "felt like my wings have been clipped." While her peers roamed across state and national borders, she lived a closeted life, literally. "This room," she moved her hand around in a circle, "was sort of a storage area, and then my parents moved stuff around to create enough space for me to have a desk and a bed. I spend most of my days in this room." Maria moved from sharing a room with her teenage brother to residing in a former closet a few weeks after returning home. "It was really isolating. I was just feeling not very motivated, I had a heavy course load, I was very stressed, I started breaking out; I've never had acne. I started getting terrible acne on my forehead. I was definitely not taking care of myself. I was perpetually stressed; I couldn't sleep.

My hair started falling out in chunks. That was super jarring, being in the shower and my hair falling out in chunks. . . . It's just stress and anxiety and isolation and sadness."

Returning home meant giving up freedom students had found only by going to college. For most students at Harvard, those freedoms have long been taken for granted: a bed of one's own, a bit of privacy, enough light to read. This forfeiture, however, left low-income students scrounging for places to call their own.

A 2018 Pew Research Center report revealed that a record 64 million people, or 20 percent of the entire U.S. population, lived with multiple generations in the same house or apartment. This arrangement was highest among those from immigrant families. Already cramped living quarters were often made even more so during the pandemic because of the need to consolidate limited resources. Bringing in additional people—familial and not—under the same roof helped and it hurt. Multigenerational and multifamily living helped to offset reduced hours or lost jobs and thus to stave off financial hardship, but it laid waste to what little space students had and opened the home to greater exposure to COVID-19.[16]

This constellation of distractions got in the way of coursework, and soon coursework started to feel even more like an afterthought to managing relationships, tempers, and expectations. Nicole (LI,L) and Michele (LI,L) lamented the distractions that arose from concentrating families in already-cramped quarters. Nicole was careful speaking about home. There were things that annoyed her, but she also knew that it wasn't anyone's fault. Times were tough and money was tight, so her parents did what they could: "We live in an apartment and it's a two-bedroom apartment, but we rent out one bedroom." The tenants in Nicole's apartment "came in a couple of months before COVID. One of them works in a deli and the guy works in a car shop. They were both laid off." The house was in constant chaos. The adults were all on different schedules. The children were all on similar ones. When I asked her if she had space to focus on academics, she responded, "Close to none. It's shared space so if one of us is at the dining room table, one of us would have to be on the bed and one of us would have to be on the couch." To make up for unforeseen expenses of everyone being home and everyone's hours being cut, Nicole's mother began babysitting: "My mom, she takes care of children. She started taking care of children again right now. I just remember the kids being there, like, 'What's happening? Who are they?' And I'm like, 'Oh, you're so cute, but I need you to go away.'"

Michelle, sharp and observant, experienced just as much commotion at home. In her house, there was "our family of four and six men living there at the same time; we rented out the rooms mostly to guys my father knew." An uneasy laugh escaped her lips when speaking on differences between Harvard and home. "Yeah, to have my own room, it's a luxury, man." Carving out personal space was near impossible. In addition to the constant stream of people in and out of the house, Michelle realized all over again how everything at home was "really cheap" and poorly maintained. "The water was yellow sometimes. I was like, 'That's normal,'" she said with a shrug. In fact, when she came to Harvard, she participated in the Freshman Urban Program, which focuses on volunteer work in the surrounding area. During orientation, they visited a shelter for the unhoused. That visit was a host of disorienting experiences. "I entered the homeless shelter, and the apartment was nicer than mine. Brightly lit, the walls were all colorful. They had a really nice kitchen and everything. I was like 'Wow, alright, nice.'"

After years of searching for cheaper housing, Michelle and her family moved about nine months after she left Harvard in March. While this relocation significantly reduced the number of people and traffic in and out of her house, it meant less space for everyone. She picked up her laptop to show me just how cramped her quarters are. Her back was to a blank wall, although there were boxes to her right. To her left was the door to enter the house. To her front was the wooden door leading outside. She could touch both at the same time if she stretched her arms apart and bent just a little. She told me, "I'm currently living in a hallway. My house is two bedrooms. One room is for my parents; one room is for me and my sister. We have a bunk bed. That's all we can really afford. The computer is in the room. I have a laptop that I was able to save up for. We can't have two people speaking all the time in one room. So, my parents cleared out this hallway. I'm literally living in a hallway! That's where I study. I was pretty good for a while. I grew to definitely resent it. A lot."

She heard everything as she tried to work, and not just her family's movements. Despite living in a rural part of their state, their house sat next to a major offramp from the main thoroughfare. Small things began to eat at her. Even the rustle of the plastic grocery bags when her parents returned from shopping became too much. Michelle grew increasingly frustrated with the lack of space and the "antiquated traditions" that underscored her "lack of freedom." She said, voice stern, "I'm not allowed to use tampons in my house or have a boyfriend, even though I'm 20. I can't leave because I don't want to give up the stipend. I also can't look for a cheaper place to live, because really there's no cheaper place to live." She longed to return to campus, even though she knew it was impossible. At one point she quipped, with barely veiled anger, "I'm willing to trade $5,000 for my mental health."

The Deepest Cut

Students lost more than the freedom to come and go as they please. They lost those who were near and dear to them. With so many people coming and going into their homes, COVID-19 inevitably came knocking. Sara (LI,W) and Mya (LI,L) both felt its devastations. Sara's father, like many men who came to New York City from the Middle East, worked as a driver: "not a great job to have during COVID," she said drily. The risks were secondary, though, since "he would try to take any job he could." They needed the money. "But we'd all be scared while he's doing it. Including himself." Their fear was soon justified; in December, he contracted COVID-19. Within days, the entire family fell ill. Her dad, who is diabetic and "not, I guess, what you would consider in shape," struggled mightily. He was eventually hospitalized. "He had a lot of trouble breathing. He was hooked up to the oxygen thing." In addition to recovering from COVID-19 herself, she said, "I was worried all the time." It showed. Sitting still, as if frozen, she recounted the five days she couldn't see him. She lifelessly recalled the hours she spent staring at the chair in the corner of the living room, the spot he normally sat when he was not on the road.

Before campus closed in March 2020, Mya made the trek home pretty frequently; she lived close, and she missed Portuguese food as much as she missed her big, blended family. When campus closed, she went home only to discover that her entire family—grandmother, cousin, siblings, and her mom—had contracted the virus. With so much traffic in and out of the house, to and from jobs that put them in contact with the public, anyone could have brought it home. The day after she arrived home, they rushed her grandmother to the hospital. And after "a week and a half just going through what people that have COVID go through, she passed." For those ten days Mya could not visit. FaceTime helped close the distance, but "by the time we did that, she was already pronounced brain dead." Fighting back tears, voice cracking from the weight of memory, she recalled their last exchange. "The only thing that happened is she handed me a bowl and I took it from her." A gesture so common, so simple, Mya never thought that the last time would be the last time.

To be clear, it wasn't that privileged students felt immune to COVID-19. Many spoke about it as a serious threat to public health, even as they traveled around the world in its early days. But what I did hear, time and time again, especially from more privileged students who were White, was a feeling that there was some distance between the virus and their immediate families. Partly, this was practical: fewer privileged students, again mainly those who were White, had lost someone close to them, and so COVID-19 was something they were seeing from afar. When they did know someone who had died, it wasn't anyone they really knew well. Everyone wanted to claim some proximity to the disease, but "a friend of a friend" or "someone who I met once a while ago" were repeated refrains. Wealthy White students like Hannah (UIW) and her family could elect to stop working or were able to work from home, had space to quarantine, and had the money for the nearly $200 at-home rapid antigen tests long before they were commonplace in Walgreens or free government testing was widely available. They didn't save these pricey tests for emergencies or important events; rather, they would use them if "we were ever coming back to the house after spending time with friends or large groups." Going further, she noted, "We weren't super worried that it'd be fatal or have super bad side effects," even for her grandfather. Showcasing her privilege, Hannah shared that her grandfather was once an active surgeon who still had hospital privileges and "because he has connections at the hospital, he could get plasma; he knows so many people at the hospital."

Grass Not as Green

To get away from the mayhem and heartbreak, and in the hopes of some solace amid depressing times, some lower-income students sought escapes. They scraped together what they could after taking care of financial responsibilities at home. They quickly discovered that not all Airbnb experiences are created equal. Aisha (LI,B) found out the hard way. Despite loving meals and TV time with her mother, Aisha grew more downtrodden as days turned to weeks. Noticing a change, Aisha's mother suggested finding a rental with friends. "My mom was encouraging me to leave and 'be great' with friends," she said, chuckling at her mom's attempt to use a popular saying. Things didn't quite work out according to plan. "The fall semester, we had a lot of housing problems."

Aisha took her mom up on her suggestion and looked into apartments with friends, all of whom came from similar class backgrounds. They decided on the DC area. There were red flags from the beginning. For everyone in her friend group to live close together, they would need two apartments; larger homes were out of their price range. Also, not everyone could see the apartment before moving in; again, the cost of a scouting visit to Maryland when she lived in the Midwest was too much. With a sour look, she explained how everything continued to go sideways:

We were in an apartment. We had a friend from Jersey go look at it. We're like, "How the hell did you say this was going to be OK? You were our proxy and you folded." There were just so many problems. First of all, thank God they got the apartment that had the leaks. But our apartment, things weren't working, constantly calling people to fix things. Towards the end, the week before we left, my window blew in. I was in the bed. And it just opened. It was connected to a fire escape. Nobody came for four days. I reported it to the city and *now* they come. It's just horrible.

Throughout, the landlord was a curmudgeon. He ignored her calls and emails and was dismissive of their concerns the few times Aisha did reach him. In addition to classes, she researched how to report him to the city, which took even more time away from both studying and socializing. It was the opposite of the relaxing environment they had hoped for, that they saw on Instagram and TikTok. "It really put a damper on the whole semester." But the apartment, with its flaws and inattentive landlord, was all their budget could provide; their limited funds were stretched between their new rent and food, on top of the existing expenses at home that Aisha was already helping with.

Away also didn't mean unavailable. Duties often followed lower-income students wherever they went. In fact, for many, it didn't even mean being that far away. Sofia (LI,L) rented an apartment just a few neighborhoods away from her family. Home was more than a bit crowded. And Sofia said, with a shy smile, that small moments of kindness from her mom turned into lengthy conversations. Her mother often brought her lunch and sometimes snacks native to Oaxaca. With a chuckle, she said, "It was never something like sandwiches. My mom is extravagant to the extent of the word. . . . My mom is a fantastic chef. She would make sopa de pollo con fideo, it's like chicken and broth with thin noodles." Sofia appreciated her mom's generosity, but she couldn't afford what it entailed: "on campus, two hours is a tremendous amount of time for me. I could finish half a p-set in that time. Thinking about what I would do back home and what I don't do while I'm on campus, it's definitely very noticeable." But Sofia's biggest—albeit most delightful—distraction was her younger brother, who was integral to her rationale for renting the apartment: "There was no one to take care of my little brother. And so, my little brother lived in the house with us. He got to interact with my Harvard friends. I was his caretaker. He would do classes in the bedroom; I would do classes in the kitchen."

Given her role as the eldest child and the most proficient in English, Sofia was the de facto parent, especially during the pandemic when "my little brother is constantly needing help with school because he also transitioned online." Her parents appreciated this help, given that they were not able to work from home. Still, "on a daily basis, I'll get a call from my parents saying, 'Hey, could you give this school a call and ask them about this,' or 'Hey, could you send this email,' or 'Could you proofread this for me?'"[17]

Although Aisha's and Sofia's rentals were not as restorative as they hoped they would be, revealing yet another difference between those with and without money, some of their lower-income peers had even more harrowing experiences.

Dangers: Grounded

It is easy to have a romanticized image of home: a place of warmth and safety, four walls cloaked in love and patience. And it is definitely true that, for many lower-income and first-generation college students, their journey is made possible because of a devoted family. However, as author Chimamanda Adichie reminds us, there is an inherent "danger of a single story." It can not only blind us to the complex reality in front of us but also direct our actions away from knowing, preparing for, and supporting those left out of that single story.[18]

The reality is that for many students across the country, home is hell, not because of the distractions but because of the dangers. Home can be downright debilitating, providing little respite from the outside world, let alone protection from who and what lurks inside its walls. Nancy (LI,M) has a calm demeanor. She takes her time answering questions, often pausing to reflect before speaking. Yet she becomes increasingly unnerved when she discussed her family, fidgeting with a black hair tie. Nancy is adamant that not all lower-income students have a familial safety net to fall back on. Indeed, Nancy is emancipated:

> Being low income to the point where I don't have any family support at all, and I'm registered through Harvard as financially independent from my parents because I don't have a relationship with my parents.

Yeah, I don't know. In first gen low income spaces, a lot of people are like, "My biggest support is my mom" and "I call my mom every day." That seems to be a really big story that people have. It's not my experience. It often feels important—when I'm comfortable, obviously— to distinguish that as an extra layer of my experience in college.

Nancy feels that some experiences are absent, even in groups dedicated to providing community to first-generation college students, like first-gen student unions that are populating more and more college campuses, hers being one of them. On the eve of her eighteenth birthday, her mother, who suffers from anxiety and depression that only worsened with her abuse of opioids, told her she had five days to move out. Her mother had done this before; manic episodes and threats of evictions were common. But this time, her mother was a woman of her word. Nancy went to high school that Friday in a daze. She could not concentrate on classes, knowing she could not return home that night. Fortunately, a teacher took her in, and she stayed with that teacher until graduation. Unfortunately, even this situation soured: "She told me at one point that it felt like I was treating her like a laundromat and a hotel. Which, to be honest, all I needed and wanted was just a place to literally sleep. She wanted more. She would joke sometimes about adopting me or that I should marry her son who was 26. I was 18."

Starting at Harvard was hard, but it was also thrilling. She had a home—a room that was officially hers. Even when the email from President Bacow went out on March 10, Nancy was sure she was safe. Harvard knew she was unhoused. Her permanent address and her campus mailing address were one and the same. So secure was she in thinking that she would be able to stay, she didn't follow emails asking students to petition to remain on campus. Instead, she spent the first three days after the announcement worried about her friends, even helping them pack. And then reality hit. On that third day, she got an email from her dean: she was not guaranteed housing. She panicked. She felt exposed. Friends offered her a place to stay, although some of them barely had space for themselves; she reflexively declined. Still reeling from the scars of her teacher, who Nancy had known almost all her life, she wouldn't let herself just move in with a friend she, all things considered, just met: "Relying on people's kindness as opposed to a legal arrangement, it can get really uncomfortable. Anything could happen. You can get kicked out and there's no reason for them not to." She felt overlooked, unseen. She scrambled, venting on social media and emailing the only dean she remembered meeting. Fortunately, Nancy was able to secure housing on campus a day before campus shut down.

The fear of going home was evident when I spoke with Eleanor (LI,M). She sat uneasily, nervously flicking her sheets of black hair over her shoulders. When the email came, she steeled herself, yet again, for uncertainty: "the space that Harvard gave me was being taken away." It was not just space, but security. She continued, "For a lot of FGLI (first-generation, lower-income) students, Harvard is a safe space away from their past, in terms of the experiences they've had, just family situations. For me, Harvard was—not a safe haven, it's very far from that—but safety from some situations from home." She was seeing a counselor to deal with "the trauma that I had experienced growing up." Her explanation was painfully blunt: "My dad verbally abuses my mom. And a lot of times it's because of the decisions that I make, if I'm a little more free in my decisions away from the patriarchal norm. It falls on my mom for permitting that liberal thinking."

Leaving campus, however, meant losing her counselor and returning to the person whose assaults she had only just started to reckon with. "The only way of living that my dad knows is controlling what he can control. . . . When COVID hit, when we were kicked out, it was his opportunity to again control my life." It also meant a more active role in taking care of her mom. At home, she noted, "I'm a protector." Her return was a regression.

Things took a turn a few weeks later after returning home, when her father lost his job as a packer at a candy company. Now he could no longer provide for his family, which worsened his own anxiety and depression. In addition to the laundry list of issues to deal with: "troublesome neighbors, a dangerous street to live on in terms of violence, and, in that part of southeast LA, drug use," Eleanor also had to contend with "a lot of fighting between my parents, constantly." But as Eleanor noted, "it's hard to live with a parent who is dealing with anxiety and depression when you're dealing with your own anxiety and depression." She said coldly, "I've gotten so used to things being hard, I don't know what is supposed to be good anymore. The days where my dad would cry were horrible because, when a Mexican dad starts crying—I need to be a daughter, to be the strongest person in the family, and I felt so weak. How do I tell my dad, 'No, dad, you are going to get a job. No, dad, you can learn these technical skills; you're not too old,' even while knowing that was probably not true."

There was no end to the responsibilities—some old, some new, all hers—that came with returning home. Eleanor found herself "paying bills, again, reading papers, translating stuff, making phone calls to companies. I did a lot of applying to jobs for my parents." She did everything in her power to help them get back on their feet. Still, it was hard to support the person who, almost every day of her adolescent life, had made her feel small.

Fear of parents was common. Talking about home brought on a physical change for Charlotte (LI,L), a first-generation college student with the raspy voice of an old Blues singer. When our conversation began, her room was pitch black, save for the glow of her laptop illuminating her face. Darkness seemed to be her blanket, comforting her as she started to cry, black mascara streaks flecked with glitter streaming down her face. Her mom left her dad when she was 14. But the abuse didn't stop, it just changed. Voice cracking, she explained, "My dad was angry about child support. He would just keep me in the car or his room for hours and just lecture me about how my mom was just keeping me for money and all these other really nasty things. When we asked him to leave, he would put his foot in the door. If I didn't make eye contact with him, he would force my face to make eye contact with him. That went on for several years."

College was her long-awaited release from "that constant state of fear." The reality of going home destabilized her; it crushed the hope that Harvard brought. On campus, she had finally started sleeping more. She even exercised. Her weight had normalized, no longer yo-yoing up and down. And then campus closed. "From March until August, I had bigger mood swings and longer periods of depressions. The symptoms were worse. . . . My body felt really heavy all the time. The emotional outbursts were a lot more frequent and unpredictable."

Marianne (LI,L) sat comfortably in her chair, a jovial smile creasing her face as we commiserated about being middle children, shouldering burdens—real and perceived—that our siblings do not. At the mention of her parents, however, she began to deflate, speaking slower and lower. Unlike Maria, whose parents supported her making her own choices, Marianne felt "bullied" into taking the $5,000 incentive to stay home. She tried to reconcile herself to another semester in which she would "lock myself in the bathroom to work." But getting work done was not her top priority. She looked away from me, and batting her eyes like a hummingbird's wings, she shared, "My dad has never touched a hair on my head." The same could not be said about her mother. "There was definitely threats of physicality, and it's gone physical before." The abuse in her house was common enough "that the transition to violence doesn't seem like a big deal when you're growing up. . . . I've definitely been hit before." It became something she expected; even the simplest disagreement would set her mom off. The irony is that it went against the life advice that her mother drilled into her children. "It's a strange thing because it's like, 'You should never let anybody hit you' was always the mentality in my house. 'No one can ever hit you.' She'd always tell me, 'If your boyfriend or any person hits you, you call the police.'" Marianne's mother didn't see her slapping her daughter as hypocrisy. It was a mother's duty to discipline her child.

Jamie (LI,W) knew this reality well. Tall, thin, and pasty white, she still looked pale from her bout with COVID-19 and complications from an autoimmune disease. Like Charlotte (LI,L), who decided at an early age that she "wanted to leave as soon as possible," Jamie counted on college to facilitate her first and final exit. As she noted, "I feel like in Carolina, I am the sick, poor kid who waitresses to help her family get by." College changed that. "At Harvard, I feel like this person who is successful, doing what she wants with her life and living independently of this situation that really drags me down."

Finances were always a struggle for Jamie and often the root cause of her family's troubles. Having very little money—aided by her parents and grandparents' mismanagement of what little they did have—left them struggling to find food and housing for weeks and sometimes months on end. With more than a hint of frustration in her voice, she noted,

> We were on welfare. We had a house in Carolina. My grandparents lived with us. And then my grandparents moved out. The house was in their name. My mom was sending my grandma monthly payments. My grandma did not use that money to pay the mortgage. So, we were evicted. We were homeless for months. After that, we jumped around houses a lot. When I turned 16, I knew I had to get a job. My finances went to helping pay bills; my mom has always struggled to make ends meet. My school used to send me home with meals over the weekend because there wasn't ever extras in my house. We had the groceries needed to make five dinners, and nothing else.

As she, her mother, and brother bounced from shelter to rental to friend's house, Jamie became determined that she would never experience poverty again. She lamented how, for her mother, "there are times when she literally has $2 in her bank account. That's true even now. There's just no safety net if there's an accident, or an emergency, or someone has to do something, or the car needs x, y, or z. There's just nothing there. And that's usually when I get a call."

Her reality—versus what the deans at Harvard thought was possible for students like her—was alarming. One of the scariest things about campus closures for Jamie was "that Harvard took their time in telling you whether or not you would be able to stay on campus. That's really hard to sit with, that feeling." She finally tracked down her dean as he left his office, and his response only amplified her pain: "Well, can't you get an apartment off campus?" The question was a slap in the face. Her eyes narrowed, and she threw her hands up in frustration.

> I'm sitting there, as someone who is housing insecure, and hearing these people just tell me, 'No, you can't come back right now. We're

going to readdress it on Tuesday. Just take the weekend to focus on healing.' How am I supposed to focus on getting better when I don't even know if I have housing? It was ludicrous. . . . I don't have to go get my own groceries, because there's a dining hall. I don't have to cook my own food, because there's a dining hall. And there's an urgent care center within walking distance. So that is the best space for me. Not off campus, alone, trying to fend for myself.

This moment fundamentally changed her relationship with the school and the people in it. "I came in feeling really special; Harvard thought I was someone worth caring about and supporting. I've just come to the conclusion now that for them, I as an individual don't matter, beyond my alumni donations."

Jamie knew what awaited her at home; that's especially why she didn't want to go back. Her mother's uncaring response came right after emails announcing closures: "Well, you can't come home. What are you going to do?" This was just the tip of the iceberg. The precarious state of her family was always on her mind: "There is food insecurity issues there, and internet insecurity." Jamie explained why "it's tough for me to go home," in good times or bad:

When I go home, suddenly there are a lot of emergencies related to money. I end up spending a lot to have necessary items. My family really relies on me. One of the last times I went home, the power was cut off. It really frustrated me, because I was like, "Mom, you should have just told me this before the power was shut off. Because now, not only do I have to pay the bill, but now I have to pay to get the power turned back on again." It's more expensive and more of a hassle.

As she noted, "If I go home, I'm going to a couch in an apartment. . . . literally. In the dining room, instead of a table, there's a futon. That would be my bed." There was no space for her, in multiple senses of the word. Her family often questioned her choices to pursue higher education. "My family has a really hard time understanding my work. In their mind, everything that I do is minimized." Although they wanted access to her wages, both when she waitressed in high school and from her many jobs in college, Jamie said that they remained dismissive of what she ultimately wanted. Jamie found herself "really masking a lot of my feelings, and thoughts, and goals, and passions, because they weren't supportive."

But homelessness and disruptions in utilities were often not the most pressing or damaging aspects of home. When she got into Harvard, it was her chance to leave not only poverty behind, but also pain. Years earlier, her stepfather sexually assaulted her. "There was one night when I walked in on my mom giving my younger brother a bath, and I said something that I shouldn't have known as an eight-year-old about anatomy." Her stepdad was arrested and imprisoned but was released after serving a reduced sentence.

Jamie's voice, weighted with anger, did not crack but fluctuated, as if her volume were controlled by a faulty knob. Decades-long trauma haunts her still. For it was not only her stepdad but also her biological father, whom she met as a teenager, who hurt her. "I used to spend a lot of time wanting to be the daughter that he wanted, because I didn't want to lose another father figure. But he ended up victimizing me as well." She explained:

> My stepdad was sexually abusive. My actual father was tiptoeing around that. I was getting ready one morning in my father's house. I walked out, and I saw a live stream of my bedroom on his computer. He was just sitting there. I really freaked out, obviously. It became a CPS issue. My father was touchy feely in ways that made me uncomfortable. But I was like, "Oh, I'm just uncomfortable because of what happened when I was younger. This is a normal father-daughter relationship." I didn't really know what that was, because I hadn't had it before. He was very interested in having me drink, asking me about my sexual life. When I was 17, I was still very much in PTSD brain. My deep fear was, I can't lose my dad *again*. I can't *not* have a father.

Try as she might, Jamie could not escape these troubles from home. Her finances were always being tapped by her mother who, now single, relied on her even more. Moreover, her stepdad, the abuser, was released from jail and lived just over the state line. She noted her stepfather "went to prison when I was eight years old for the sexual abuse. He was released from prison my sophomore fall. One of the things that I was working on that semester was going to the courthouse and getting a restraining order so that he couldn't pop up anywhere." Her other victimizer, her biological father, never saw the inside of a jail, at least for how he treated her, and lived mere bus stops away from her mother.

Campus closures breathed new life into old fears. A thousand miles separated Cambridge from Jamie's family. The college gates felt like added security. One email erased that. A thousand miles gone in a second of recognition that Harvard might not be home anymore. Moments like this, and the ensuing loneliness took Jamie to some dark places. She stayed up until near dawn one day. Her service animal had just died: "It was like me and my dog against the world." Her mother needed money again. She felt devastated by the university's decision not to punish a harassing mentor. Her only companion was a bottle of wine, a cheap California pinot noir from Trader Joe's. After finding a clean SOLO cup in her room, she poured herself a drink. And then another. And another. She finished the bottle in less than an hour, and then headed outside.

Her feet took her to the Charles River. Jane Chopin's words from *The Awakening* rang out like a siren's call, providing clarity to her cloudy mind. Standing on its banks, too tired and too numb for tears, she thought of one sentence in particular: "The voice of the sea is seductive, never ceasing, whispering, clamoring, murmuring, inviting the soul to wander in abysses of solitude."[19] Jamie's voice was unflinching as she described this moment to me, her words unfiltered:

> I felt this really deep urge to just jump in and just be done. I was sick. I was sick of being a fighter. And feeling alone. I was like, "I don't know why I'm pushing through all of these experiences anymore." The thing I liked most about this book was it wasn't like, "Oh, this person is depressed and they're going to get through it or this major trauma happened in their life and they're going to work through it." It really is just this woman who is living a life that is not satisfying to her. And she just slowly decides that she doesn't want to do it anymore. It's a really interesting look at a slow break, a slow longing for something that is just more peaceful and calmer than what you currently have.

There is cruel irony in Jamie's words. Jumping into the Charles River, especially from the Weeks Footbridge, is a rite of passage for Harvard students. It is on the list of "4 Things to Do before You Graduate" that gets passed down from student to student, right next to running buck naked during Primal Scream, having sex in the stacks of Widener Library, and giving the John Harvard statue a golden shower. It unites those who have been through the crucible of Harvard. But unlike her peers who, sopping wet and a cold from the chilly waters, would wade to the banks with screams of jubilation and joy, she would surrender to the current, slow and steady. For her peers, the dive would be their entry into the wild possibilities of their futures. For Jamie, it would have been her exit from the inescapable burdens of her past.

Conclusion

When campus closed, some students thrived. Others survived—and a few just barely. Students' testimonies offer a window into the menacing dangers that some were navigating long before the pandemic hit. What we learn is more than just the difference between how the rich and poor experience life. We learn more about how privilege is exercised within a college community. We also learn more about the contours of poverty.

Privileged students had many freedoms and exercised those freedoms in remarkably creative ways, whether in choosing where to do "Zoom school" or where to spend their gap year as they waited out the pandemic. In line with sociologist Elena van Stee, I find that wealthy students' parents supported them in their endeavors in various ways.[20] Some of that support, of course, was ready-made: their homes had ample space or they had access to additional rooms that they could turn into personal offices for studying. Parents lightened their already limited responsibilities at home. Other modes of support were more intentional. They offered second homes to their children and their friends or paid for rentals in cities across the country and world for that matter. At each turn of the pandemic, privileged students had a plethora of options. These students were nearly all aware of how fortunate they were, and yet their voices were often blasé, even bored. Such is privilege.

Lower-income students did not have such liberties. They went home to an array of distractions and disruptions. The cramped quarters they returned to, more often than not, became even more cramped when parents either rented bedrooms to members of the community or families moved in together, whether to consolidate resources or to help the most vulnerable among them. Students had little space to and for themselves, whether for class or simply to decompress. They felt the need to be constantly on guard, even at home.

Lower-income students also weathered greater exposure to the outside world. The greater number of people in the house, and the imperative for all adults to work however they could, meant more risk of contracting COVID-19 and bringing it home. The need for students to contribute meant that they, too, ventured in the virus' crosshairs.

There is also that population of lower-income students for whom returning home would have been unimaginable, unsafe. There were real traumas in their past that did not go away when they left for college. These traumas waited for them, in the same bedrooms they slept in and around the same dinner tables they ate at before college. The mere threat of having to return home was destabilizing. Harvard was a chance to experience stability, to make a new community; distance brought some relief. And then students had to confront just how temporary that relief could be. The thought of going home, with all the other things she had to contend with, was what took Jamie to the river, willing to cast it all away to finally be able to rest.

But it was not just their families that students returned to. Students' homes were not islands on to themselves, divorced from the outside world. When campus closed, they traded one community for another. As we will see in the next chapter, although COVID-19 affected each neighborhood across the country, it did so unevenly, immersing students once again in the generations-long inequalities that they had either fought so hard to escape or had long been oblivious to. The pandemic has been a particularly blunt reminder of how the communities we inherit continue to shape so much of our lives.

2

Beyond These Walls

LIKE VEGGIES, fresh air does the body good. The mind too, many experts say. Hannah (UI,W) and Samantha (LI,M) are both runners, both slender yet toned, both eager to extol the joys of exercise. They especially cherish running outside. Their paths never crossed at Harvard, but they both crave the singular joy that comes with easing into a meditative state and watching the mile markers pass by. Not marathoners by any stretch, but a quick midweek 5K, especially after a long day at the computer, was a welcome treat. A two-hour hike to usher in the weekend was equally satisfying. They came to Harvard already hooked: cross-country and competitive running filled their high school schedules. When campus closed in March 2020, Hannah gleefully returned to her passion. Samantha did not.[1]

Hannah, blue-eyed and dirty blonde, lounged in her spacious bedroom with its patterned window shades and matching bright orange accent wall behind her. But she had a nervous energy at the same time, like she was eager to get started or, perhaps, like she was counting down the minutes until her next run. Just a few minutes into the conversation, she shared how running outdoors is a family affair. Her parents introduced her to running in middle school. It was a way to spend more time in nature and a way to bond, growing closer as the runs grew longer. She and her siblings joke about how their "parents are in better shape than us. They're the most fit 55-year-olds you've ever seen." But now Hannah gives them a run for their money.

When Hannah realized that Harvard was going to close, she had no doubt about where she would go. She booked a ticket to San Francisco hours after the president's email. Despite the speed of her departure, the actual leaving was brutal; Hannah was angry about everything she'd be missing, from completing problem sets with friends to dancing with them at Yardfest, Harvard's spring concert. But all that frustration was tempered by what she had to look forward to. Hannah relished the idea of more time with family, especially because "we do a lot of hiking, running, and biking." She missed her family dearly, but she missed the outdoors of Northern California even more. The chill of the fall, not to mention the dreary New England winters, clashed harshly with her California sensibilities, undercutting both her mental and physical health. All that changed when she left the airport and drove past familiar landmarks of home. Their not-so-small corner of the world was quiet, wealthy, and stunning, a few miles outside of San Francisco, butting up against Muir Woods. Her father went "running or biking every single day." A named partner at a law firm with three decades of service, he easily transitioned to remote work. And it was easy for Hannah to join him on his outings, making up for lost time.

As the world locked down, she ventured out often. "In my backyard, we would go on trails, go on runs." From her dining room table, you could see the start of the paths that led down to the park. And she knew them well. "There's lots of redwoods everywhere," Hannah noted with a smile. Muir Woods is famous for its old-growth pines; she loved taking in the near majestic rays of sunlight bursting through the tops of aged trees and listening to the soft crunch of the earth beneath her feet. Time walking under their canopy was too good to pass up. When her dad did have to work, she left him at home, opting to head out on solo journeys. Returning to the miles-long trails gave her both an emotional boost and sense of stability in an uncertain time. Her backdoor was her wardrobe; the woods beyond the house, her Narnia. She only had to walk through to enter a world that felt all her own.

And it was just that: her own. On March 17, just days after her return home, the National Park Service closed Muir Woods. It stayed closed until June 29. But Hannah, living so close and knowing the trails so well, had a built-in workaround. The joy in her voice was pure and palpable as she described sneaking into a national park: "They shut down the state parks, even national parks, at one point during COVID. For us, that was actually not the worst thing. There's no parking there, but we can walk up. We can run or walk or whatever in those parks. They were basically empty, but we were still able to access them, which was really nice. If anything, we had even more of an incentive to go outside, to take advantage. I could be the only one in these beautiful spaces." Hannah admitted, almost in passing, and without any real conviction, that "maybe we shouldn't have broken into Muir Woods, but we would be the only ones there, which is super rare. . . . It's usually just packed with people." Hannah took restrictions as an invitation, even calling closures an incentive. COVID-19 transformed public land into a private oasis for Hannah.[2]

Not all students were so lucky: Samantha, who loves finding new alternative musical artists for her runs, was not. While Hannah kept her head toward the horizon when she returned home, Samantha kept her head on a swivel. She hails from a small town nestled between Toledo, Ohio, and Columbus, Ohio. "We don't walk around my neighborhood," she states with a knowing look. She and her siblings didn't do so when she was growing up. And it was as much habit, and protective strategy, now as it was then. "Even nowadays, I'm 20, almost 21, I wouldn't walk a half mile down my road for safety reasons."

Samantha is a runner's runner. Distance was—and remains—her forte. "I was a very serious cross-country runner back in high school. And middle school," she noted with pride. The joy remained. "I still continue to do leisure running, especially up and down the Charles River," she said. Coming to Harvard brought unexpected bonuses to her outdoor excursions. The clean air was a big one. Samantha traded the chemical plants of her small Ohio town, and their perpetually billowing grey clouds, for the tree-lined paths along the river. Fall was her favorite time; her chosen route lined with reds, golds, and yellows. Except for the bothersome geese that sometimes nip at your ankles, and the bells

BEYOND THESE WALLS   55

of aggressive bikers, Samantha said that there is nothing like hitting your stride along the water. Deep breaths and long strides came easy.

Our conversation then took a somber turn. "It was kind of a shock coming to Boston and Harvard." The order of her words—city then school—was significant. Looking deflated, Samantha said home is "very desolate, a lot of empty buildings, not much downtown life"—the kind of place that allows delinquency to grow unchecked. Although she lives adjacent to what the uninitiated would consider a beautiful bike path, she dares not stray too far from her front yard. While others might focus on the roses, she saw the thorns. Leaning forward to the point where her black and white hair obscured her face, Samantha repeated her fear of not going "too far away from my house for safety concerns." Sitting up, stroking her furrowed brow, she continued, "I run about a quarter mile down and a quarter mile back. . . . I kind of lap around a few times. A quarter mile down a few times, like I said, because of safety concerns. . . . There's gang violence, as well as robberies, as well as Toledo is a big sex trafficking capital. There's a lot of stuff with that. So, especially being a younger female, it's not the best idea. It's just known to *not* be outside alone."

From running miles along the Charles River, with its bends and turns, to quarter-mile clips, going home for Samantha meant a more circumscribed existence. "It's a big difference," she bemoaned. Samantha had no illusions, as she prepared to leave, about what awaited her. "Home was more unequal and more dangerous, to put it bluntly, than areas like Cambridge," Samantha explained. In fact, one of the largest sex-trafficking stings in the state's history would happen a few months later. She knew her return would be more of a regression than a retreat. After all, she knew her city well—it was the only place she had ever known. And yet, when she did return home, she was still surprised at just how small her world became, just how closed-in she felt.[3]

Two students. Two communities. Two different worlds. Hannah got more exercise, relieving herself of the stresses brought upon by the pandemic. Samantha got less exercise, and the reasons why left her more troubled than tranquil. It is safe to say that most students at Harvard take the ability to walk through their neighborhood as a given (even if that neighborhood isn't a national park). But for a growing number of students at Harvard, and other elite colleges who aggressively recruit first-generation and lower-income students, to stretch one's legs is a luxury laced with danger.[4]

Previously, we explored students' unequal returns to the families they were born into. Now we'll explore how they navigated the family that they inherited—their communities. Some at Harvard take for granted that community and security are synonymous, that their streets and sidewalks provide sanctuary from social ills. Others know that safety can never be presumed. While students all occupy one physical campus, they come from depressingly different worlds.[5]

Knowing more about the intricacies of the communities that students come from—and remain connected to while enrolled—permits a more nuanced understanding of the inequalities that continue to shape students' lives when they come to campus, especially the worries that tax their minds and undermine their well-being. For many, closures equated to a one-way ticket to communities that—long before the pandemic—were struggling with unemployment, crumbling infrastructure, and violence. COVID-19 disruptions made all those things worse, amplifying structural failings and making it nearly impossible to focus on classes and coursework. As we'll see, no matter where students are, whether they are taking classes in person or virtually, what happens at home affects what happens on campus.[6]

Out and About

When I asked affluent students about leaving campus and returning home, the first thing that several mentioned was a sense of calm from being out and about in their neighborhoods. For many, it had been years since they rode their bikes down nearby streets, played in the treehouses of neighbors' backyards, or jumped on the trampolines that allowed peeks above the manicured hedges. This throwback to childhood was joyous, a bright spot of whimsy amid mounting uncertainty. One student even unknowingly quoted the theme song from the sitcom *Cheers*—he realized more than ever before that his neighborhood was "a place to take a break from all your worries and where everyone knows your name."[7]

More than anything, though, it was a heartening reprieve from Zoom. As March turned into April, this sentiment grew. May brought more than flowers; final exams and end of semester projects inched ever closer. Logging in—for what quickly felt like all day, every day—was exhausting, physically and emotionally. Having an exit strategy from the computer, especially one that took them outside, was a lifeline.

Hannah (UI,W), for example, felt especially safe going out. Or perhaps better said, Hannah never even considered the possibility that she would be unsafe. It was not just the woods that helped her feel comfortable venturing outside of her spacious home. In addition to enjoying the vastness of nature, her sprawling neighborhood was a wealthy, White enclave offset from the city—accessible to San Francisco, but a world away. Soon after reminiscing about Muir Woods, she offered one of the rare instances of wealthier students acknowledging their privilege. Hannah explained, "I live in an incredibly safe area. And I'm a White woman." Going further, she shared, "I've always felt pretty safe in that identity. So, I think living in a safe area and being White, I can't even begin to say I would experience any of the things that so many people in America, especially right now, have been experiencing."

Although Hannah focused on her being White and a woman, it was also her parents' considerable wealth that made other protections possible. Her neighborhood was a shelter—it made pandemic living possible, even easy. Her streets were wide, open, and tree lined. She had enough neighbors to not feel alone, but never so many to be worried about feeling crowded. Those harrowing early months were a little less daunting when you could still walk your dog and chat with your neighbors at a comfortable distance. From early morning runs to late-night walks, everyone there was free to move about the community.

The word "quiet" often came up as privileged students talked about their communities. Hope (UI,W) comes from a "little neighborhood" about thirty miles outside of Chicago, where everyone was White, wealthy, and "I think people were just friendlier." As weeks turned into months, Hope started to feel a little closed in. She was used to being on the go, coming and going as she pleased; high school had been one extracurricular after another. College reinforced this independence. She is a three-sport athlete, accustomed to rushing between not only classes and clubs but also practices. When she moved back home, she pleaded with her parents to let her go to the exclusive gym two miles from their home. She made her case. They refused—too crowded, too dangerous. Tensions rose. Then they offered an olive branch: a Peloton bike. Hope's training was back on track—delayed but not derailed. Shrugging her muscular shoulders, she joked how adding the Peloton really helped "transition" their workout room into "more of a home gym situation." She extended her indoor cycling with outdoor adventures with her family; especially in the "summer we got to do a lot outside and go for long bike rides together."

There is an intimacy in the way that Hope speaks of home. "My parents are my best friends," she said. But it was more than her parents that made her return easy. She recalled falling back in love with her local community as if she were reunited with a high school crush. "We've got great neighbors," she said with the sense that she couldn't imagine anything else. "If you walk out our back door, you can see right into our neighbor's backyard." And what she saw made her smile then as it did during our interview six months later, "Over the summer, they built a trampoline!"

Moreover, Hope ventured out, first alone and then with family, first for short periods and then long. Her spirits lifted as simple hellos blossomed into opportunities to "stand on opposite sides of the of street" or "sit and chat for 30 minutes, just chatting, seeing how everyone's doing, because no one really had anywhere to go." It became her new ritual with her parents. They did not go alone; they, like many of their neighbors, took the four-legged members of their family along. Hope enjoyed passing all the "big yards. Everything's pretty spread out. There's a lot of dogs! We would go on a lot of walks. We would take our dogs! Every night we'd go on about an hour to hour and a half long walk with our dogs. And we would just pass so many people walking their dogs." When asked about how her community fared, Hope didn't have any specifics but was confident in her declaration that people fared well because "mostly everyone I talked to just transitioned to remote work." As she knew more concretely, most of the neighborhood was like her parents—a lawyer and a consultant—and had the option to work from home. Even the possibility of getting COVID-19 didn't seem like it would disrupt their lives much: "I'm from a pretty well-off town. There's some incredible hospitals around, too. Everyone had good access to health care should they need it."

Alice (UI,W), like Hannah and Hope, also found great comfort in being outside. The pandemic was not easy for Alice. She found herself inexplicably tired and more stressed by online classes than she ever felt when she was on campus. She was an in-person learner and thrived off contact with others. When asked what she did to cope, she looked on quizzically. "I've just sort of continued living my life," she retorted. In addition to working out, sleeping seven hours a night, and journaling, Alice would "take a lot of walks . . . these are things that I've always done to deal with stress." When she wanted to get her heart rate up, "I would go for runs around my neighborhood. There's enough space in my house to work out. It was not a problem. It changed my exercise routine not at all." Her walks and runs were therapeutic and continued almost completely uninterrupted. Alice and her father would walk their dogs and see people out. The accounts she got from her mother, who was on the neighborhood council, were also positive, both economically and physically. "A lot of people have jobs that are COVID-stable, if you will," she said. As an afterthought, she mentioned that, according to reports, no one in her community contracted COVID-19 in the early days, and she wasn't aware of many cases since returning to campus almost a year later.

As we talked in March 2021, Alice reflected on the first year of the pandemic. Revealing the protective power of privilege, Alice shared that it was only when she returned to campus, after almost a year away, that COVID-19 seemed like a perilous presence. Walking through Johnston Gate, one of the main entrances to Harvard Yard, was when the virus seemed, for the first time, "extremely close" to her own life. The university's COVID-19 protocol "rules literally every action," she said with a scowl. Home had been free from such restrictions.

Privileged Asian, Black, Latino, Native, and some mixed-race students spoke about similar protections granted to them by their more affluent communities. Unlike their White peers, however, there were caveats. With a mix of emotions, although mostly anger and sadness, they shared how racism, interpersonal and structural, pierced even their relatively sheltered enclaves. Emily (UI,B) comes from an affluent community in Austin, Texas, that is like an eye: Black at the center with a White periphery. Her neighbors are "doctors, lawyers, people in finance." One thing that Emily loves about her community is that everything is at her fingertips: the "post office is right at our disposal, policemen patrol our streets to make sure we don't have any security issues," and there are "tons of food places within walking distance, local grocery store, banks." With a smile, she noted, "We honestly have everything. We have more than you could need. It's a pretty safe, well-off community, I would say." People were doing quite well. She noted, "It just speaks to the type of neighborhood we have, we felt comfortable and safe to be able to go out of our homes and walk and enjoy ourselves given the pandemic." The pandemic, however, was not always her biggest worry.[8]

Emily knew that privilege doesn't protect all those with money equally. Even with her high school varsity letters for track and field, Emily was nervous to run down the open, public roads. Even something as simple as getting exercise, a light jog to end the day, felt shaped by race. She went out, but with hesitation and a gnawing feeling at the pit of her stomach. "For me, Ahmaud Arbery, his death was the one that really shook me the most," Emily said when speaking about her evening runs. "I go running outside my neighborhood all the time, and the fact that you could just be running, minding your own business, and someone could shoot you? That's scary. Like, don't go running by yourself when the sun's about to go down."

Arbery was a high school athlete just like Emily, which made it hit even closer to home. He was killed on February 23, 2020, but the video surfaced online on May 5, launching the local case to national news. Learning of Arbery's murder, at the hands of three White men, and watching the video of their brazen vigilantism, made the dividing line— invisible yet detectable—between her little community and her larger neighborhood even more pronounced. Emily wanted to get some exercise, to try and stay fit. Yet that simple act was laced with worries that her White peers did not have to consider. Her disdain deepened as she considered how much her parents had worked—to overcome disadvantage in their own childhoods, to own their own home, to achieve financial security. "Even though you live here, you have a house here, all they see is your skin color."[9]

Emily's words remind me of what so many children of color have heard at grandparents' knees: "Outside is for White people." Not because people of color inherently dislike the great outdoors, but because of a learned fear of what it means to be in any—let alone the wrong—place at the wrong time. We saw this in 2020 in Central Park when Amy Cooper verbally accosted Christian Cooper (no relation), an avid and accomplished bird watcher, and even called the police on him with false allegations of intimidation all because he asked her to leash her dog, which the Central Park Conservancy mandates in "A Dog's Guide to Central Park." Accounts such as these abound. Moreover, the history of U.S. national parks—"the best idea we ever had," as novelist and conservationist Wallace Stegner famously put it—is littered with the policing of Black and Indigenous people, especially as Jim Crow–era policies prevented people of color from using public spaces and punished those who did. It is haunting how Hannah (UI,W) felt comfortable roaming a closed Muir Woods, a park named after John Muir, a documented racist and segregationist, while Emily was scared to jog just a few streets beyond the boundary of her little Black enclave.[10]

Similarly, Mary (UI,B) recognized the undefined yet ever-present boundaries of her community. She is a daughter of the Deep South and is keenly invested in studying racial inequality in the region. Her neighborhood is "definitely walkable, definitely one of those upper middle-class, out-of-a-magazine type of neighborhoods." According to her parents' telling, it was entirely White until the early 1990s, when there was a wave of White flight and Black resettlement. By the time she and her family moved in, it was a full-on, well-to-do, connected Black enclave. Every BBQ and birthday party, by default, included everyone on the block. The parents, like their children, were extremely close and remained connected even as the children went off to college. Mary was as much at home at her house as her neighbors' and at the local park. Like Hope (UI,W) and Julie (UI,W), she and her parents "started taking a lot of family walks together and bike rides" to end their long days. Her mother, ever the one to take things to the next level, would challenge everyone to keep up with her. "She's like, 'I'm going to run.' We just wanted to walk. Nobody's trying to race you right now," Mary said with a healthy laugh. But Mary also knew that she lived in a Black quarter of a White town: "When you leave our neighborhood: the glances from the older, White people or 'I'm walking on this sidewalk; I'm not going to move.' Like, what!?! Stuff like that. It's very interesting the type of community we have within our neighborhood."

While their White counterparts talked about the neighborhoods as one entity, a general collective of sorts, affluent students of color spoke about pockets of protection. Their immediate streets, or a certain collection of houses, were where they felt safest. Yes, there were cute boutique shops selling knickknacks and specialty ice creams. Yes, the streets were kept clean and the lampposts adorned with seasonal decorations. But proximity to home mattered; danger still lurked just beyond invisible boundaries.

The experiences of Emily and Mary, in turn, are the exceptions that prove the racial rule. Their relatively protected neighborhoods surely would have felt like a dream to most families of color with just a bit less money. Because of the deep-set racism of American real estate, middle- and upper-middle-class families of color do not have the same purchasing power as their White counterparts. Moreover, as historian Keeanga-Yamahtta Taylor shows, banks, regulators, and real estate industry leaders continued to exploit Black families long after redlining and other discriminatory practices were banned in the late 1960s, further undermining the mobility of Black families across the country. Even when families do have the resources, as sociologist Karyn Lacy shows, wanting neighbors that looked like them more often meant more mixed-income communities than the more exclusive enclaves of their White peers. One result is that they do not have as much distance from places with higher rates of disorder.[11]

This was true for Angelica (UI,B). She was an avid tennis player. She preferred the hard court but had a soft spot for clay. These are where she had spent most of her adolescent days. But she lost all that when she came home, and not just because she no longer had access to Harvard's well-kept facilities. "My dad was like, 'You guys need to get out of the house. Do something.'" Sure, everyone wanted to get out of the house. The question, however, became, "Do what?" The question was not just a result of the pandemic. The local area was not always the safest. The loitering men made her feel uneasy; too-long looks from their red-tinted eyes made her skin crawl. "What we did, my sister, my mom, and I, we'd go on a walk at the park right across the street. The park, it's a little dangerous. It was good that she was there to supervise, making sure we're not going near anyone. . . . She was watching." Their walk in the park was no walk in the park. They had to be on alert. Angelica really wanted to find time to play tennis. But it wasn't always possible, even under her mother's watchful eye. "I play tennis; I didn't play for a long time. That's the longest time I've ever gone without playing."

Shelter in Place

Lower-income students, as we know, had no illusions about what awaited them at home. After all, Harvard had been their way to escape—not necessarily home itself, but the conditions that made being home hard. While their more affluent peers talked about night walks and evening bike rides, lower-income students offered no such reverie. They knew not to let the streetlights catch them out. Instead of families walking dogs that invited pats, they avoided stray animals that patrolled the streets.[12]

For Samantha (LI,M), the uncertainties of home were always on her mind. In high school, violence was common enough that the local school board changed its dress code policy "due to issues concerning colors and associations with gangs." Officials mandated uniforms, a first, because "kids were leaving school wearing a regular T-shirt and being stopped, questioned, and assaulted." Sometimes calls from her family reminded her that, even though she was now 2,000 miles away on

Harvard's campus, with both Securitas security guards and campus police patrolling the area that warded off some types of dangers, her family
remained in harm's way.

Poverty doesn't stay in one place. Long before the pandemic closed
campus, problems at home made their way to Harvard. As poor students
across the country can attest, even getting into one of the most acclaimed
colleges did not spare students, or their families, from local terrors. With
a wry smile Samantha shared a "funny" story: "I get a call from my family.
They were about to go to bed. Suddenly they hear a loud noise. Turns
out there's a bullet hole in the house. A stray bullet went into the house.
Luckily, no one was injured, but it was in a path that could have injured
someone. It went through the outside wall, went kind of across the stair-
way, and got lodged into the other side of the wall."

Samantha laughed, albeit halfheartedly, but when her phone unexpectedly rang that night, late and loud, she was not laughing. Samantha
knew something was wrong. And so did her roommates, seeing the
color drain from her already pale face. All the previous calls that came
in like that almost always brought bad news. It was a pattern, as regular
as it was disruptive. Her mind went straight to the worst-case scenario.
She was not that far off. Fortunately, no one in her family was physically
injured. Nevertheless, the scars, emotional and physical, remain. She
would run her fingers over the hole just a few weeks later, when campus
closed. When Samantha got off the phone and told her roommates,
"who are from more well-off areas of Boston," what happened and how
often stuff like that happened in her neighborhood, one of them responded, without thinking, "I've only heard of that in movies."

Another student, August (LI,L), lightly tanned with a chiseled jaw-
line, is pierced and curly haired. His tattoos connect to his Indigenous
Chicano roots. His mane, effortlessly loose, is just his style. Like
Samantha, August waited, albeit subconsciously, for calls from home.
He knew his community on the South Side of Chicago struggled. "For
me, I don't live in a fairy tale world like a lot of privileged students at
Harvard do. I'm very well aware of the ill nastiness in the world and how
a lot of things have manifested historically." He also knew that his family
would sometimes not tell him things as they happened, wanting to spare

him of the details of life outside their four walls. But he got the updates, nonetheless. August downloaded Citizen, the mobile app that provides community safety updates and notifications. It sends alerts if there is fire or water main break, but more common for August were the notifications about gunshots, robberies, and stabbings. In more ways than one, the app almost never brought good news. Just different types of bad. It highlights "when literally people are dying." August told me, "I literally get at least two notifications a week of a gunshot within my radius. Whatever. I'm not trying to portray Chicago like that, but where I live, it's like that. Literally, a week ago, at 2:00 in the morning, got a notification that there was a woman screaming in the middle of the street, shaking a machete."

While at school, the app helps him keep up with what is happening around his family. When he returned home, where he remained for a year and half, the app helped him keep up with what was going on right outside his window. Some people use the Citizen app as a heads up on what places to stay away from or what roads to avoid. In other words, where not to go. For August, that was not possible. His house, his block, was right in the middle of constant activity. There was no alternative destination. No detour. It was just home. Throwing his hands up, he said, frustrated and tired, "That's normal to me. That's normal to me."

What is normal to some is unthinkable for others. This experience was especially true for Snow (LI,N). Snow sat perched on her chair, holding one knee to her chest. She was comfortable, as if she sat like this often. Her long, dark brown hair fell loosely over her shoulders. She adjusted it frequently, arranging it over one shoulder and then the other, braiding and unbraiding the ends with her nimble fingers. She cherished a glimpse of home, a single feather, a kaleidoscope of cool blues and greys, a symbol of her tribe and a most treasured possession. It was one of the few traces of home that she held dear. So much of home consisted of other things—things that she wished she could, not necessarily forget, but wished no one had to experience. Shifting both her hair and seating, Snow tried to explain the challenges of going home. She said, "It wasn't so much the schoolwork or even being virtual. A lot of Native students feel this—this is a documented phenomenon—but it's walking in two worlds. When I'm at Harvard, home seems like this abstract place. And when I'm at home, Harvard seems like this abstract place. It was really weird and just unsettling to have them mix together." As Snow's worlds collided, she felt stuck in the middle.

The Great Plains were her home. Pastoral and peaceful, at least from afar. It was where her reservation, which sits on the border of the United States and Canada, resided. It hurt her to return. Her voice dipped as she started and restarted her explanation of what made home hard, a prelude to her pain. She loved her community. They looked after each other; everyone knew everyone and was willing to help. The problem was that so many people needed help—help that went beyond what any neighbors could provide. They were living in the long shadow of a brutal history: land theft, forced resettlement, political disenfranchisement. Unemployment was high. Substance abuse ran rampant. Fights were common. Each a legacy of the pain of past generations:[13] "I come from a reservation. It's a very poor community with a lot of violence, drug, and alcohol problems. It's a very unique community. Obviously, in my life, I've had my own traumas. To have to be home, trying to do my Harvard school work while being surrounded by all these negative factors really proved to be weighing on my mental health. I actually ended up just taking three classes last semester. I just—it was really hard for me to find balance between home life and academic life."

Snow's only recourse was to take the next semester off. Home didn't give her many options, and the options she did have there came with their own set of challenges. "It's very, very rural. There's not really rental properties; I ended up staying in this really rundown house. The people who lived there before me were drug dealers. It was really bad. It was not safe." When asked why she rented instead of staying with family, she stated, words catching in her throat, more from anger than sadness, "That's where I had to live; I didn't want to expose my grandparents to anything." She was adamant about her grandparents isolating, even though she could not. She had to work.[14]

Snow revealed that she couldn't live with her mother, despite her being in the same sleepy town. It was too risky. She got a preview, or perhaps more accurately, a reminder, of just how dicey things could get when her mother, for a time, moved into the house next door. They had not seen eye to eye for years. Snow invested in her studies. Her mother focused on her drugs. Her mother's actions, aided by pandemic closures, brought a host of other problems, literally, to her doorstep.

> The pandemic, the isolation, and the stress of it all has been more difficult for different people in my family. I live next door to my mom, and I think it's caused her to make a lot of bad decisions. My biggest concern is her proximity to dangerous people, and the danger that she could bring into my life, my grandparents' life, my little cousins'. . . . Her and her friends are involved with drugs. There would be people pulling in and out in the middle of the night. One time, I was in class, and one of her friends was looking for her. He came and knocked on my door. I was home alone. And this was a really rough-looking guy. I just remember being very scared and obviously unable to continue with the lecture that day; I was worried about this drugged-out dude outside my house. Just a lot of little things like that, and just always being on edge, and feeling like I never knew when something could go wrong because of her and the people she was choosing to engage with. That just threw a wrench in my academic life.

It was hard for Snow to focus, at least on schoolwork. Instead, her attention often traveled away from Renaissance art to knocks on the door, the real ones and the potential ones. She knew just how many people traveled down their street and up her steps, looking for their daily fix. The coming and going of her mother's friends kept her up at night and on high alert all day. She missed more than the one lecture, forced to hunker down in the house out of sight.

Neighborhood woes kept many students up. Dawn (LI,B) is a huge devotee of all things theater, from melodramas to musicals. She talked excitedly about pretty much everything, especially Black artistic expression. Dawn showed similar excitement speaking about her natural hair journey. She just started Sisterlocks, and within five minutes of meeting me she began explaining why I should lock my growing hair, too. Speaking about her rough home life and the emotional upheavals she had witnessed dispelled a little of that enthusiasm. She had "lived in six different apartments in my lifetime, and four of them in the same neighborhood" near Cleveland, Ohio, one that had long been in a steady state of decline. That count omitted the three homeless and domestic violence shelters that she and her mom had spent months living in since Dawn was young.

When I asked Dawn how the transition to Zoom classes was going, she brushed off the question. That transition was easy compared to dealing with the rest of her life. What she wanted to talk about was how constricted she felt. Dawn fixated on what leaving Cambridge had meant for her. "I would see nothing but poverty." But it went beyond that; the fear of harm was ever-present. Echoing Samantha (LI,M), who forfeited therapeutic runs upon returning home, Dawn said flatly, "I purposefully don't walk around my neighborhood alone." In 2019 the Bureau of Alcohol, Tobacco, Firearms, and Explosives (more commonly known as ATF) designated her community as a "high violent crime area" because of the number of shootings and the amount of gun-related activity. Things have only spiraled since then. The way she felt at Harvard is a world apart. When she described being at Harvard, her words were slow and steady, weighty with reflection:

> I feel relatively, quote unquote, "safe" here, even though no part of the world is really safe. The same things that go boom in the night in my neighborhood, don't go boom in the night up here, you know? There is a level of safety up here; I can move around more freely. When I heard the notification, it was just, *OK, I know I don't feel safe walking around my neighborhood. That means when I go home, I'm going to be at home, in our two-bedroom apartment, for 90 percent of every day for who knows how long....* That was just disconcerting, to go from having as much freedom to walk around to immediately being back in that constricted space. I didn't have time to prepare for that mentality.

COVID-19 pulled the rug from under Dawn's feet. Dawn's words speak to a reality that many lower-income students face year after year: the breaks in a semester can mean breaches in security. The pandemic was not the only time that students are asked—or mandated—to leave. As we know, many schools shut down their campuses for shorter breaks like Thanksgiving and spring recesses, and many more shut down their campuses for longer intervals, like winter break and most of the summer. The difference, as Dawn noted, is that those days are preset, known long in advance. Students have time to develop a game plan. COVID-19 was different. And it hit harder.

Importantly, what makes home "that constricting space" goes beyond there not being "much room" in their tiny apartment, where the kitchen is "just the stove and the counter" and too small for her and her mom to fit at the same time. It was, just as important, the consequences of living in a segregated community with "dilapidated, grungy buildings" where "I've seen people arrested; I've seen cops just sitting there watching the building, seemingly waiting for something to happen." She dreaded the stray dogs that prowled the streets, searching for scraps. She feared the men, breath stale with alcohol even early in the morning, who had catcalled her since she was thirteen years old, as she made her way to the library.

Her angst also spawned from neighbors handling private disputes publicly. Dawn and her mother developed inventive strategies to stay safe. They literally mounted their defense. In one apartment, Dawn shares that "whenever there were arguments in the hallway or gunshots outside, we would roll our couch up in front of the door. If anyone came trying to get into the door, they would have to go through the couch. And then we would go sleep on the floor in my mom's room."

For Dawn, such disruptions were nothing new. They were the one constant in a consistent stream of changes. In fact, closures captured the reality of her neighborhood. She spoke tenderly of spaces in her community where life once thrived. She lamented how her community seemed to be emptying out more and more rapidly. "Every time I go back, I notice that things are not as kept up as they used to be, like the recreation centers I used to go to." The Dollar General, robbed numerous times, was not the only building with wood planks as stand-ins for busted windows. Dawn admitted that "obviously, because of COVID, things are affected, but all the public pools were closed over the past five years. Recreational spaces for inner-city kids to go to have been shut down." These places weren't pretty or well maintained, but they were crucial features of her life, places she went to study, exercise, and see her friends—places that were quieter and safer than home. These were the places where she discovered her love for reading and learning, where she won the library's "Best Reader" award when she was in elementary school. The money for these centers started running out long before the pandemic started and all but evaporated during lockdown. The one program that remained is the soup kitchen that occurs every Tuesday and Thursday, where the lines were getting longer and rowdier each week.

"Just the memory and uncomfortability of those things made me less likely to walk outside," she said, seeming to deplore the reality of this statement even as it came out of her mouth. Dawn sat stiffly on her bed, squeezing a black-and-white plaid pillow so tightly that it looked more like an hourglass than a checkerboard. "There's always something going on. Every week." As she talked, her voice rose; she was practically yelling, although I'm not sure whether it was out of anger or sadness. While home, in just one week's time, "a kid had gotten shot as he was playing with his dad's gun, somebody got robbed, somebody's house got broke into. There's always something going on. Always on the news."

COVID-19 compounded those problems. As in many communities across the country, there was an uptick in crime. Reports show that firearm-related homicides in 2020 hit heights that the nation had not seen since 1994. But shootings have always been a problem in Dawn's community. She explained, "There is just a lot of gun violence where I live. Since the pandemic, it's been increasing. A lot. They've seen a 50-percent increase in gun violence over the past year and a half. But prior to that, there was a lot of it. It's not to say that every time you're walking outside, you're going to hear gunshots, but it's every other day or maybe twice a week."[15]

For lower-income students, we often focus on how hard leaving for college is. We chronicle not only the tearful goodbyes but also the fraught relationships with a tempestuous place and the difficulties of maintaining a connection with home. We pay too little attention to what happens in students' home communities, as the ripple effects of local problems reach far upstream. It is not just about the people. Place matters. College and home, as students noted, felt like two different worlds. Lower-income students were exposed to a host of dangers that their more affluent peers were not. As Samantha (LI,M) noted, she sees things in her daily life at home that her Harvard classmates only see in movies. The students I spoke with had all started to get accustomed to college, albeit in different ways. Some students, especially those from lower-income families, came to like it, not only because of its privileges, although they were important, but also because of the basic security it provided them, something their peers generally took for granted.

(Not So) Sick and Shut In

For some students, the virus that caused all this disruption was a distant worry, even at the height of the pandemic. For others, it was a constant presence, even as things began opening back up. This unevenness, not surprisingly, was directly related to a student's degree of privilege. The area where Hannah (UI,W) lived was, as she put it, "doing super well," both before and throughout the pandemic. Starting in March 2020 her neighborhood definitely moved at a slower pace but generally was free from the burdens of lockdowns and distant from reported cases. In fact, Hannah did not know of a single case in her community. As with the rest of the United States, and the world for that matter, COVID-19 was less successful at infiltrating sprawling, multimillion-dollar houses. Spacious backyards and access to outdoor space, it turns out, proved a remarkable vaccine. Her neighbors—"a lot of people work in Silicon Valley, in tech, or in banking. I have a few friends whose dads are lawyers"—like her family, had ample resources to be nimble, to change habits and sched-ules, to account for the pandemic but not radically alter their lives. They also had the resources to fortify their houses against the virus. Access to masks was easy; adoption was near universal. They had the flexibility to work from home. Many were already getting groceries delivered from local butchers and specialty stores. They had the space, both inside and out, and both for work and for pleasure, to spread out.

The simple absence of COVID-19 from these communities—or at the least, from students' perceptions of their communities—was par-ticularly striking. Thomas (UI,W), head tilted in a way that threw his five o'clock shadow into greater relief, described his historic Boston neighborhood with great fondness. When reflecting on how his neighbors fared during the pandemic, he said, "I think people have fared pretty well. People were concerned about getting it. But I don't know if a lot of people did." With similar nonchalance about what was going on around them, Piccadilly (UI,B) noted that his neighborhood fared "pretty decently." He knew "some people," but there were no tell-tale signs of crisis. "There wasn't—my neighborhood was never, I guess, a hot spot for COVID-19. Of course, some people got it. Some people got sick, but I don't actually think—I mean, people probably did die in the area. But I don't know of anyone who did die of COVID-19. But I'm pretty sure some people definitely did get it." For all his certainty, Piccadilly remained unsure. But that combination—only a hazy understanding of what was actually happening to the people around him but a certainty that things were pretty much okay—spoke volumes.

Another student, June (UI,A), loves color. Her fondness for vibrant tones is evident in the acrylics she uses for her paintings—chronicling intimate moments exploring her Asian American identity. She offered a similar refrain as her privileged Harvard peers: "We lived in a town where people were doing well enough that our hospital wasn't overflowing and at capacity." This wasn't just hearsay. She heard it from her dad, who is a doctor at the hospital. "My dad would come home and say, 'We have three floors dedicated for COVID patients, and we barely filled up one part of one floor.'" In general, COVID-19, the virus, did not enter June's immediate world, although the rise of animus against Asian Americans did give her pause. Her assessment was simple: "We had a decent amount of scares," but none of them materialized into actual cases. In fact, when speaking about those who contracted COVID-19, it was as if she were playing Six Degrees of Separation—COVID edition. "I knew a lot of people who just knew someone else, but I didn't ever know that person."

For Black, Latino, and Native as well as mixed-race upper-income students, COVID-19 was more successful at infiltrating their communities, although not at the rates of their lower-income peers. Although they have more money, long-standing patterns of racial residential segregation made their networks more susceptible to the virus than their affluent White counterparts. Denzel (UI,B) enjoys exploring cities. When he travels, he gets off the beaten track to understand how people move through the winding streets. Like many middle- and upper-middle-class Black families, not all members of his own family were as financially well off. Denzel's parents were the first generation in their family to earn a comfortable living. Not all of his aunts and uncles, whether blood or fictive, could say the same. Not surprisingly, his family lived in communities—and went to churches and belonged to community organizations—that were more socioeconomically diverse. This diversity translated into a much wider range of exposure to COVID-19. As we talked, he grew frustrated, thinking back to that early belief, common in communities of color, that COVID-19 did not affect Black people.[16]

> We definitely knew of family, friends, church people who were just dropping like flies. We were like, "Man, what is going on?" I distinctly remember that transition from, for whatever reason it was, you know, "Black people don't get Corona." It didn't seem as though any of us were getting sick, and then all of a sudden those communities—our communities—start getting hit the hardest. We're like "Oh, whoa, when did that happen?" So yeah, there was definitely that reality. And then with older grandparents, too, how do we take care of them? How are we able to get things to them? Should we stay over there at their house or do we just deliver food from a distance?

Denzel's world became a series of realizations and concerns. COVID-19 is here. How can we take care of this person? What do we do about that situation? The mental and emotional weight of trying to figure these things out left him reeling, distracted from classes and focused on how to take care of those in front of him. As the old saying goes, he didn't know if he was coming or going. The decisions were so numerous and came so quickly that he and his family didn't have much time to process what was going on.

Affluent students generally spoke a lot about COVID-19 in the world but infrequently about it entering their own corner of it. When they did, like June, it was at some distance. June described how her local hospital was overprepared and underused—a strange inversion of the horror stories that dominated the news. More affluent students of color, especially those who live in Black and Latino communities, however, felt it closer to home. COVID-19 spread through their networks. As Denzel noted, there was an initial delay that gave a false sense of security in many communities of color. But that feeling didn't last long. Reports of people contracting the virus, and of dying, weren't constant but were consistent enough to stoke fears and undermine well-being.

Everywhere You Look

My conversations with lower-income students could not have been more different. COVID-19 was unavoidable—a potent part of their communities. But that's not all. Their descriptions of the virus's impact on their communities were inseparable from the impact of, well, everything else on their communities. Problems of all kinds, virological and structural, became much more entrenched during the pandemic. There was no buffer from any of it. The emergent public health crisis simply exacerbated the already existing crises, and vice versa.

The twinned nature of COVID-19's chaos was clear as soon as lower-income students returned home. They saw it not just in their families but in almost every aspect of neighborhood life, even as they sheltered inside for protection—both from the pandemic and the problems that predated it. As Samantha (LI,M) noted, her community was already dealing with "small and big inequalities, even before COVID." Many of her neighbors did not have jobs. And among those who did, many lost them. She said, "I feel like everyone—a lot of people went home" from their jobs. One neighbor, a truck driver, went from always being gone to always being home. By the time we spoke in February 2021, many of the people on her block had already contracted COVID-19. Partly because of their jobs on factory floors that had terrible ventilation and partly because of "their actions," as she put it—"I feel like they're not really adhering to guidelines." In addition to knowing "a number of my neighbors, just within like 10 houses, have contracted COVID," her aunt and

uncle also contracted it. As service workers, one a manager at a local
Chili's and the other a front desk worker at a Holiday Inn, they had no
choice but to go to work. They faced threats of termination if they failed
to do so. However, the precautions in place and the protective equipment available were weak and in short supply, respectively.[17]

Similarly, Sofia (LI,L) shared how COVID-19 "definitely feels very
close," even as no one in her house contracted the virus. "Coming from
a community where a lot of our family friends are essential workers,"
she explained, "a lot of them were contracting COVID. It definitely was
a very constant thing in our lives." One of her favorite families was hit
particularly hard. Quarantining wasn't always possible for them because
"they have three kids, and their husband's always at work." The mother
babysat community kids to bring in needed money. Sofia and her family
stepped in to help them out. They made dinners for the family and care
packages for the kids "and small things like that." With mixed emotions,
half fondly and half sadly, she recalled running up to their front porches
to drop off the packages. Each trip from the car to the front door had an
audience: the kids looking on, waving eagerly from just beyond the window. Sofia's generosity was not a one-time thing. "Our community is
definitely very tight-knit, family friends. It was much more likely that
they were going to contract COVID because of just the jobs that they're
in and the people that they come in contact with." Working from home
was not an option, especially as many of the men in her community
worked as day laborers.

Dawn (LI,B) was less connected to those in her neighborhood than
Sofia, but that didn't change the fact that she saw the toll COVID-19 was
taking on them. "When I got back, I could tell people are feeling it."
Going further, she said that "when I'm looking at my community, I'm
looking at my own family." Her aunt contracted COVID-19 early on, and
it scared Dawn. But she continued that what "is really interesting to me"
is that "I felt the economic impact of the pandemic a lot more than I felt
pathogen-based aspects of this pandemic." Sheltering in place likely
limited her exposure to the virus, but the main reason she stayed inside
was out of fear of being caught up with the fights and robberies that
had become all too common. Her community, as early as April and

May 2020, had two to three times the number of COVID-19 cases as the wealthier, whiter surrounding areas. Dawn may be able to distinguish between firecrackers and gunshots, but differences between sirens are not so clear. She could not tell if the siren's source was the solo from the patrol cars she was used to hearing or if the persistent, piercing wail was really a duet of police and EMTs.

What was very clear, however, was the ripple effect through her extended family—"everyone in my family has been economically impacted by it." "Precarity" is the word Dawn used to describe their situation. Her aunts and uncles "lost their jobs, their kids had to get pulled out of school, and they had to figure out how to teach them while they're also doing their jobs." The few family members who were still employed "have to work all these crazy hours just to keep their jobs." And for those aunts and cousins who worked the "crazy hours," Dawn and her mother were their lifeline. Dawn, on top of being a student, became teacher, disciplinarian, and cook.

Marianne (LI,L), whose dimpled smile usually adorns her face, grappled with similar fears. For her, there was no escape. She lived in a small New York City apartment with her sisters and parents. Her room, which she shared with her sister, had one window. Usually, the curtains, which cast the room in muted tones, were closed to give them some sense of privacy. Those curtains, however, did nothing to block out the symphony of sirens from the streets below. Her window overlooked the primary route that ambulances took to the hospital. Sometimes she would catch herself looking out in wonder, sadness filling her heart, making it impossible to focus on classes. She saw the steady stream of ambulances speeding through the streets, like ants hurrying back to the colony. But it was the sounds, rather than the sights, that had a lasting impression.

Marianne's face was a study in despair as she reflected on the sirens. "It would be endless. It was heartbreaking. It was all people who live in Queens." She thought of her aunt who braved crowded soup kitchens to feed her baby cousins. She thought of her uncles and older cousins who had to use the subway and public transit to go to work. Queens, for Marianne, was family. "When we didn't hear them as much, we'd say

'Oh, tonight was a good night.'" She and her family participated in the tradition of banging pots at 7:00 P.M. in support of health care workers and to give them all, workers and her family alike, a bit of light during dark times. But she knew what awaited her a few hours later, when the pots and pans were placed back in the oven and her head found her pillow. For months, Marianne "went to sleep to sirens." They were both her lullaby and alarm clock.

Like Marianne, Snow's (LI, N) love for her community stayed strong. In some ways, it deepened during the pandemic. She knew that the traumas manifesting themselves around her were a legacy of the generations-long oppression and colonization of Native people. So often alcohol and drugs were an escape more than a malediction. Still, she hated seeing her community struggle. Unfortunately, she bore witness to some of the worst of it. With a proud look on her face, she shared that, despite limited resources, "our tribe has actually done a really good job with COVID-19 response. Whenever somebody does get COVID-19, our tribal leaders will bring two weeks' worth of supplies for them and their family." She proudly contrasted her reservation to the rest of the state, noting that "our community . . . was so different from the rest of the state; we're a sovereign nation. Our tribal council makes all the rules for us, so we had a mask mandate on the reservation. You have to wear a mask anytime you're in public on the reservation. But when you leave the reservation, the state did not have a mask mandate." An instant later, however, the smile slid from her face. "There was all these conspiracy theories that Native blood is immune to coronavirus, which is obviously just dumb. But once it did come to the reservation, it was really bad. People were getting sick. A lot of people died right away." The weight of the pandemic, made even heavier by longstanding poverty, crushed the tribal council's efforts.[18]

Her reservation, like many across the country, experienced death due to COVID-19 at alarming rates. Residents of reservations and Native communities were contracting the virus and dying at twice the rate of White communities. This is why some entities like Seattle Indian Health Board, exercising sovereignty, elected to lower the minimum age for the initial round of vaccinations from 65 to 50 based on the chronic health disparities present in urban Native American populations. Similarly, it was why tribes like Standing Rock Sioux Tribe and the Cherokee prioritized Native language speakers to preserve culture. Valiant efforts though they were, disparities in contraction and death continued. The disparity was especially great in the Midwest, where Snow is from, where the death rate was almost four times higher. But Snow did not need CDC statistics to know this fact. From solemn to angry, Snow shared how it felt like a double gut punch because the pandemic seemed to skip over the "White community adjacent to the reservation. I remember, at one point, this nurse said that ten people from the reservation had died, whereas none from this White community had died." The disparity made the losses in her own family stand out even more. "There were three deaths in my family, or very close to my family." The thing is, as Snow noted, everyone was family. "In my community, we're all very close knit. Everybody knows everybody," she said, the pride mixing with the pain.[19]

Just like life, death was a communal affair, too, one that brought on additional responsibilities for all members of the community, and especially Snow. Pulling her hair back to reveal a grimace, she shared, "There's rites that our culture partakes in whenever somebody passes away, and one of those things is a four-day, four-night fire. And, especially as a Native woman, I'm expected to help with the fire, to keep the fire even all night long, that kind of thing. And so, at that time, it became very difficult to balance school, and to say, 'I can't make it to class basically this whole week because I need to be fulfilling these roles in my community.'"

It soon became too much. Snow's grades began to drop. In addition to the ominous knocks on the door and her mother's illicit dealings, Snow's proximity to death deepened the heaviness of her fears and worries. Life was not the only thing that was surrendered to the pandemic. Elders who were often the first to die were also the culture bearers, those who kept oral traditions and language alive. She could not simply be a bystander. She did not want to sit on the sidelines, no matter how brutal it was to be at the center. Just as the tribal council helped those who contracted COVID-19 with food parcels so that they could stay home and recover, Snow, with pride and grace, fulfilled her community and cultural responsibilities by diligently tending to the fires. She was right there, day in and day out. With so many passing away in the community, the traditional fires were near permanent features on the bucolic, hilly landscape. Snow returned home many nights smelling of the smoke that accompanies this final rite of passage, lingering reminders of just how much her community had lost.[20]

Conclusion

Returning home after campus closed was tricky to navigate for everyone. It was a blow for all students. It is just that the severity of that blow differed. When scholars speak of home as it pertains to college, the conversation usually focuses on a specific spot—the house or apartment students live in—or a particular set of relationships. Neighborhoods and communities are often left out of these conversations. But to understand what influences undergraduate life, especially the hurdles that pop up along the way, we must account for both students' immediate families as well as neighborhood dynamics. This is not to say that one supplants the other, but rather to highlight that there are dual processes at play. Both family and community shape the fundamental aspects of undergraduate life.[21]

Wealthy students came from and returned to places that could absorb them back in the fold, both quickly and safely. More than that, they found places that were less disrupted by the pandemic. The consequences of the pandemic were kept largely at bay. Hannah (UI,W) and June (UI,A) ventured out without much worry. Yes, closures of businesses and public spaces happened and annoyed them to a certain degree, but the world was generally open to them. They experienced minor inconveniences instead of true disruptions. Of course, there were exceptions. Wealthier White and Asian students felt freest to roam. Black, Latino, mixed, and Native students knew limits to economic privilege their peers did not. Their neighborhoods were not all isolated, affluent enclaves. The people in their communities had varying degrees of shielding from the pandemic. And not all survived, as Denzel (UI,B) shared. Moreover, the country's larger racial unrest sharpened the attention of some students, like Emily, to the dividing lines between their community and the larger neighborhood.

Lower-income students came home to not just a different set of circumstances but practically a different world. The reality they returned to was even harsher and harder to navigate than the one they left at the start of the semester, before COVID-19 hit. Sociologists have long documented the weighty burdens that segregation and concentrated poverty place on the lives of undergraduates. Lower-income students, and especially those who are Black, Latino, Native, and mixed, experience more disruptive life events in college than their more privileged peers, especially those who are White. Lower-income students' testimonies not only speak to the magnitude and frequency of these events but also provide insights into their strategies to deal with them—a complex set of experiences that universities must contend with. These testimonies also show just how connected students are to their communities: neighbors are often indistinguishable from family, and the resulting bonds bring deep joy, deep obligation, and for some, deep heartache. August (LI,L) uses his Citizen app in the way most people use The Weather Channel to prepare for and to move through the day. Students are no longer waiting for calls from home or even social media posts by relatives; notifications of homegrown dangers find their way to campus in greater number and at faster clips. Apps like Citizen help students stay connected, on the one hand, but also keep them hyperattuned to local dangers, helping and hurting in equal shares. August's attentiveness and his search to find ways to track local troubles underscore how this fear, this anxiety, is not new. He learned long ago to track what is happening in his city. Trauma has been and still is a constant companion on his journey to adulthood. And this reality is both when he is on campus and at home. For even when he is away, his family is not.[22]

The COVID-19 pandemic further exacerbated these divides. Entrenched inequalities grew even more glaring during the pandemic— or, to put it differently, for low-income people everything just got harder. There's a psychic tax that colleges must account for. In returning home, some students felt more protected than ever. Some felt rubbed raw and exposed. Students' words not only underscore the pain of the moment but also speak to the trauma that they and their communities were dealing with before 2020 and will be dealing with for years to come.

Learning the nuances of community life, how poverty and privilege in students' families—both the ones they are born into and those they inherit—shape so much of students' everyday reality, answers as many questions as it poses. One such question is, what do colleges do now? The task now, for scholars and college officials alike, is to adopt policies informed by this more nuanced understanding of just how rooted these inequities are in students' lives and just how much worse they got. To build an inclusive community, we must meet students where they are, or more accurately, where they need us to be. This requires not only creating new policies that promote equity but also weeding out old ones that undermine it.

3

Help in Hard Times

DURING THE PANDEMIC, universities made it easier for students to apply to college. The rationale was simple: stress and inequality, twin problems that they are, were growing across the country; applying to college was already difficult, especially for those with fewer resources. So, shouldn't universities do what they could to make the process less of a burden? One such change was making the SAT optional. The move to dethrone the SAT—from its long, undeserved place at the center of the admissions process—was already well underway, but that slow shift suddenly no longer seemed sufficient. The pandemic prompted more and more colleges to figure out if there were better ways to evaluate those students graduating high school in the throes of unprecedented disruption. Evidence of these difficulties was abundant—the stories of high school students without sufficient internet access, sitting in the parking lots of McDonald's and Starbucks after they had closed, using the free Wi-Fi to try to finish their homework, were just some of the many difficult stories that emerged in the spring of 2020. In December 2021 Harvard announced that the SAT would not be required for the next four incoming classes. Many other influential schools did the same in the months before and after.[1]

This change is laudable—after all, we know the SAT is riddled with biases, and there is an argument that the admissions process would be more equitable if we abandoned it entirely. Yet I fear this change, while useful, is actually a symptom of a larger problem. Here is another example of colleges going to great lengths to remove barriers at the beginning of the college journey—the application to enter—but ignoring the many barriers that remain once students arrive on campus.[2]

This shift—relatively small, and potentially temporary—is like trying to fix a blown-out tire with a patch. It is not just in the exceptionally hard times, those that are publicized for the world to see, that students need help. Getting into college is not the only problem. We need corresponding policy changes to help students make it through college. The same rationale applies across the next four years: the same stressors, the same inequalities, that haunt students as they apply to college nearly always endure as they move toward commencement.[3]

We have gotten a glimpse into students' lives by exploring how they navigate the family they were born into, and then their home communities, the family they inherited. We have seen that no matter how rich or poor you are, what happens at home and what happens when you step outside are shaped by much larger structural inequalities such as poverty and segregation. It is time for campus policies, especially at elite colleges, to account for these entrenched inequities, not only in hard times but also in quieter moments when we think, almost always incorrectly, that things are alright. For lower-income students—and especially students of color—quieter didn't mean life was any less perilous.

Lower-income students are more likely to have disrupted tenures in college than their wealthier peers. Many critics argue that this disparity is a sign of academic underpreparedness—that these students have bit off more than they can chew and are struggling as a result; that they are "mismatched" and aren't ready for the rigors of college life. But this deficit-oriented way of thinking assumes that students' lives are only about what is happening on campus. In the same vein, it assumes that academic performance is only about how smart you are—as if the college gates provide some sort of panacea to the world's troubles. The students I spoke with make clear the absurdity of this idea. Leaving home and walking through the college gates offer many things. A reprieve? Yes. Some distance? Sure. A cure, a true fix? Absolutely not.[4]

We see this inequality perhaps most clearly in an often-invisible moment in a student's college career: taking time off, whether voluntary or mandated. Academic leave, however, provides a window into understanding how campus policies amplify inequality. Many of the reasons students take leaves of absences from campus is because of how much of their attention is being monopolized by what is happening off campus—both what is happening in their homes and around them. These worries tax them emotionally, making it harder to study. One consequence of these disruptive events is that their grades slip. This is especially true for lower-income Black and Native students, who come from neighborhoods with the highest levels of concentrated poverty, segregation, social isolation, and disenfranchisement. We need to be very clear: this more delayed path toward graduation is not necessarily because of academic preparation.

Snow (LI,N) spoke of the duality that Native students experience, navigating such drastically different communities—Harvard and home—with the weight of history making the disparities even more of a burden to bear. As Snow shared, she had to drop a class because she was so distracted by the knocks on her door, and the worry of who might be on the other side. On top of this fear, as COVID-19 laid waste to the reservation, economically and otherwise, she was also dealing with the pain of her duties helping elders transition to the great beyond. These twin burdens of home and community sat on top of traumas from adolescence that she dared not relive in full during our conversations.

Latino students, especially those from lower-income families, experience similar levels of disorder and violence at home as their Black and Native peers. The call that Samantha got, the one that announced a bullet ripped through her house, was utterly foreign to most of her classmates but was sadly all too familiar to her, her family, and members of her community. She had received similar calls before. Her fear of going outside for a run, something she lives for, was not new. She likened avoiding the outside to a morbid form of self-care, even as it ate away at her during each of her returns home, and especially so during a global pandemic that forced her to take on the additional duty of parenting her siblings.[5]

When grades slip, universities are quick to place students on academic probation and mandate time off, which also means leaving campus. Yet these types of policies run counter to what college psychologists and psychiatrists advocate for in their best practices to help distressed students. Mental health professionals, those who help students at their most vulnerable, push for lowering barriers to reentry, rather than adding on additional responsibilities. Today's policies work in the opposite way, and they do so in starkly unequal ways.

If a student at Harvard elects to take leave because of an internship, or because they want to explore the world, they must inform their resident dean or another member of the office of the dean of students that they are leaving; at some unspecified later time, they must tell the university what semester they intend to come back. That's it. To make things even easier, these students do not lose privileges. In fact, according to the student handbook, students who take a "voluntary leave of absence may be permitted to apply for Harvard funding, including but not limited to summer grants." Even if a student pauses their classes, they can continue to build their resumes with the help of the university. In other words, students who elect to leave are free to fill their days as they see fit.

Students asked or mandated to leave do not have the same freedom. They lose campus privileges, from grants and summer research opportunities to the services that would help them manage the gap. What's more, these students face numerous and far more daunting requirements to return.

So many college policies effectively penalize students further for being put on leave. The result is that students are punished for the insecurities that structure their lives—things that are by definition beyond their control.

While public universities are more likely to charge you a fee to return to campus—usually about the same amount paid to apply to college—private colleges tax you in a myriad of ways. Students who've been booted must prove their mettle to get back in. Akin to welfare work requirements or parole guidelines, selective colleges like Harvard and Yale require students to be "constructively occupied" to prove themselves worthy of return. The student must provide "a written statement describing how the student's time away has been spent." This first criterion alone is already more than their peers have to do. The other requirements are even more demanding, especially for students from poor families and/or disadvantaged communities. Students must show "evidence of stability," which includes a work mandate requiring "a substantial period of regular employment at a nonacademic job and a suitable letter of recommendation from the employer."[6] Vanderbilt University requires students to submit two letters of recommendation, which include one from an employer that addresses "your readiness to return to Vanderbilt and successfully complete your program of studies (e.g., by discussing your maturity, work ethic, sense of responsibility)." Notre Dame is even more blunt, practically prompting students to divulge their traumas. There, students have to "describe two situations, one personal and one academic, when you sought help and utilized positive coping skills to deal with a stressful situation while home." Sometimes university requirements are concerned less with student progress or well-being and more about assessing financial liability. New York University requires "bank statements proving you have sufficient funds to pay for one year at NYU or the remainder of your study if it is less than one year."[7]

Stability, of course, looks different to different people. The definitions these universities use simply presume the trappings of a middle-class life. The various requirements read like a wish list from some imagined vision of 1950s living. Needless to say, the conditions of home and community for nearly all of the lower-income students we have learned from thus far would make complying with such definitions laughable, a tortuous exercise in futility.

The work mandate, which requires students to attain a full-time job or two part-time positions, deserves particular attention; the disruptions of COVID-19 exposed the ridiculous blind spot baked into this notion that all students on leave have equal access to not only a job but also whatever jobs the institution deems good enough. Where are students like Samantha and Snow supposed to work when their communities—their aunts, uncles, cousins, let alone their parents—have struggled with employment throughout their lives, long before the pandemic? And for many of the jobs that a lower-income student is able to get, asking for a letter of recommendation is a tall task. Again, the university assumes that any and all bosses are familiar with this kind of formality. Many of the lower-income students I spoke with were not only the first in their families to go to college but also one of the few in the community to do so. Who writes your recommendation letter when you are running your parents' restaurant? Or when the people you do odd jobs for have limited English proficiency? Yet failure to comply with these requirements means further delaying one's time to a degree.

To make this fraught situation worse, Harvard, like most colleges, does not help students with the transition off campus after making them leave. Here too we see an additional loss of campus privileges and the resources that come with them. This means that students do not get support to help them find employment upon returning home. In fact, during the time I was doing my interviews, a handful of my interviewees on leave lost access to precisely those offices on campus—like the Office of Career Services—that could support their compliance with the rules governing a mandated leave.

These requirements feel like the cold calculations and bureaucratic hurdles we would expect of a large corporation, or a government agency, rather than an institution of higher education. But perhaps we have an overly rosy view of universities? After all, Harvard is, fundamentally, a large corporation. Harvard, like every other private entity, needs to protect its investments. Anytime a student leaves campus, the university risks losing money. But punishing these students for going through a hard time surely is not worth whatever minimal cost savings these policies create.

Georgetown University is certainly just as much a corporation interested in the bottom line as Harvard, but it demonstrates that punishment is not the only option. Their discussion about leaves underscores membership in the college community, putting different leaves on equal footing and centering them as a part of the college experience, as moments that are a sometimes necessary and often useful part of the path toward matriculation. The warm wording from the dean's office at Georgetown is a refreshing divergence from Harvard's crisp, official language that focuses only on requirements: "We support the idea of taking time off if you have a good reason to do so—an intensive internship, a work opportunity, a special family circumstance, or simply a desire to change the scenery and recharge. The door does not close behind you; we are here when you want to return. A leave can be clarifying, inspiring, challenging, fun, relaxing, and an important change of pace. A leave can also sometimes be necessary, and when that necessity arises, we will help you find your way." And when a student is ready to return, they simply write a letter to their dean to start the process.

Removing punitive policies is a major step in supporting students who are already dealing with so much. Even establishing parity between different types of leave would be more equal than what is currently in place at many colleges across the country. There is no need to open old wounds if you're not going to help students heal from what initially caused the damage. There is no point sending students on a wild goose chase to find jobs that haven't been there for a generation or more. Moreover, continuing rather than restricting access to support services would help students not only comply with the return policy, but also lead to more curated leaves that still helped them progress toward achieving the job or career they want upon graduation.

But the particular requirements for return are just the beginning. Exploring the inequities in students' lives demands that we have a larger conversation, one that goes beyond which boxes students need to check to be allowed back on campus. Does putting a student on leave need to automatically mean their removal from campus? When campus is no longer home, we can unintentionally place students in more dangerous situations, and with more unrealistic expectations, both of which can further undermine their mental and physical well-being. Here again, students' narratives provide the best way to understand the problems they face.

Nancy (LI,M) came to Harvard with severed familial ties and a teacher who tried to force her son on her in exchange for housing. Marianne (LI,L) endured her mother's hypocrisy and violence. Michelle (LI,L) said in no uncertain terms that she would give up $5,000, more money than she ever had in her life, for her mental health when speaking about the fork-in-the-road moment of being home. Her dad, with his own mental health issues, was leaning on her more and more and since she wasn't whole herself, the cracks were growing deeper with every one of life's blows. In all these examples, we are doing a disservice by simply sending students home, abdicating responsibility to students when they are the most defenseless.

In that same vein, given the uneven exposure to durable inequalities in their communities, is the "four years and out" model of college—especially beloved at elite colleges—even equitable? Students of color, especially lower-income students of color, endure more destabilizing life events than their peers, a pattern that has only increased since 2020. The testimonies reveal the everyday reality and power of those disruptive events. Expecting all students to progress toward graduation at exactly the same rate is yet another example of the bias long built into college life. Stanford University and the University of Rochester could serve as alternate models here. Stanford allows students to "apply for additional quarters of aid if you require extra time to complete the minimum requirements for your first bachelor's degree due to academic or personal difficulties," which includes disruptive life events. While Stanford's program is responsive, the one at Rochester is proactive. While a four-year degree is still the goal, Rochester created the Take 5 Scholars Program in 1986, which supports a select number of students to take five years to complete coursework. Given what we've learned about students' family life, both programs offer alternatives that are more equitable than the current system at the majority of residential colleges.

Providing students with the opportunity to remain on or connected to campus in meaningful ways while on leave is necessary but still insufficient to deal with the effects of savage inequities in the rest of their lives. If support services, and especially mental health counselors, are not trained to understand and provide support for those who live in poverty's long shadow, can colleges ever truly support the students whom they so actively recruit? Snow lived in this gap, which only served to eat away at her mental health and relationship with the school. As she noted, voice cold and clear, mental health providers at Harvard "are not at all trauma informed and can't give the kind of help I think that Native students need whenever they are in an institution like Harvard." Making matters worse, she lamented how counselors at Harvard "are pretty unwilling, I think, to discuss trauma. My therapist—she told me that she doesn't want to talk about my childhood anymore. She just wants to talk about test anxiety and my stress about assignments. It just feels like they don't really care about that kind of thing. They just want to help you get past your Orgo exam."[8]

As Snow noted, students don't just need help with classes and coursework. For her, it was everything else. Colleges should expand mental health trainings that, for example, understand, promote, and adopt practices like traditional Indigenous healing and grassroots cultural interventions. This shift to more complete wraparound support for students can be done by partnering not only with Native and Indigenous therapists but also with the particular tribes and councils that students are connected to. Such a tailored approach with community members could go a long way in connecting students who are trying to navigate an otherwise disparate world. This expansion also calls for greater appreciation for and training in the principles of American Indian Historical Trauma, which centers an understanding of the lasting legacy of settler colonialism, providing opportunities to help students address present-day anxiety as well as work through generational trauma.[9]

Students' narratives provide evidence for the changes needed to make campus more supportive. Some adoptions need to be more targeted, informed changes that take into consideration the unique experiences and circumstances that undergraduates face. Some policies, like the specialized trainings for counselors, will look different for different groups; this is part of acknowledging the troubled racial history of America. Still, there are more elements to change that require a universal approach. From building out mental health services to diversifying the training of those providing the services, these are examples of what can be done to get colleges closer to that goal of supporting a broader swath of the college community.

Students are resourceful. For lower-income students, being resourceful is a learned necessity, a skill often essential for survival. Colleges should be supporting that resourcefulness, not testing it. Students' trials are ongoing. One way students often try to minimize the gaps in their lives is by helping their families make ends meet. They do so by managing their finances in creative ways, especially how they approach working and earning money in college. As we will see, students' employment strategies in college are just as divergent as their experiences with home, producing uneven returns.

PART II

Finances

4

Pink Slips for Some

LIKE EVERYONE on campus in March 2020, Gertrude (LI,W) and Carmen (UI,B), both spirited juniors, waded through the flood of emails about campus closure. Most were from administrators with fancy titles but unfamiliar names. Eventually, Gertrude and Carmen each found a familiar one: the supervisor of their on-campus job. The messages they received upon opening those emails, however, were as different as left and right. So were the emotions the messages prompted.

Gertrude wore her politics on her sleeve, literally. She almost always sported political swag from past campaigns—from T-shirts to Nalgene bottles—as she traversed campus. Her MacBook, too, sported candidates and progressive causes, a parade of stickers that obscured the iconic Apple logo. Outside of canvassing and classes, Gertrude worked a lot. She wanted to be financially independent in Cambridge. She felt like her parents, and especially her contractor dad, had done their job to get her to college, and now it was her job to make it through. This striving to be independent shaped not only her decision to work but also the jobs she sought.

Like many lower-income students, Gertrude was not comfortable engaging with adults, and that went double for faculty. "I don't ask for help very often or enough. . . . I like to be able to figure out stuff on my own." When it came to finding a campus job her first year at Harvard, Gertrude sought out work that allowed her to clock in and clock out without much interaction. Harvard hosted a job fair, but it was so overwhelming. A lot of options but no direction. She left. Instead, she chose dorm crew. The job was simple: servicing the bathrooms in the student dorms. Mainly cleaning toilets, counters, and showers and delivering rolls of toilet tissue when needed.

She had been doing this job ever since the fall of her freshman year. The work was certainly not glamorous, but that didn't bother Gertrude. Her father worked with his hands; she grew up valorizing a hard day's labor. As she reflected on the work, she recited a quote from Taylor Caldwell's novel *Dear and Glorious Physician*: "Work of any kind was not degrading unless it became so in the mind of the worker."[1] Cleaning bathrooms was respectable work. Moreover, it was one of the few things at Harvard that reminded her of home. And she made good money doing it—more than most of the office jobs across campus.

When rumors about closures began percolating, Gertrude worried. Dorm crew was her only job and sole source of income. Then came the email, as tone-deaf as it was debilitating. Its subject line said it all: "It goes without saying, but don't worry about work this week." She continued, describing that moment in greater detail, circling back again to the email as if repetition would help her make sense of it all. She remembered that day well—the routine of it all, "waking up and checking my phone, like you do." Pulling her hair into a short ponytail, she continued, "I read it. It was just a lot of shock. I was like, 'I don't know what to do.' It hadn't fully set in; I just got dressed and went to class like normal. After the email went out that Tuesday, one of the various emails I got included an email from my manager with dorm crew saying, 'Focus on staying safe, staying healthy, getting home to your families. Don't worry about cleaning any bathrooms this week.'"

As she told the story, tears began to well up. Her hazel-brown eyes seemed to grow even bigger against her cherub face. Her twelve hours a week went to zero. It makes sense that she lost her position. Even she admitted, a hollow smile breaking through, "You can't work from home cleaning bathrooms. I effectively lost that job at that point." Still, Gertrude felt dismissed, unceremoniously, and a bit uncaringly. "Don't worry about emailing me," her boss's email began. "Thanks for your great work this year," it ended. She allowed herself to be annoyed but not angry. She recognized his struggle. He was a student too. He was in the same boat. "My boss barely had time to send a quick email to update us amid struggling to figure out what he would do. It felt clear that there wouldn't be any resources available, that he was already too strained dealing with his own issues." Still, Gertrude fixated on the directives. The president of Harvard told her to go away. Her boss told her to stay away. And she didn't know how long this limbo would last, a heartbreaking reminder of what little security she had in life, a further fraying of her already frail safety net.

Carmen, however, received different news. An easy smile spread across her face when she spoke about working at Harvard, a smile that highlights her plump cheeks—the kind a grandmother couldn't help but pinch. She loves art the way Gertrude loves politics, especially the digital humanities. Carmen dedicated most of her time in college to classes and clubs; of the latter, there were many. However, she made time for one job on campus, as an undergraduate pedagogy fellow at the Bok Center for Teaching and Learning; she found it "fascinating." Carmen couldn't believe she got paid to "make professors understand the identities of their students." Perking up, she shared, "I speak to instructors, which can be museum staff, but mostly TFs (teaching fellows) and instructors, about structures of power and privilege in the classroom." As a biracial Black student, this work was central to her own personal development.[2]

When Carmen got the emails about campus closures, her first thought was getting back to her family quickly—she was hoping to have a little fun before settling in for what she presumed would be an extended stay. Though saddened to leave campus and friends, an email from her supervisor, a full-time administrator, lifted her spirits. Smiling broader than ever, she explained, "Because of where I worked, which was the only place that I was working at the time of school closure, the Bok Center, part of our work was going over the COVID-19 website about classes restarting. Because of that, they were like, 'We fought really hard for you guys to not be fired and be able to continue working. We are trying as hard as we can to adapt this work remotely.'"

Her position—not only flexible, but also aligned with her academic and personal interests—evolved with the pandemic. And it did so quickly, with the support of her superiors. Carmen felt empowered. "The first presentation I ever gave for this job," she shared, chin high with pride, "was the semester that we went home, about how COVID-19 exacerbates underlying issues that are identity based but not identity caused." Going further, she underscored how her work was "very transferable" because "they worked very hard to make sure that it was able to be remote. . . . That's part of the job anyway, to help professors, and other people on campus, move things over remotely." Carmen was even able to increase her hours, from five to fifteen hours a week. There was higher demand, and she had the time; her responsibilities at home were minimal. Amid the vast changes of the spring of 2020, Carmen came to feel even more valued. And even though she was remote, she felt right there in the thick of it, buoyed by her supervisor's support.

The contrast between Gertrude and Carmen is stark. One got sympathy; the other got solutions. This pattern echoed across campus just as it reverberated across the nation. Those from less privileged backgrounds lost out on opportunities as campuses, business, and other institutions closed. Gertrude was from a working-class family. Their reserves were barely that; they had enough for a little while but not for the long haul. And her boss, as cool as he was to work with, was a peer, powerless to help himself, let alone her. Carmen was the child of two professionals. They were financially secure; her parents transitioned online as easily as she did. Her supervisors, full-time Harvard administrators, navigated the university's byzantine bureaucracy to keep her position going.[3]

The student who needed to work, couldn't. The student who needed the money more was offered less. Less support. Less income. Less security. And the student who needed less—again, at least financially— was given more. More hours. More money. More support.[4]

The point here is not to cast blame on Carmen or on the administrators who enabled her to continue working. Within the awful uncertainties of the pandemic, and amid the terrible restrictions that the disease required, staff and students alike made incredible adaptations to maintain some semblance of normalcy. The point, instead, is to interrogate why some students were given these options and not others.

Just about three out of every four Harvard undergraduates hold an on-campus job at some point of their college career. These jobs, however, vary enormously. From baristas and ticket collectors to teaching fellows and course assistants, these jobs all provide a host of resources—financial to social to institutional. Just as important, they provide schedules that are more flexible and stable than their off-campus counterparts, whether stocking shelves at a department store or slinging burgers at a fast-food chain; as a result, they are a lot easier to integrate into the competing demands of getting a degree. But working on campus is not just about the here and now. Education scholars Anne-Marie Nuñez and Vanessa Sansone argue that these paid jobs can be a revelation to students, especially lower-income and first-generation college students; on-campus jobs enable students to not only develop a sense of community but also to "incorporate new conceptions of work and careers beyond what they had been exposed to through their families."[5]

Yet not all campus jobs are created equal. And neither were they protected equally when the COVID-19 pandemic hit. Campus jobs like Carmen's—those that attend to the "life of the mind," as administrators at Harvard are fond of saying—were far more likely to continue when campus closed. This inequity was of course a product of the vagaries of a highly transmissible disease. Remote work was possible, while most in-person work was not. Yet the inequities run deeper because who gets these different types of jobs was—and remains—unequal. Getting a campus job is not as straightforward as it might seem. Harvard's approach to helping students find jobs is laissez-faire; they offer lots of information but little guidance one way or another. Sociologist Jessica Calarco calls these kinds of situations—in this case, the ways that students look for a job—"interpretative moments," when no set rules or guidelines exist for the "right" way to behave or act. Within this void, you fall back on what you know—and for low-income students, this often means what you *don't* know.[6]

What COVID-19 closures exposed is a labor market at Harvard that was largely segregated by social class. Those students who arrived at Harvard already comfortable—read: mostly wealthy students—not only felt more at ease navigating the slew of job opportunities but also were strategic in matching academic or personal passions with campus work. Those less at ease—read: mostly low-income students—sought out the kind of jobs that felt safe or convenient or familiar, jobs that were often, in one way or another, connected to home. These differences in approaches to work are relatively small, and yet together they snowball into radically different trajectories.

Needed More. Got Less.

For lower-income students, money is nearly always tight. Once they arrived on campus, finding a job was just as much a part of life as decorating their dorm room. A campus job was a near-universal given. In fact, only a handful of lower-income students I interviewed did not work, aided by outside fellowships and scholarships. And among these students it was most common to not work in their first year but then to take a job the next year. For those who worked, much of their money earned was earmarked for home, whether sending it directly to parents or holding it in their savings accounts for those all-too-often rainy days. Gertrude referred to the money she earned on campus as a security blanket. "I feel far more comfortable when I have a lot of money saved up. That comes from growing up during the 2008 recession hitting my family really hard. I really don't like to not have a lot of money saved up." In her neighborhood in Arizona the subprime mortgage collapse was devastating. She remembered the blocks around her house filled with U-Hauls and the backseats of friends' cars too full of their stuff for even a small child to sit comfortably. She remembered having to pack up her own stuff and move.[7]

In the months before the pandemic, just as in the years prior, lower-income students tended to flock to jobs that were familiar to them, either because of similarities in the work itself or because of the route to get the position. Harvard was complicated enough, especially for those who were the first in their families to go to college. At least some things were simple, or so it seemed.

You go to class. You go to work.
You get grades. You get paid. You send money home.
You repeat.

As at colleges across the country, there are tiers to the jobs at Harvard. From the most prestigious—research assistants and teaching fellows—to the mid-level work of office assistants, to the most menial work—cleaning toilets, cleaning the dining halls. For jobs like course and research assistants, and even some office positions, however, applying went beyond submitting an application. Often there wasn't a formal application at all. Contact with gatekeepers—faculty and administrators who coordinated hires—mattered. Knowing faculty, and, even more important, faculty knowing you, was how you got the job. Yet, for some students, schmoozing and networking with professors and administrators wasn't just foreign, it felt fake and uncomfortable. There were so many unwritten rules. There was a dress code. As Nicole (LI,L) exclaimed, throwing her hands up in the air, "I didn't know what business casual was. I still don't."[8]

But sometimes it went deeper than unfamiliarity with khakis, loafers, and button-down blazers. Charlotte (LI,L), voice harsh, noted, "I don't know what it is, but I have a fear of people getting too involved in my personal or private life." And work, especially working for money that would support her family, was deeply personal. Charlotte never could see a search for a campus position through. "Every time I had to answer another question or talk to another person, it freaked me out. I would always chicken out at some point in the process."

Lower-income students often drew bright boundaries between coursework and paid work. They did not look to link paid work to classes, beyond ensuring that shifts and class did not overlap. In fact, many voiced concerns or even shock that their peers "gamed the system" by blurring the line between what you get graded on and what you get paid to do. What resulted were often jobs like desk clerk in the library or delivering laundry. These are, to be clear, great positions. They are flexible and pay well enough to support students at school and fill the ever-present financial gaps at home. The students I spoke with talked about their jobs like necessary chores that had to be done, but they rarely complained about having these jobs. Some of these positions even allowed students to do homework while on the clock, which they saw as an acceptable bonus. These positions are also easier, or at least simpler, to get. You just apply. No schmoozing required. However, most of these positions, because they needed to be in person, could not withstand closures. For lower-income students, therefore, closures meant more than just a scramble to get off campus; it made the lifelong race for security—a terrain they were already way too familiar with—even more treacherous.[9]

Helping home, even when away, was paramount. In fact, because students were away, they often felt even more of an obligation to support their family. August (LI,L), with a sharpness to his voice, felt obligated to help his mom, "My mom doesn't have a retirement account. My mom doesn't have siblings. I'm the savings account." What he made on campus helped out at home. Speaking about money problems, Jackie (LI,A) said simply, "That's always something that's been on my mind since I've been growing up." Similarly, Melissa (LI,L) shared, "My mom just takes money when she needs to pay bills and stuff." They share an account. Melissa has direct deposit. Her mother has an ATM card. Melissa puts money in. Her mother takes it out. Trips to the ATM are regular, if not frequent. That is why, Melissa explained, "I worked all through college, and I worked all through high school. . . . It was like, you know, this will directly impact the ability of my family to pay for food and pay for bills and stuff."[10]

Mia (LI,M) knows what it means to not make ends meet. Her parents didn't work. One couldn't, and the other one always had some excuse. "High school was like fighting for my life, fighting for any sort of opportunity to, in the future, not be so poor, where I had to worry about things like housing." It was not always easy. The weight of taking care of everyone sometimes got to her. The long days and even longer nights when she and her family lived out of their beat-up Volkswagen, moving from empty parking lot to abandoned mall and back again, are memories that she can't shake. They haunted her early days at Harvard. By December of her first year she was brought into mental health services after peers and professors alike saw a decline in both her mental and physical well-being. "I've been footing the bill for my family for a long time," she began, "It's just been frustrating. I have other family members who could. That frustrates me, because I don't have the option to give up. Those are my parents." She paused, her voice catching. "If I die, there would be no one to help them." Mia didn't give up. She focused on school and work and shelved everything else. As she put it, "You gotta grind."[11]

And grind she did. Mia took on two jobs when she got to Harvard and grabbed additional gigs whenever they arose. And not many escaped her attention; she stayed glued to websites that announce psychology and business school studies, investing almost as much time looking for paid studies as she did participating in them. Speaking about her work history, Mia said, "I started being an usher at the Institute of Politics, which was a very inconsistent level of income, but they fed us. We would have to stay super late and the dining halls would close. But that wasn't enough money. . . . I also took up a poster posting job. Gotta grind. What else did I do? I would also take place in studies, at the business school or any other school for that matter. They would offer quite a bit of money. I'm OK with being a guinea pig as long as I get paid."

The opportunity to have an influx of money was important for Mia, especially since shifts at her main job were sometimes "kind of sparse." She needed to work as often as she, or rather her family, needed her to. She stretched herself thin. But she kept pushing. She had to. "I depleted all of my savings helping them stay in motels; my savings account got closed because there was no money." I asked Mia whether she applied to the many research and office positions on campus. Hours would be steadier, and the pay would be roughly the same or sometimes more. She wouldn't have to scrounge for studies to be in; instead, she would be paid to conduct them. Mia shrugged her small shoulders and mentioned that she wasn't terribly familiar with research. More telling, however, she said she didn't "feel qualified."

This feeling—of being unaware and underqualified, and, I would argue, unwelcome—was common among lower-income students. The feeling itself was amorphous, not always clearly articulated, yet its impact was anything but. It shaped the jobs they considered, and more importantly, those they didn't. Jackie (LI,A) earnestly noted how, although she knew people could do research and work in different offices, "It felt much less accessible to me. I just didn't develop personal connections with professors freshman year. I didn't even really know how people found those research jobs. I guess it was just a lack of knowledge, a lack of experience."

Kevin (LI,W), clean shaven with a buzzcut, offered a similarly earnest review of his first three years. Without skipping a beat, he called his inability to connect with faculty "the problem" that plagued his undergraduate time at Harvard, blocking his access to the supposed life-changing experiences that Harvard brochures promise. He lamented how "nobody told me to do that; I had to figure it out later on. And I think that's the issue. It's not that the professors themselves are inherently out of reach. Some of them are, but who cares about them? It's very hard to know that you're supposed to do that." Kevin did get a lesson on connecting with faculty, and the bonuses doing so can offer, but it came later in his college career and from a rather unlikely source: his partner. But even then, the lesson proved too hard of a pill to swallow. Reflecting on the difference between the jobs he and his girlfriend went after, he noted,

> My girlfriend, her jobs are interesting because she was doing research with a professor and has done that for a while. She gets paid a lot more than I do! I had no idea how to even get that job. She had known because a friend had done it. It's an informal network that you feel like you're not a part of. If you don't know people that go here, you don't have that sense of being here. I just went for what was obvious, which is doing work for money. I didn't know you could research with the professor, make money while also advancing your own academic interests. I didn't know you could combine all that stuff. When you're trying to make money, you don't have a lot of time to go career shopping.

Flexibility was important, but so was familiarity. Kevin reported "not having that perspective." He separated "doing work for money" from doing research. But it wasn't just about perspective. It was also about comfort. Kevin shared that his girlfriend was used to places like Harvard. Unlike him, she was wealthy—"movie-theater-in-her-house" wealthy. Moreover, she had friends at Harvard that she knew before college; her high school wasn't a feeder school, per se, one of those high schools that sends scores of students to Harvard each year, but her school sent a steady stream, nevertheless. They gave advice about best strategies that supplemented her parental guidance. Kevin was all by himself.

Kevin began to rub elbows with privilege during his junior year, even dating a daughter of the 1 percent, but he was unable to shake his working class roots. As he noted, "Manual labor is something to have pride in." While he begrudgingly accepted her offer to pay for plane tickets so that he could visit her during break, chumming up professors for academic help, let alone work opportunities, was a no-go. During his first year, he went to office hours for help on a tricky practice problem. And after just one visit, Kevin "thought it was for smart kids who could make their own theories." The way everyone, including the professor, seemed to know each other and speak the same language—one that was foreign to him—was off-putting. Flushing a little red, he admitted, "I never went back." He made connections elsewhere. "When I think about all the adults at Harvard, honestly, the adults that I have the most connections with are dining hall workers or people that work in the house." Going further, he noted, laughing a little, "We can relate on a lot more topics than faculty members here. So, I've actually felt like I've grown deep relationships with most of the people that are here working." There is a tenderness in how Kevin spoke about those who labor but also a sadness in how he drew a distinction between those who profess and those who cook. It was clear whom he valued more in making Harvard feel like a place for him.[12]

Combining disparate interests was something Kevin never considered. Connecting with faculty in their offices and over coffee to secure a job and earn money was not in the realm of possibility until he saw how different his partner's time at Harvard had been from his. But it goes beyond his initial lack of awareness. Kevin, like Jack, acknowledged how using personal connections to get a job on campus was as off-putting as the work was new. And it was time intensive. Kevin lamented not having time to go "career shopping"; he needed money now.

Playing an unfamiliar game in this already unfamiliar arena was, for many lower-income students, deeply unsettling. We must remember that for many lower-income students, move-in day was the first time they had ever set foot on a college campus, let alone one older than the United States itself.

Laura (LI,A) felt the weight of this history and how much it contrasted with hers. She and her family are new immigrants, she and her siblings being the first born in the United States. She calls herself Asian American, and the two words sound equally weighty on her tongue. But even though she felt fully American, so much was new, especially when she stepped onto campus. "This sort of relates to never really having met people outside of Alabama, or in the position to become long-term friends with different people. The culture shock was massive, both from the South to the Northeast, from a poor neighborhood to an elite institution, and everything that was never covered in terms of building relationships with teachers in high school to building relationships with mentors here on campus." This reluctance influenced her academics; she was hesitant to ask for help and fearful of even the thought of asking "for a re-grade or anything." She still sounded astonished as she explained, "Whenever I talk to peers who have asked for a re-grade, I'm just like, 'Is that really a thing?' Oh, you're making this up. But it's real! I didn't find that out until much later." It also closed the door to certain positions on campus. When speaking about working with faculty or the different administrative offices, Laura said, "I didn't feel like I was qualified. I don't know. I didn't really think about it, didn't really know about it until late, I guess sophomore, junior year. And I was like, I don't even know if I have the skills. I guess it was also self-doubt and lack of confidence in my own skills."

Out of all the lower-income students I spoke with, few explicitly connected the jobs they sought and their academics. Michelle (LI,L) was one of those few. She explained that there are "two components" to her job search process. "One, I started working on campus because I thought it was the best way for me to contribute. I didn't come to Harvard with money, and I wanted to become financially independent. . . . I really didn't want my parents have to pay anything, both for selfish and unselfish reasons. . . . And the second component is a way of me building up skill sets and references to be able to have a pretty good resume for whatever I want to go into in the future." Her peers found solace and stipends elsewhere.

The plan lower-income students adopted with respect to finding work was akin to a patchwork quilt. They prioritized stitching together jobs that fit their schedules, paid well, and, if they were lucky, both. Their craftwork often included an ever-changing mosaic of one-off gigs and temp work. Sometimes this patchworking was a skill learned from their parents. Many students described how their parents always pieced together multiple positions to support their family. Dads often had two jobs on the books. Moms usually had one on and one off, typically adding babysitting or housekeeping to their hourly wages. UberEats had in the last few years become a more and more reliable side hustle (at least for as long as the car held up). Being a shopper for Instacart was another option. Students saw nothing wrong with the strategy, even if they abhorred the toll it took on their parents. It kept them fed and kept the lights on. And besides, if their parents made it work in more difficult situations at home, then adopting the same strategy during more settled times on campus was a no-brainer.[13]

These jobs, by their very nature, were easy or rather straightforward to apply for. They didn't necessitate building any relationships or require contact with administrators or faculty. They were also almost completely taken out by campus closures. In fact, for some students, these one-offs constituted the only type of work on campus they felt comfortable pursuing and having. Gabrielle (LI,M) "did like tons of random things," from brand ambassador for eateries in Cambridge—which typically meant handing out a lot of fliers—to studies in the Psychology department. Elliot (LI,B), his boyish brown face adorned with the beginnings of a scraggly mustache, noted, "I always have side things. I didn't have a job-job, per se." Similarly, Betty (LI,B), the child of African immigrants, flocked to campus websites to find one-time opportunities. "One-day jobs and stuff like that, I'm pretty comfortable navigating that, but not exactly reaching out like, 'Hey, I need a job.'" Contrasting her approach with that of her peers, she noted, "That's a bit out of my comfort zone and something I've never done." With a laugh and smile, she explained that from housekeeping to being a nanny, "I do side hustles. And my side hustles have side hustles, basically."

Sometimes the jobs students took attracted them not only because they were one and done but also because they looked fun. Ella (LI,A) didn't work her first semester; the shock of Harvard monopolized her thinking. But in the second semester she had to work. Perusing campus websites, she found a match. She applied and took a "job just selling hot chocolate outside of the Science Center" off and on "for like three months or so." Sharing her rationale, she said, "It was just because I just saw the job and I thought it would be fun to do and make a little bit of money while I'm at it." Sampling the hot chocolate as the temperatures began to dip was an added perk. Her studies were interrupted by the need to take a year off, forestalling her ability to apply for other jobs on campus. It was not until her junior year that she mustered up the courage to apply to an office job. Yet here again she was thwarted. COVID-19 hit. They weren't taking on new people. They were focused on keeping those they already had.

For Laura (LI,A), working with students came easier. She worked five jobs to support herself and her family, including cooking at The Grille in one of the undergraduate houses, serving as a peer advising fellow and student mentor, and acting as a scribe, someone who takes notes for a student who can't physically take notes for themselves. These jobs allowed her to send money to her family; she may have been away at Harvard, but help was needed at home. The joy she got from these positions was evident in the sunny smile that spread across her face; her multicolored Google calendar—with its constant chirps, letting her know her next shift was starting—was her secret weapon. Closures threw her well-organized world into complete disarray. "It meant half of my jobs were being cut. And the jobs I still had, the hours were being cut. So, it definitely meant not making, I guess, the threshold I had for myself and my family." Her joyous smile melted from her face. "Yeah, in terms of getting new jobs, that wasn't going to happen." There were no jobs to be had, at least any she felt comfortable applying for.

The college transition can be difficult. It can be downright distressing. While many people focus on the big changes, sometimes it is the most routine things that trip students up the most. Finding a job on campus is just one example. That was Monica's (LI,W) story. "I'm the first one in my family to kind of navigate the higher education process." She quickly added, "right now"—already anticipating the moment, a few years down the line, when her sister will follow in her footsteps. Monica is keenly interested in exploring the history of race and medicine, especially in the Global South. She is the pride of both her family and the larger North African community that called the thirty-mile stretch between Lakewood, Denver, and Aurora home. Their dedication was her strength, fueling her to excel. But pride doesn't help you fit in or figure out the details. "Harvard was a massive culture shock for me. I had never been around such affluence, such wealth. My exposure to wealth was *Gossip Girl*. That's what I knew of wealth. Harvard, for me, represented all of that. But, in a way, that snuck up on me."

Monica's voice cracked as she fought back tears. The difference between Harvard and home was painful from the start; just a few weeks into her freshman year she was thinking "about leaving, tucking my tail between my legs and just starting over." When I interviewed her a few months later, Monica was still adamant about transferring to a state college, writing off schools like Harvard—elite, White, and privileged—altogether. When asked what made Harvard so uninviting after it being a life goal, she paused. She looked like she was searching for examples to illustrate the problem; there seemed to be too many to choose between. What her brain finally landed on was her struggle to find work. With another heavy sigh, she explained how she ended up at Starbucks: "I thought that if I had gone to a job fair and gotten a couple of business cards, I would have been fine. But that wasn't the case. I was terrified by all the different booths. I didn't know who did what, how much they paid, where was Federal Work Study offered, where wasn't it offered. I grabbed a couple pamphlets. I'd applied for two or three things, and never heard back. . . . I tried to look for jobs on campus."

Monica's words speak to how already feeling uncomfortable colors one's experiences. There was little direction in how to handle a job fair or what strategies are best to make sense of the cornucopia of opportunities present. Already a little lost, Monica saw it as just another reminder of just how different she was from her peers. When everything was new, going back to what was familiar seemed like the only choice. For Monica, however, there were drawbacks. As she tried to fit the familiarity of working into her new life, she struggled:

> I fell back on something comfortable, something I had done before. I ended up getting the Starbucks job. It was very inflexible; it was very stressful. It was very in my face all the time. I was working about 25 hours a week; I didn't realize that was a lot until I would talk to my friends. They would be like, "I work 10 hours a week." I'm like, "Well, I work Friday, Saturday, Sunday closing shifts." I would always work closing shifts, from 4:00 to 11:30. If you've been in that Starbucks before, you see how chaotic it is all the time—I wasn't used to that. When I started people were like, "This store has terrible turnover." I didn't understand why people were dropping like flies so quickly. And then I started working. I understood. After my shift, I felt like I had gone through a full body, intensive CrossFit workout. I was always exhausted, always tired, but I needed a source of income.

Monica tried to limit the stress work brought in her life by choosing shifts no one wanted: weekend closings. It helped and it didn't. Although she knew, more or less, when she would be working, the physical demands of those marathon shifts compounded the anxiety she felt around missing out on college. And even twenty-five hours of chaos each week at Starbucks didn't feel like enough. Monica still looked for other work. She states matter-of-factly that "I've worked multiple odds and ends since I matriculated." She soon became a barista at the Barker Cafe on campus. The one silver lining: the process of getting the job there, she found, was easy. No business cards. No small talk. You just apply.

When campus closed, Monica could not continue working. All her jobs stopped, and she returned to Colorado. There, she had to reassess. Harvard made a valiant effort to provide virtual work, but they didn't consider the difficulties of accessing those jobs. For Monica, like several other students I spoke with, the thought of going through a virtual Harvard job fair produced as much anxiety as did the one held in person all those months ago. "It was very harrowing for me to consider at the

beginning because I did not know if I would be able to find employment. I didn't know if that was possible." Her mind was always on
home, "especially with all of the uncertainty with job security on my
family's end." The uncertainty around if she would find work "spawned
a lot of existential dread." Monica found herself "reapplying for jobs at
home in the health care sector, whether it be room service or cooks or
housekeeping" at the local hospitals and searching for "odds and end
jobs that I had before, like fast food restaurants and things like that."

The agita she felt over finding work increased when thoughts went to
bringing home more than a paycheck. Fanning her fingers, she counted
how many family members got sick. Her aunt and cousin, both frontline
workers, contracted COVID-19. Her grandmother got so sick her family
began making burial plans. The family was divided: honor tradition and
bury her in the West Bank, her homeland, or keep her body here in
America? Then she mentioned her father. Her quick counting slows. He
contracted COVID-19 at work and had to be isolated at the hospital.
Monica abruptly stopped speaking. She broke eye contact. After a pro-
longed pause, she said, "Walking by rooms where people are fully
strapped to huge ventilators and it's visibly evident that they couldn't
breathe, that they are fighting for every breath, never leaves you."

Gertrude (LI,W) is a hard worker; like many of her lower-income
peers, she got her first job in high school. She, like Monica, worked as a
barista at Starbucks. Gertrude used almost all of her wages to help her
family. The bond she had with her grandfather was especially strong,
something that her parents teased the two of them about. Talking about
returning home after campus closed, and then returning to frappe-filled
days, Gertrude looked flattened. Her characteristic bounce was gone.
Tears began running down her face. Her voice shook worse than her
hands. "My dad and I both continued our in-person jobs during the
pandemic, especially aware that if we got sick and brought COVID into
our household, my grandpa's life would be at stake." Taking a moment
to compose herself, she continued, "Gramps had so many underlying
conditions; I had little doubt that if he got the coronavirus, it would've
killed him. . . . I was so afraid that I would get COVID. That I would
spread it to him. That I would cause his death."

Gertrude faced so many competing demands. She felt like she was worker and provider first, daughter and granddaughter second. Student came third. Gertrude explained how in her three years of working for Starbucks, she had never seen as much drive-thru activity as she did during the height of the pandemic. With so many restaurants being closed, her store did sales that surpassed even holiday season totals. She was able to get a discount on food at work and was even able to sometimes bring food and drinks home—a small way to lighten the burden of the extra groceries her presence in the house demanded. That made her feel better. But she was tired and scared. Nothing eased "the fear of inadvertently bringing death upon someone you love so much."

Of course, not all lower-income students lost their jobs when campus closed. Although relatively few found research and course assistant work compared to their more privileged peers, some did. Those who held "life of the mind" jobs were more likely to have graduated from boarding and day schools, those who I call the *privileged poor*. Their comfort with engaging adults and navigating elite spaces influenced their strategies for securing employment; even though earning money remained a major motivation, their strategies—and ultimately the jobs they secured—matched that of their privileged peers more than their lower-income counterparts.[14]

Sam (LI,B) entered Harvard focused on physics and with some research experience. His posh prep school provided him access to wet labs that just about all of his public school peers never knew was possible. And he wanted more in college. This yearning was bolstered by his introductory chemistry professors—"just two amazing professors and people who I learned a lot from, obviously academically, but also more about myself and what I want to learn." Spurred by such positive experiences, Sam made up his mind that it was "time to get some experience" in the lab. And so, he did what his high school trained him to do: he reached out. "I looked for chemical physical biology labs in the area. And I reached out to the PI. I was like, 'I'm really interested in like, whatever. I really want to get some lab work, some lab experience." He assured me that his email was more articulate than he was in our conversation. Nevertheless, his cold call paid off. "She's like, 'Oh, that sounds great. You can come by.' And then afterwards, I got hired, and I was working." When campus closed, he continued to do work for the lab, albeit remotely, for 15 hours a week. As for hours and pay, he said, "I saw no real change."

Maria (LI,M), small in stature with a big smile, also served as a research assistant. At the age of twelve, she made two big transitions simultaneously. She left the West Coast, where Spanish and seasoned food were common features, for New England, where, as the old saying goes, the weather is cold and the people are colder. She left her public school, with friends she had known since pre-K, and started at an elite boarding school; diamond-studded Van Cleef and Arpels jewelry far outnumbered the ombré rubber band friendship bracelets that were more popular back home. If interacting with her peers was novel, doing so with her teachers was even more so. Just the fact that they had time for students seemed bizarre to her—even discomforting. They actually *wanted* to talk to her! She lamented how that just wasn't the case back home.

The transition to boarding school life was rough, but gradually she figured out how to navigate this strange, elite space. Reflecting on her progress, from her boarding school to Harvard, she described the evolution as obvious and inevitable, but also continued, "I'd say I'm pretty comfortable. I had to become very comfortable, or else I would be failing. I had to very quickly swallow my pride and ask for help, and realized that asking for help is not a weakness, it's actually a sign of strength. Just because I need help in this moment, because I'm doing poorly, does not mean I will be doing poorly at the end of the semester."

When Maria got to Harvard, she flexed the muscles she developed over the four years at her boarding school, building a network of faculty whom she liked, trusted, and admired. And she didn't hesitate to reach out to them for work opportunities. As an aspiring doctor, working with her science professors was a win-win. Working in a lab checked boxes and provided checks every two weeks. She would be the first person to say how much steady income mattered to her. "Earning money was definitely most important." But it wasn't all about the money. She explained, "I got the research job because, for medical school, there's a big emphasis on research. You didn't necessarily have to work in a science lab, but the head researcher at the lab, she was my professor, and she announced that there was an opening in her lab if you wanted to apply, while we were in that class." And Maria, liking her professor, her research, and the fact that she was a woman in STEM just like she wanted to be, applied. Like Sam, she got the job after reaching out to her professor and having meetings with the rest of the team. By the time the COVID-19 pandemic hit, she had held the position for over a year; "fortunately my job did continue online and that definitely alleviates some of that stress I was feeling." Her dad "wasn't working the extra hours that he was working" at his side jobs before the pandemic, and now she was an extra and unexpected mouth to feed in a house that was barely treading water. Virtual work kept her engaged, kept her employed, and helped keep her family safe.

Even when the privileged poor lost out on work on campus, they activated networks to secure employment. And they were comfortable doing so. Dima (LI,L), tall and lanky with a blunt demeanor, shared how he used connections to secure work. Help came not from Harvard but from Prep for Prep, the educational nonprofit that helped to get him into boarding school six years earlier. Before campus closed, Dima worked in a campus library "because I needed a job that was low key and I could study while working." There was an added draw; he liked the people. Calling the staff a real "community," he said, "they're really kind. Every time I get into the office—I feel like I can relax a little." When campus emptied, Dima lost this retreat "away from the academic intensity of Harvard." Closures, he noted, "definitely just cut out any avenue of money, because I could no longer work. And my mom lost her job shortly afterwards, too. At that point we were parched for money. But I found something through Prep, thankfully."

Prep, which he said changed his life when he was little more than a kid, threw out another lifeline, securing him a position as an analyst for a major television network. "I was doing analytics for them." Even though his position ultimately was away from campus, his willingness to enlist others helped in the long and short run. Dima didn't hesitate to reach out to the Prep's administrators, even though he had "graduated" from their program years prior. They were his security blanket then and now. The network asked him to stay on beyond the semester.

It is this difference, in both strategy for seeking employment on campus and approach to college more generally, that we see how powerful a force familiarity is. We tend to gravitate toward what we know, whether it is a crushing job at Starbucks or a cushy job with a professor. For the privileged poor, that familiarity with elite institutions provided some, albeit incomplete, shielding from the full effects of closures, at least with respect to earning money, but it also provided access to institutional resources that give students a leg up in their postgraduation plans.

Still, most lower-income students were like Jade (LI,W), who had taken whatever work felt familiar, and who gave up extracurriculars because "I was worried about having a job, getting some income." She willed herself to "work as much as humanly possible." She found herself repeatedly checking the online job board and taking all available shifts. This manic search for hours all came to a stop, swift and hard, in March 2020. "I didn't have a job anymore and I couldn't find a job" when campus closed. Looking defeated, she said in little more than a whisper, "I tried."

When campus closed and work stopped, financial cracks were laid bare. Anxiety and insecurity spiked. The jobs that they felt comfortable seeking were those that were the first to be dissolved. Working with faculty and administrators was off the table for most, not because of ability but because of comfort. The anxiety of attending a job fair or interviewing—let alone working—with a faculty member one-on-one was overwhelming for many. And the jobs, for most, remained elusive, just like the security they sought. Lower-income students like Kevin saw their peers work for professors and even saw them continue doing so during closures. This proximity didn't ease their fears, even as they saw the benefits of doing so. For lower-income students, the ability to have flexible jobs, and especially those that reminded them of home, made the adjustment to college easier, even if only by a little bit.

Needed Less. Got More.

The ruptures of the COVID-19 pandemic were numerous, of course, for both the privileged and those with lower incomes. But where and how those ruptures were felt, as we have seen, varied widely. Roughly

30 percent of Harvard students don't work while on campus; and most of them come from money. Sociologist Nathan Martin finds that upper-income students "are more likely to have a job out of choice than necessity." I saw this in students I spoke with too. For those well-off students who do work, it was often for the "extras." For Carmen (UI,B), money wasn't the main or even secondary draw to the undergraduate pedagogy fellow position. Although, she reported with a smile, the extra money allowed her to become a connoisseur of Cambridge's many Indian restaurants. "I love Indian food. Any of the different tiers of Indian that are there." Smiling, she said her money goes "mostly to food, eating, just general stuff in the Square." The transition online, and the extra hours and extra pay that came with it, were an unexpected boon; as she put it, while home she was "definitely more frivolous."[15]

The choice to work, however, went beyond the desire to, as Evelyn (UI,B) put it, "have my own money that I can use to do what I want to do with, literally just for shits and giggles." Yes, it was about increasing their freedom to do what they wanted. But it was also often about double dipping, getting paid to access institutional resources that would grow their personal and professional networks. In other words, working today would facilitate success tomorrow.

Upper-income students are typically more comfortable engaging with adults as equals and are more intentional than their lower-income peers at connecting their academic or career interests with their jobs on campus. This dovetailing came easy to them. They strategically enlisted faculty and staff at Harvard to make sure that their own interests were furthered—that they earned experience as they earned money. Sometimes faculty did the enlisting, and they were as happy to accept an invitation as they were to submit an application. What resulted from this ease is that privileged students were more likely to have what academic researchers call high-impact positions, on-campus jobs that promote connections in addition to pay. Such jobs deepened the bonds they already had to faculty and staff, adding a professional dimension to academic connections. And when closures became a reality, these burgeoning networks were swiftly activated. With fewer worries about moving back home, and greater freedom to say yes, campus closures were less debilitating disruptions and more navigable detours.[16]

Again, the need to work was lowest among privileged students, before and during the pandemic. This gave them freedoms that their lower-income peers did not have. One such freedom is the option to work for pay or for course credit, a practice that predates the COVID-19 pandemic. Taking this option allowed them to lighten their course load, substituting interesting research for a course. And many privileged students opted for course credit. When asked about getting a job on campus, Teddy (UI,W), whose blonde curls almost reach his unkempt brows, explained that his parents supported him fully; money just wasn't a worry. As for work, finding a job wasn't a top priority. "I just didn't put enough time to do so. I didn't feel the financial need to get one."

Similarly, Mary (UI,B), the daughter of healthcare executives, was upfront about her priorities. "I was looking forward to post grad," she stated, matter-of-factly. She worked to ensure that she dedicated herself not only to her classes but also to clubs that deepened her understanding of policy reform and the law. Moreover, she prioritized making connections at the many events around campus, especially political forums, which working could prevent her from doing.

Just because students didn't have to work, however, did not mean they didn't work. Many did. Like Carmen, they reported continuing to do so when campus closed. Manuel (UI,L), a double legacy at Harvard, sported rectangular glasses with a sparse mustache and goatee. Before college, Manuel kept himself busy. In addition to school clubs and honor society, he held a host of positions, from landscaping to office work—character-building stuff, as his immigrant parents teased. He said, "That was a very unique set of circumstances; I'm glad I did it. It gave me a new appreciation for . . ." He paused, as if searching for the right word, before shifting course: "It's not fun." At Harvard, he purposefully sought out more "life of the mind" positions. Although an intentional move, he counted himself fortunate for making this shift, since "tutoring is one of the easiest ones to convert to the online format." In a similar fashion, Claudine (UI,B), an evolutionary biology major with a passion for global politics, noted how "at home, online tutoring became a great option if I wanted to do any form of tutoring. I found an online service that does that and that's been pretty seamless for me." Going further, she shared that "I think it was an immediate work opportunity during school, during the semester. And one that was made easier by the fact that it is fully online. It was more conducive to being able to work during the semester."

For Meredith (UI,N), venturing into the lab was something that gave her singular joy. To maximize her college years, she reprised her role of course assistant over many semesters, twice teaching for the same chemistry professor, while also training with local EMTs. One of her favorite classes was Organic Chemistry, an infamously difficult course. She had grown up sitting around a biologist's dinner table: "My dad works in pharma." Test tubes and beakers were as normal to her as Legos and American Girl dolls. She explained, "I've been a course assistant, last spring and this spring. I'm here to make money. So yeah, I actively sought them out. My friends were doing it for other classes. I was like, 'That sounds fun.' I like teaching too. I was a teaching assistant for the EMT class after I did it. So that's why. I actively sought it out. No one was like, 'Hey, you want to do this?' I was like, 'Please, professor, I loved your class,' that kind of thing." Meredith wanted to further develop not only her understanding of the material but also the strong relationship she had with her organic chemistry professor. It helped that her friends were serving in similar positions too. Meredith then told me about campus closing: "At the time I was course assisting for Orgo. I just had to switch to online. It was weird doing office hours. Much fewer people went to my office hours. Before, I'd have fifteen or twenty people swarming me with questions. Then it was one or two or no one. My friends that were taking the class were reaching out to me to ask questions, like private help, which we get paid for. It was fine. Yeah, nothing that bad." Meredith's enthusiasm was evident when speaking about her time teaching. She went after these positions, reaching out to faculty to secure positions. When campus closed, her services were still needed. And her transition online was easy—even liberating. Sitting next to that joy, however, was some sadness. She chuckled nervously and said, "I'd be lucky if I had one person." Nevertheless, her position, and pay, continued even as the steady stream of students dwindled.

Alice (UI,W) lamented campus closures. She missed connecting with professors. She served as a course assistant, or CA, starting her sophomore year and continued until her senior year when things transitioned online. She didn't stop there, she added research to her schedule. "Last semester I was a CA again; this semester I'm a research assistant. I always have a job." When asked about what campus closures meant for working, she shared,

> It was a bit sad, because I was a research assistant. I would go over to the business school and meet with my professor. He would take me into the staff lounge, where they have all the nice food, and get snacks. My professor will give me a topic, and he's like, "I want to understand this topic." And I will go understand it for him, distill it down into a memo, and explain it to him. It's such a fun job. I don't think he's ever given me a boring topic. Now, being on Zoom, it's a little bit less fun, but not that different.

Alice missed the accoutrements of the "swanky" business school pantry. The work continued, however, maintaining both her hours and her interest. Moreover, she appreciated engaging with a faculty member interested in hedge funds, which is where she was hoping to land a position upon graduation.

Transitioning to remote work was easy for privileged students for several reasons. They were more likely to have space at home to utilize however a job might need. And their parents were more likely to leave their days unencumbered by household responsibilities. These two reasons are obvious. But a less obvious reason was how the pandemic spurred already existing networks of privileged students into action. As with Meredith, and many others, staying in touch with professors after taking their class and being open—even willing—to reach out to them when needed proved critical. Yes, these connections meant that they were more likely to have and keep whatever teaching and research position they already had in the spring of 2020. But there was more. Students spoke about how they were sought after once campus closed. Faculty reached out to them directly, to fill gaps brought upon by the pandemic. While some of this reaching out was sparked by students' performance in a course, many noted how being known from office hours, teas, and departmental events was an even surer way of getting these calls, and thus to securing positions they didn't even apply for.

Johannes (UI,A) was the recipient of this kind of support. In the fall of 2019, he started as a research assistant for a project on democracy. When campus closed, "They decided to keep me on; I'm still a research assistant there." Despite so much uncertainty, Johannes said, "Actually, it was even better for me, weirdly enough." The relationship he developed with his supervisor made the assistantship particularly rewarding. His professor, in one of their casual conversations, asked, "'Hey, you want to still continue this semester?'" It was a no-brainer for Johannes. He liked the professor and the project. Moreover, Johannes appreciated being looked out for. He explained,

> It was a $2,000 blanket stipend and about seven to eight hours a week. I could finish it in four. I was like, "OK. Cool. Done." During the year, my supervisor was like, "We have you at about 10 to 15 hours a week." I was like, "I've only worked six hours a week." He was like, "You're a working college student. This comes from grant money. If we don't spend this money, it just goes back. Just put 14, 15 hours." *That* for a whole semester was absolutely amazing. I was like, "Thank you so much. I love you." This semester, it's changed. Unfortunately, he left and I have a new supervisor. She's like, "Please report to me your hours each week." Which is like, "Oh no." Rest in peace to that era.

There's an easiness to his story, an awareness that he was in the right place at the right time, but just as important, a confidence that this is just how life works out. This sense of ease about such an opportunity was generally absent among lower-income students.

Despite Johannes's breezy tone, we should not discount how much work goes into developing relationships with faculty. Attending office hours. Asking questions. Demonstrating your own interests in a way that's just shy of bragging but still sounds like you are smart. Showing interest in the professor's research and life beyond what they teach. Sure, it was easy for Johannes, but it was still work. But the reason why this work felt effortless was because connecting with adults was a skill honed by Johannes, and nearly all other privileged students, long before coming to college.

Angelica (UI,B) offered a glimpse into how networks, even when not intentionally called into action, can help students in times of disruption. Now a junior, she had fully come into her own. Or to use her words, "less shy." Before I could ask her to explain, she said, "Freshman year, I didn't go to office hours that much. However, I was still coming into myself. And so, my sophomore year, I did go to office hours more. I went to a 'Classroom to Table,' which is dinner with my professor. It's free. It's fun. You get steak. I loved it." Free food, even for the child of professionals, is a plus. But the real draw was connecting with a professor she thought was cool. After that, she explained, "I go to office hours more and I try to utilize it. And I'm not sure if that's because I'm just older and I realize the importance of it or it's because that's the only time you can speak with your professor and the time where you're having more social interaction."

Angelica sought out more than help in office hours, whether they were held in a professor's office or at her new favorite restaurant in Harvard Square. She wanted to make connections. This more personal and engaged contact helped her secure a position when so many of her classmates were losing theirs. She had an "in" and was comfortable making the ask of her professor to become his teaching fellow. "I just emailed him, and he was like, 'Yeah, of course. Be a TF.'" She continued, "The TFs are grad students and there's a lot of undergraduate students. I'm a junior, so I don't know if I'm qualified to be teaching a class of juniors and seniors what I learned last semester. COVID had a lot to do with that; they didn't really ask me for anything. I told him, 'I got this grade in econometrics and I loved your class last year. I don't have any teaching experience. Can I be a TF?' He was like, 'Yes, let's put you on board.'" A true economics concentrator, she framed becoming a TF as supply and demand. Still, even she couldn't help but laugh at the clarity of her path: she knew what she wanted, went after it, and secured it.

The pandemic sometimes cleared the way for even better opportunities, or at least ones more fitting to students' larger plans. Teddy (UI,W), laid back with a wild sense of humor, was a case in point. For him, the COVID-19 pandemic was like a palate cleanser. "I had only two jobs prior to COVID. I was a tour guide, and I was a Peer Advising Fellow."

Closures meant "no more tour guiding, but that opened up the opportunity for me to take on more academic-centered positions." Teddy became a course assistant for a professor he really respected. He didn't apply; he was offered the position. With a smile, he noted, "He liked me. And I liked him. So, he asked me to come on to the team."

Clark (UI,B), tall and toned with an easy gait, is no stranger to the academy. His parents are professors, and so are some of his extended family members. He inserted himself into the life of the university, from booking appointments at the Office of Career Services to attending office hours. With respect to work, he actually delayed it until the pandemic hit, filling his days in what he saw as a productive way to invite some "accountability" into his life. Clark noted that he didn't go looking for jobs per se; it was more like they found him. With high marks in his classes, his knowledge of economics was in high demand. He explained, "I get emails about it, you know? Like people reach out to me to tutor, so it doesn't feel like I have to do as much job searching." And equally important for Clark, he liked the work because "it puts me in a learning mindset."

This is not to say that the campus jobs of privileged students remained cocooned from the impacts of the COVID-19 pandemic. Some privileged students opted for jobs that were more "chill" and "relaxed," like at libraries, where they could get work done same as their lower-income peers. These positions, of course, shut down just like the rest of in-person work. Yet it is the impact (or lack thereof) on the rest of a student's life that makes the real difference. Mariel (UI,M) enjoyed long walks, especially under Cambridge's canopy of trees. Her interest in poetry connected to her attachment to nature. Her calm veneer broke, however, when she spoke about working on campus amid closures. She became visibly annoyed when I asked her about the wave of notifications. She had just signed up for extra shifts at the box office, where community members purchase tickets for campus events. Once the dust settled, she had to undo what she had just done, a loss of not only the extra money from the extra shifts but also her usual six hours. "I remember just going through my Google Calendar and having to delete the shifts that I was scheduled for. It just felt sad; that made it so much realer." Similarly, Mark (UI,W) worked at a coffee shop because he wanted some space from the academic grind and to see more people than those he would see in class.

Erica (UI,N), earnest in her own way, worried desperately about Zoom fatigue and debated if it was best for her to keep her teaching position after being home for a few weeks. These are very real concerns. But each of these students, not always willingly, admitted that they had a family to fall back on that was largely "unfazed" financially by the pandemic. As Meredith, the organic chemistry enthusiast, shared, "My dad's side of the family has a family business where they do machining, and one of their clients is Clorox. They're doing well—business as usual." Speaking about her dad's work, she noted with a smile, "And you know pharma is doing well too, nothing crazy there. They weren't really affected." Many, if not most, of these wealthy students were like Julian (UI,W); all their needs taken care of meant that any money they made from campus jobs remained "largely discretionary." Rahel (UI,B), unable to stop herself from chuckling, worked as a course assistant in order to "not eat in the dining hall." Sharon (UI,B), who worked as a course assistant, shared that she worked so that she can "go on dates and give donations" to different causes or nonprofits. When the former stopped, she doubled her contributions to the latter.

Importantly, while lower-income students were leery of the process of securing jobs, some privileged students criticized it outright even as they benefited from it. Julian, never one for holding back, revealed both the mechanics of securing work and his strategy for playing the game. "It's this faux interest in people, in their lives, be it professors that you take out to dinner and are chatting with them about opportunities. And somehow you work in your interests." Julian even modeled how he broaches the subject: "'Oh, have you heard anything about a lab that might'—things like that." Julian doesn't like this method, instead preferring to be more direct, almost transactional but not quite so, in his engagement. Perhaps earnest is a better word. It is not that he doesn't engage. He does. "I still know plenty of people doing plenty of different things that I can and do reach out to if I'm curious about something, or I'm looking for opportunities in this specific sphere." He just doesn't feel he has the energy for "the second rat race." Julian was critical of the fact that students generally have to do so. "I am not interested in just talking to people just to talk to them," he began. "If I like you, I'll talk to you. If I have a question, I'll reach out to you. If I want to go to dinner with you, I'll ask. But there's another element of it where it's people are just doing things to do things because they know that's the steppingstone to furthering their access. . . . The people who are really good are really good at faking interest."

Students from more privileged homes generally returned home with jobs in tow, if they worked. Indeed, some of these students even found themselves in higher demand than when they'd been on campus. Several of the students I spoke with had worked as research assistants somewhere on campus, but then as professors transitioned online they were recruited to serve as course assistants. This was especially common in STEM courses, which use more course assistants than other departments. These positions were overwhelmingly able to transition online. For some, these once-coveted positions were being handed out like audience gifts at a taping of *Oprah*. You had to be in the room to get one. Again, connections matter. The professor had to know the student first. Bolstered by their ease at engaging faculty and staff, more privileged students not only maintained their pay but deepened their connections, and now had stories to tell about professors and mentors and employers in recruiting calls and in applications for jobs and graduate school, or whatever else these students wanted to do after graduation.

Conclusion

Students' departure from campus in March 2020 was not just frantic packing and emotional goodbyes. The logistics of life had to be figured out. And working was a big one. The COVID-19 pandemic revealed an unspoken reality: the labor market, at Harvard, like almost everywhere else, is segregated. It is shaped by social class, layered by the ease of privilege as well as by the burden of poverty. Students most comfortable with adults, and with Harvard, were more likely to participate in the knowledge economy, specifically research and teaching. More affluent students like Carmen (UI,B), who forced professors to interrogate their biases, were aided in their endeavors by professors and administrators who asked them to join their teams or advocated for them to continue working in their offices during the pandemic. Upper-income students matched campus positions to academic and even personal interests, seeking out faculty to make this connection a reality. Through their existing connections they gained access to institutional resources and exposure to even broader networks—people and places and positions they might be interested in after graduating.[17]

Lower-income students had a different experience. They were generally not familiar with Harvard and felt uncomfortable navigating things like academic job fairs, let alone office hours and one-on-one sessions with faculty. Like Gertrude (L I,W), they looked for work that was familiar in an unfamiliar place. And connecting with faculty in this more intimate way was not something they had practiced. It was as uncomfortable as it was new. Sometimes we grasp at semblances of home when we feel farthest away. So, not surprisingly, lower-income students were content with work being transactional. Jobs were about making money; wages for hours. Their earnings helped them close the gaps between what they needed on campus and also what their families needed back home. Linking labor to academic interests was often not even on the radar. The fact that the privileged poor—those lower-income students who went to private schools—adopted behavior more like their affluent peers and secured similar positions, underscores this reality. Knowledge of an elite environment provided insights and pathways to work that buffered some, but not all, of the uncertainty brought upon by closures.[18]

This division was most pronounced when looking at STEM, because of the availability of work, who wanted those jobs, and who was invited to take on those positions. STEM courses and labs are associated with a disproportionate amount of hiring. One science lab can hire ten to fifteen undergraduates, as many as entire departments like the Bok Center where Carmen worked. Yet STEM, across the country and even the world, is known to be a boy's club. However, it goes further than that. It is also classed and racialized. Women, students of color, and first-generation college students are more likely to feel ostracized in STEM courses, especially introductory courses that many departments use to "weed out" students.[19]

In fact, New York University made headlines in 2022 for the antagonist culture in STEM courses. One underexplored dynamic of this chilling effect, and one that the COVID-19 pandemic exposed, is how, for a wide array of students, this culture renders an entire sector of work on campus as "Need NOT Apply." Students must make it beyond the introductory classes to advanced-level courses to be able to return as a course assistant. Even Maria (LI,M), with years of practice connecting with adults in elite spaces and who sought out and secured work as a research assistant, faced issues with a male science professor who was "condescending" and "looked me dead in my eyes and he said, 'It sounds like you don't know what you're talking about'" when she asked a question in office hours. She persevered, knowing one professor did not speak for all. But many of her lower-income peers, especially those who already experience those moments with greater trepidation, do not.[20]

Understanding students' motivation for working and strategies for securing jobs deepens our grasp of how inequality is reproduced on campus. But not all work is paid work. Often students take on roles and responsibilities they are not compensated for, at least financially. For many, taking on these duties is elective, a choice. For others, it is not. To more completely understand how work shapes undergraduate life and mobility prospects thereafter—and how the pandemic exposed and exacerbated inequalities therein—we must account for unpaid labor as well. This too-often-overlooked dynamic of undergraduate life is what we explore next.

5

Free to Labor

LIKE MANY of us during the pandemic, students flocked to social media as a form of escape, a reprieve from the monotony and uncertainty of lockdown. Like always, there were drawbacks to the dopamine-induced high that came from our tiny screens. Switching between TikTok, Snapchat, and Instagram into the wee hours of the morning makes getting up the next morning for work hard. Hannah (UI,W) and Sofia (LI,L), both booked and busy, knew the feeling of waking up early for work after a night of liking posts and sharing memes. Hannah decided not to enroll in the fall of 2020 and instead took a gap year that she curated with intention, using family connections to secure an internship at a venture capital firm. Sofia remained at home and enrolled virtually; in between, and sometimes in lieu of classes, she supported her dad with his pool-cleaning service.

Both young women woke up groggy, phones half-drained, a battery of questions demanding their attention. Hannah, as she left the Newbury Street brownstone her parents rented for her and made her way along the few bustling blocks to the T, had her choice of pick-me-ups. Would it be Starbucks or Tatte? The baristas at the former were a little blunt for her liking, but they got her name right. The latter, however, had better pastries. Or perhaps something from the new spot that was getting rave reviews. She wondered which had the shortest lines, hoping to be only a few minutes late. The culture at the firm was busy but lax; no one was really policing time. The questions continued. Which podcast to put on to drown out the screeches of the Green Line? When is my boss's meeting with the client? When does he need the updated spreadsheet? Will he let me sit in on the meeting this time?

Sofia, back at home in Texas, now sharing a room with her sisters that was once hers alone, grappled with a different set of questions. She and her father also needed fuel, but of an industrial sort. Do we have enough gas to make it across town to our first cleaning? Which station is cheapest this week? Which has the shortest line on Mondays? Being late just once, just by a few minutes, could mean the loss of a client, especially that new one who required multiple phone calls and what seemed like a whole day reassuring him they could handle the additional job. Do we have enough water and Gatorade? She knew her dad wouldn't admit it, but she'd noticed him getting tired in the unrelenting Dallas humidity. Who is handling pickup from daycare? Am I missing class or just office hours? Are the new buckets, nets, and scrubbers I ordered already on the truck or still by the back door? Who has the addresses and itinerary? Are we zigzagging across the city or making one big circle so we end closer to home and make it back in time for mom's chicken molè?

One question that both Hannah and Sofia knew the answer to was how much they were getting paid for their work. Nothing. When campus closed, Hannah went home for a spell, decided on the gap year, traveled with friends for the summer, and then got the unpaid internship back in Boston. Sofia returned home and took on additional—although old—responsibilities on top of classes. For students of means, choosing unpaid gigs was just that—a choice. Which firm to apply to? Which internship to take? These students typically found a position that would maintain their momentum, something that would fit with their broader postgraduation plans. Each internship was a building block to the career they sought. Less privileged students like Sofia had a choice too, albeit one with very different consequences. It was either help out or go without. Without lights, without food, without shelter.

We know that unpaid labor spiked during the COVID-19 pandemic. Commutes may have gotten shorter for some, but the days got longer for many. This reality hit women, especially mothers, the hardest. As sociologist Caitlyn Collins noted, women simply worked more in all areas of life, taking on unparalleled amounts of care work in addition to home management and their regular day jobs. College students were no exception. But that reality, no surprise, was different for students like Hannah compared to students like Sofia. While we have just explored the obvious benefits of—and uneven access to—paid labor during the pandemic, there were many reasons why taking on unpaid labor was, for some, a calculated choice, and for others, the only option.[1]

This difference in labor—both amount and type—shapes students' present and has implications for their future. Who gets to weather enormous disruptions unfazed—keeping the ball rolling not just toward graduation but toward a resume chock full of experiences that employers value? Whose time is confiscated by the Sisyphean task of keeping poverty at bay? And how are those very different kinds of labor valued—by professors, by employers, and by the students themselves?

Amid the tragedy of this moment, the disruptions of the pandemic also permitted exceptional opportunities, for those who could afford to take them. In the years to come, privileged students like Hannah will prominently feature their COVID-enabled unpaid experiences on their resume; this kind of work will help launch their careers after college. Others like Sofia, whose work keeps the utilities on and the landlord away, typically see what they do for their families as just doing what is needed; some of those students will even try to hide it. And even if they wanted to take pride in such accomplishments, there's no space for such information. Social scientists, university officials, and recruiters at companies of all stripes alike ignore the work that lower-income students do on behalf of their families, remitting it to a proverbial black box. We undercount the hours they dedicate to this work. We underestimate the skills needed to complete the myriad tasks placed at their feet. We undervalue their labor. And, to make matters worse, students do too. This is a double discounting.

Ignoring the unpaid labor of lower-income students is a mistake. Doing so limits not only our knowledge of the ways in which social class—and specifically, money—dictates how students use their time in college but also our awareness of the skills they can offer to the world. We must recognize that a resume can conceal as much as it reveals.

Show Me the . . . Experiences!

The COVID-19 pandemic may have closed campus, but it also opened new doors to new opportunities. And wealthy students more so than any other had freedom to take on different opportunities to expand their repertoires. Many took time off—a gap semester, or even a gap year, to avoid "Zoom U"—but choosing to take time off was one that just about only the rich could afford. Still, for those who remained enrolled, as we saw earlier, their lives at home were mostly unencumbered by household duties; they had space—whether at home or in their Airbnb rental—that was wholly their own, and time to focus on both school and internships. As Thomas (UI,W) noted, he "took on a host of volunteer gigs." His reasoning was simple: "I wasn't doing anything else," he said earnestly, "I'm not working to feed myself or support anyone or anything." Privileged students lived without worrying about how they would support themselves. When it came to getting a foot in the door, they tapped their networks to make entrance into different industries and fields easier.[2]

Hannah (UI,W) pulled her long, blonde hair behind her ears as she talked about her internships. "I had my resume reviewed" by the Office of Career Services, she shared. But it was clear from her tone that it felt more like a formality than a necessity; after her travels yet still early in the pandemic, she secured two internships, both unpaid, through personal connections. "One was actually through a family friend who works at the company. My brother worked at this company the summer after he graduated; he said he really liked it. So, I reached out to this family friend and asked if they were looking for interns." The second came about because "I was lucky that one of my roommate's dads knew the guy who worked at this company, and he had heard I was looking for a similar type of job. He threw out an email to the guy who worked at that company and put me in contact with them." As if describing an exchange between an old acquaintance rather than a new professional connection, Hannah said that they "emailed back and forth" until this new connection said, "Alright, if you want to come in, go ahead." Apparently, Hannah wasn't alone.

Without skipping a beat, she continued, "I talked to the other interns and that sounded like how everybody there had gotten their internship . . . a little back and forth and some sort of connection to somebody at the company."[3]

One of Hannah's unpaid internships took her to a venture capital firm that "helps grow fairly early-stage companies and do the M&A of selling them." After going on for a few seconds she doubled back to explain her "M&A" shorthand—"mergers and acquisition"—to show that she was used to translating for the layperson. Her firm was one of the 43 percent of for-profit companies in America that do not pay their interns. The fact that the position was unpaid didn't faze her, though. After all, her parents were paying for her apartment in Back Bay, one of the priciest neighborhoods in Boston, helping her with food, and providing a little spending money as well. "What they would be spending towards Harvard room and board," she explains, went toward "whatever expenses I had at the apartment. They covered the apartment and then they gave me the amount that I would spend on the Harvard dining plan for food. So, I was just allocating that towards whatever I wanted to buy, and that was plenty to cover any of my costs." Tuition being what it is, even a Back Bay rental was feasible.[4]

Moreover, proximity was paramount; she wanted to be in a nice (and fun) part of the city and also close to work—no more than a few stops away on the T was all the commute that she wanted. In fact, she was so unbothered by money that Hannah did not even ask if the position was paid or not. When asked about compensation, she chuckled, saying, "I don't think so, as far as I've heard, no. But you never know." The expectation for pay was completely absent. "I haven't asked," Hannah admitted, even though she had already started to work. "I'm pretty sure the answer's no, but it could come as a surprise."

Another reason that Hannah was not worried about the money, in addition to her parents supporting her, was that she was focused on the experience she was gaining. She wanted a front row seat at a firm that "combines the growth part, that's more venture or private equity, with the M&A part, which was really interesting to me because I'm thinking what part I'm more interested in. And I'll get exposure to both."

Like Hannah and her more affluent peers, Hope (UI,W) approached internships for the experience they provided. She is interested in genetics and is adamant about maximizing her time in the lab. Payment for her time was not on her mind; deepening her understanding of life behind the bench was more important. She had long been interested in medicine and curated her time at Harvard so that each action, from courses to internships, placed her closer to the next goal: attending medical school. She wanted to follow in her mother's footsteps, albeit by traveling a slightly different path: same degree, different specialty. From her meetings, both with her parents and staff of the Office of Career Services, she knew how much lab time matters for medical school admissions. In fact, Hope took advantage of no longer having a commute to the hospital lab for work after she "was able to move my stuff home . . . I was actually able to up my hours because I didn't have the travel time." In finding an extra "hour here or there," Hope shared how "it was easy to just log in, do some work." The simulations she was running didn't require her to go in. As she explained, "I just know it's something that medical schools expect." Armed with these important insights to the admissions process, Hope secured different opportunities and wasn't looking to or "even expecting to get paid for it. I just started doing it to boost my resume and kind of tick off another one of the boxes that the med schools want to see."

Amy (UI,B) has a bubbly personality that immediately puts people at ease. She speaks with a light lisp; her voice coming through like a whisper on the wind. She pairs her love for film and culture with travel. She journals, blogs, and even writes about each in her classes, marrying her personal interests with academic rigor. Tiny white Christmas lights border the framed, vintage film noire poster on her wall. Like Hope, Amy is intentional, especially as it pertains to how she navigated Harvard, both before and during the pandemic. Bucking the trend of her fellow Ivy Leaguers, she did not put her name in the hat for an internship at the management consulting firms (Bain, BCG, McKinsey), or any of the investment banks (Barclays, Goldman Sachs, JP Morgan) that her peers flocked to. "No judgement," she began, although her words contradicted the look of mild disdain that shot across her face. "I don't hold judgement for people that do. I just felt like the things I did were not the path of least resistance. . . . I want to be creative."[5]

Like many of her privileged peers, when the COVID-19 pandemic hit, Amy walked away from campus, finished the rest of the spring 2020 semester over Zoom, and then took the next year off. At least off from school. "I used my gap year to get more preprofessional work and experience in journalism, media, and entertainment, careers that I didn't know how to get my foot in the door fully." What was top priority for Amy was that her gap year not result in a gap in her resume. Even as a sophomore, Amy was already anxious about keeping up with her peers; she told me, "I felt like I had nothing on my resume." Yet in the same breath she shared the joy she got from the many things she did to keep busy: from her on-campus job, which she took so that she could have unfettered access to Harvard's massive art collection to the multiple student organizations—two of which she has senior leadership positions in—that provide her community to the two volunteer gigs that connect her to communities outside of Harvard. She even wrote for a student publication. "I was totally in organizations, but I felt behind," she explained. A chance encounter made her particularly anxious: seeing a senior's resume when their appointments at the Office of Career Services bumped up against one another. Amy admitted having "neurotic Harvard student energies." She knows that this feeling spawns unhealthy competition as students try to outdo one another. Perfectly arched brows now knitted together, her angst showed as she got caught in a loop: she told me three more times in the next ten minutes about "not having anything" on her resume. So, with her parents' emotional support and financial backing, Amy chose to explore her creative interests and the arts.[6]

Amy curated a set of experiences that "actually gave me a lot more academic and preprofessional confidence because of what I was interested in and how I approached my different internships." Her work at a nonprofit media organization promoting gender equality in South America deepened her interest in culture and politics. It brought her closer to the feeling of being on campus a bit; some of her tasks reminded her of class, especially when she was tasked with "academic research, like reading articles and then summarizing them in outline form, looking up specific topics of eco-feminism, environmental justice, and looking up scholars who are doing work on the area of women empowerment."

In total, Amy did three unpaid internships. And not all of them required a lot of her. In fact, her time in film production, where "companies did not pay students; even some of the big ones didn't pay," wasn't particularly rigorous, even if carried a lot of cache. She and her friends, who were also interested in film, "did *all* the same stuff. Script coverage for low level execs." Seeing the confused look on my face, she patiently explained that "script coverage is when you read scripts, give summaries, give feedback. . . . Sometimes, it was truly no work, sending out the newsletter at the end of the week chronicling Hollywood news." Rolling her eyes, she continued, it "required no intellect."

Amy saw two benefits of the work during her gap year. First, these curated experiences inspired even "more intention, especially when it comes to academics and my post grad plans as well." Second, and perhaps more telling than the direction it gave her, Amy loved what they signaled. "It was good they were part time" because the different positions not only allowed for more and varied opportunities and, ultimately, a more robust exposure to the industry she wanted to enter but also filled out the perceived blank spaces on her resume. It may have been a "big hodgepodge type thing," but Amy constructed a narrative in her mind about how immersing herself in media three ways—film, TV, and journalism—would make her a strong candidate upon graduation. The COVID-19 pandemic helped her to transfer this story from her mind to her resume.

In a similar fashion, Denzel (UI,B), stocky and stoic, wanted to be in control of his own story. He became excited when talking about his internships. And there were many. He took a year off from Harvard to pursue different opportunities and to build his resume. His efforts did not disappoint. In fact, his excitement was partly because of the work he was doing and partly because he was able to get it all done. Like Amy, Denzel filled his days with a trio of unpaid internships. Free from classes and responsibilities at home, or at least financial ones, he held the three internships concurrently. Forever thinking several moves ahead, Denzel wanted to do all he could to successfully traverse the uncertain terrain of a pending graduation during a global pandemic. "There was definitely a lot of questions we had to ask ourselves, things to figure out," he said earnestly. To steady himself, Denzel became hyperfocused on accumulating experiences and making connections that would set himself up for success. A broad, confident smile spread across his face as Denzel reflected on "this pretty busy time of my life": "During the summer, especially for the sake of getting experience for consulting, I worked three internships—three virtual internships—which I don't know if I recommend doing. I was working three of those at the same time—all unpaid. My parents were like, 'You doing all this without pay?' I had a very—I've had a very busy gap experience."

Unlike his parents, Denzel did not focus on the pay or, rather, the lack thereof. He sought bigger prizes: experience and connections, not to mention a little professional and social capital. All these are building blocks for a successful college-to-career transition. He carefully curated his internships to give him insight into the future he sought: two of them at a boutique consulting firm and at a startup created to promote network development for young, Black, Latino, and Asian professionals interested in business and finance. Even in the virtual environment, Denzel scored face time with "representatives of various big name companies to collect their stories and resources." Some of these meetings placed him with current young professionals of color who had positions that he wanted to hold, permitting him insight into the life of a Black consultant. Other work calls placed him in contact with supervisors and recruiters who were trying to grow the diversity of their respective firms. From these meetings, Denzel turned personal testimonies into blogposts for the social media platforms of the company he worked for. It was simple work, but Denzel believed he was setting himself up for success. And he was right. Never one to rest on his laurels, at the end of his gap year he secured two paying internships for the summer of 2021, after making connections and learning about new opportunities in his desired field through his unpaid ones.[7]

While Denzel focused on industry, Johannes (UI,A) focused on culture. He braided professional interests with personal discovery, beginning with understanding his family's cultural heritage. He always wanted to deepen his connection to Southeast Asia. Something more innocent than envy but just as strong crossed his face as he explained that "my brother and sister both went to Cambodia before, but I never had the chance." Like Denzel, whose schedule was pretty free because of taking a gap year, Johannes "not only did a study abroad remotely with Arabic and got eight course credits from it, but I also had two internships" that allowed him to explore his Asian identity. "It was more volunteering than interning," he joked. "There was nothing paid at all." In the mornings he ran an "eight-week long curriculum for a critical English and rhetoric course for Cambodian students" and then "did a lot of social media and a lot of data marketing" as an intern for a queer Asian activist in the evenings. He was busy, but he loved it. "So that was really great for me, because it rededicated my love for education" and, because of the work, got to meet a US ambassador, who spoke at the course's graduation ceremony. In his social media intern work, he grappled with what it meant to be Asian American during such turbulent times. "This was right during Black Lives Matter as well as during a rise in AAPI hate crimes," which monopolized his mind. He noted, "It was a lot of really important work. A lot of it was also just activism and connecting with other people who were involved in the community. That got my foot in there."

Just about every college student, especially those at elite colleges, comes in already knowing or learns quickly that internships are important. Internships were discussed at Harvard as par for the course, something you did. For some, whether the position included an income was no big deal because all of the students' other needs were being cared for. Privileged students treated unpaid internships like they do course prerequisites: as stepping stones. You have to take Introduction to Chemistry before tackling Thermodynamics. They constitute a necessary part of the hustle of securing paying work in subsequent summers, and desired careers in subsequent years. In fact, only Amy (UI,B) was critical of unpaid internships, the exception that proved the rules. And even her criticism came from a privileged position. Despite being able to check off boxes and explore creative outlets, Amy called unpaid internships "ridiculous." She equated them to a trap. "Once you buy into doing unpaid stuff, there's no boundary that you can justify." And admittedly, from the sour look on her face, I expected Amy to launch into a diatribe denouncing the inequality that an unpaid internship creates, absent from conversations with her wealthy classmates. But her concern was not for her peers. Instead, her fears were for small film companies and organizations that can't afford to pay student interns. The villain in her story, it turns out, was the big Hollywood studios, not the unpaid internship itself.[8]

I Work Hard for My (Family's) Money

The old saying goes, "What's mine is yours, and what's yours is mine." Lower-income students spoke of a third reality: "What's mine is ours." This sentiment applied to not only to money but also to time. We know, from decades of social science research, as well as generations of familial stories, that lower-income students invest significant amounts of time working to help their families, far more than wealthy peers do. And according to the students I spoke with, that trend only intensified during the pandemic. This investment consists of anything from babysitting siblings to translating at different offices to paying bills. The benefits are abundant, not the least of which is the satisfaction of helping your family, but the downsides are also numerous. It is easy to feel overworked and underappreciated by your family, even as you see the immediate fruit of your efforts. Also, working for your kin can get messy; boundaries at times are either nonexistent or not respected. While students are very aware of both the joys and dilemmas of working with family, many of us are not—and that is a problem, as we'll see, in multiple ways.[9]

Sofia (LI,L) sported a rich tan that accented the copper notes of her skin. She smiled as she explained how she couldn't remember a time when she wasn't working on behalf of her family. A native Texan, Sofia returned home when campus closed and stayed there for two semesters. Before campus closed, she helped out a lot, from proofreading emails to translating documents. Being back home made this "situation a lot smoother," but it also made the work more constant. "A lot of things happened when I got back home; my parents needed more help with work." The main issue was that her father was getting older. Her parents divide duties: while her mother manages the home, her father does pool maintenance. Long, humid days lifting and carrying equipment, with the sun on his back, were getting to be too much. He was not the young man he once was, a process hastened by an accident years earlier, when he worked construction. "Dallas gets hot from March all the way through October." And with the exception of emergencies, "it has to be in the daylight. And it takes from 30 to 45 minutes to clean one pool. And its outside. It's very taxing. And that's why I would make the effort to help my dad because I knew how hard it would be for him to do it on his own, especially in the heat." With a sense of determined urgency, she explained, "They have to follow a schedule" to earn enough to cover the bills. "He definitely needed the second person." It was a role she filled more times than she could count growing up; when she returned home in March 2020, she didn't think twice about doing it all again.[10]

In truth, Sofia's time is almost always split three ways: helping with the pool maintenance service, taking care of her younger siblings, and whatever school—whether high school or Harvard—throws her way. And sometimes the first two took precedence. "I would have to go help them in the middle of the week. And so, I wouldn't be able to attend class. It was just a lot of constant communication and letting the class heads know what I was going through and whether or not I would be able to attend class."

She didn't hesitate to leave her Zoom calls, because she and her father were a team. They moved in lockstep as they carried supplies and equipment in from the faded green pickup through clients' side gates that lead to the pool. Their routine at each pool was improvised but well rehearsed. "We do all of the things together," Sofia noted.

Someone scrubs the pool, all the tile around the edge. Another person vacuums the bottom of the pool. You just kind of transition from those two. Sometimes I would do the vacuuming. Sometimes he would do the scrubbing. And then, grabbing the net and making sure you get everything on the top, cleaning out the filter in the pool,

FREE TO LABOR 137

cleaning out the baskets that lead to the pressure system, cleaning out the equipment, the bigger equipment—the filter machine—and ensuring that the timers are set. And just cleaning up around the pool in general. Yeah, we would kind of split those based on where we were in the process and how we were feeling.

Her father had long pushed himself beyond his limits. His reasoning was as simple as it was heartfelt: he didn't want his daughters to have to work. "My parents were really against us working. . . . That's something that they've really pushed ever since I was in high school. I was not allowed to pick up a job while I was in high school, and even before that." Sitting at the dinner table, laden with *arroz con pollo* and *plátanos fritos,* he was fond of telling his children, "Yo recojo el martillo todos los dias para que tu solo tengas que usar tu lápiz." The loose translation is "I pick up a hammer every day so that all you ever have to do is to pick up a pencil." She loved her father for how adamant he was about this. Not just because it meant she could focus on work, but because he did it for the future that he was determined to give Sofia and her siblings. The irony of the situation is that Sofia did pick up her pencil. And used it to chronicle pH levels at the many pools they visited.[11]

Almost as one, lower-income students shared stories of the very adult responsibilities they had as kids, many of which followed them to college, what sociologist Stephanie DeLuca calls the "expedited path to adulthood." Several students I spoke with contended with going to school while taking care of different family members at opposite ends of life. While Steven (LI,B) cared for ailing grandparents, one who was recovering from a life-preserving surgery that COVID-19 had already postponed, Jessie (LI,N) endured the terrible twos of siblings and cousins when parents and aunts braved the outside for work. Sasha (LI,B) even served as the home health care aide for her father, who has diabetes and travels to dialysis three days a week.[12]

Similarly, Monica (LI,W) served as her parents' unofficial health care proxy long before her first year at Harvard. "Before I left for college, I was the point person for a lot of things, and there were a lot of things that I was doing," she explained. Her family peppered her with questions, requests, and favors from afar, before she even handed in her first college assignment. "My parents, my family, would still call me every day asking me to help them with things that they were dealing with at home." When campus closed and Monica went home, she said, "Apart from class, I'm responsible for other stuff at home. It's not necessarily cooking and cleaning anymore, but it's going with my mother to follow up appointments or making sure that my father's unemployment is done on time, making sure that he's going to the appointments that he has set up and logging him onto his telehealth appointments." It was difficult "having to repossess the role of, 'OK, everything comes through me, and I will be the point person for all of this.'"

Alexa (LI,W), rosy-cheeked with dirty blonde hair, told a similar tale. She likened herself to a one-stop human resources shop. She was still figuring out how to live with her mother, because as a kid she rarely did. In fact, Alexa can't remember how many schools she attended as a kid because she was "moving around from foster home to foster home" after her grandmother saw the pain that her daughter and then boyfriend were putting her only grandchild through. "My parents struggle with addiction and mental health issues. And kind of growing up with that, that was always really difficult. We were jumping around from apartment to apartment in different parts of the city and going to different elementary schools or middle schools." A combination of drug use and untreated manic depression fueled what felt like a perpetual downward spiral. They would get high and then fight. Her father would go to jail. And around and down and around it went. Determined to get her daughter back and her life back on track, her mom got some help and cleaned herself up. She finished school, secured a job, and was finally able to keep the job longer than the probationary period. She eventually got custody of Alexa back.

Knowing how to navigate mainstream institutions, however, was still foreign to Alexa's mom. That's where Alexa, superhero sans cape, came in. She translated the outside world for her mother. She googled forms that her mother had to fill out. She searched YouTube for videos on personal finances to fill in her own blind spots. She drafted her mother's resume, slim though it might be. She researched flexible spending accounts to figure out how much her mother should put away, given the lifelong health issues brought upon by years of drug use. She even completed her mother's taxes, with crossed fingers hoping it would not lead to an audit.

Scott (LI,B), whose tortoiseshell glasses always seem to be in danger of slipping off his nose, is ambitious in all his endeavors, academic and personal. He rose early when he was on campus: "I taught a class, from 7:30 to 8:45 in Boston, about different topics in health care, how students can improve their mental health." He prides himself in staying busy with work but also in making time for his little sisters, who look up to him. As he shared, there is nothing he would not do for this family. He hated seeing his parents struggle. More than that, he wanted to shield his siblings from rising tension in the house, brought upon by the pandemic and increasing financial strain. When his mother was let go during one particular wave of pandemic layoffs, however, even his efforts sometimes were in vain. Luckily, his mother discovered that she was eligible for unemployment after a blast came through a WhatsApp group chat of local immigrants from the Middle East and North Africa. Without so much as an affectionate "Habibi" or another tell-tale sign from his mother that he was needed, she sent him an iMessage. It contained just two things, a link for unemployment and a question, "Can you do this for me?" Laughing about it all, Scott said, "There really wasn't much of a discussion, at least from my end." Even though he now calls the process "straightforward," it was stressful and time consuming. He had to collect "a lot of details that one wouldn't choose to remember, or like, you have to go into specifics. Like, what was your last job? What were your last two jobs? And it was a lot of clicking, like, no, no, yes, yes, things like that." He and his mother sat down to reapply each month. As time went on, it became just him. "We had to renew it every month. But, on the whole, I was the one who did the entire process." Scott now has his parents' taxes and work history saved on his computer. Sitting up straighter with his chest raised, he said, "I did it all."

When not at the computer for his mother, Scott was at the counter for his father. Helping his dad at the gas station was something that started at a young age but carried through until he returned to campus a year and half later. It was like revisiting his high school self, when "I used to work . . . to help at the gas station a little bit" to lighten his father's load. "Over the pandemic, I did work. Just because I was home, so I was like, I might as well work at my dad's gas station again a little bit to raise expenses since I'm living at home again." Several of the other employees called out, some to avoid exposure to COVID-19 and others because they were already sick. His dad took "more shifts, so he earns more money." This meant more time at the station for Scott as well. Wanting to be a good son, Scott stood behind the "bulletproof glass and all that," a necessary precaution to deal with neighborhood woes, and took orders. "$20 on pump one." "Three quick picks for the Powerball." "Change for a dollar for the vacuum." "Trojan ribbed and a pack of Benson and Hedges Light." Scott helping his father out, however, did not do him any favors, especially as his science professors were not accommodating to the additional responsibilities he had to take on at home. "I had a shift to work at the gas station and I had the exam at the same time. I tried to ask my professor can I have a different time to the take this exam? He's like, 'No, take it at work.' So in between being cashier, moving boxes, restocking shelves, he used the store's shoddy Wi-Fi to log on. "I took it at work," he said, looking dejected. The constant noises broke his concentration: the change rattling in the metal drawer of the register, the drawer sliding back and forth beneath the plexiglass. But he was not mad at the shop nor at his dad. He was doing what he had to do, what he always did when home. His frustration was reserved for Harvard. Scott said, "Through this entire experience, I always feel that, even from the beginning, they never really cared."

Amanda (LI,A) also spent time in a shop. In fact, she shared how homework was almost never done at home. The more she spoke, her featherlight voice became uncharacteristically harsh, matched by a stony look that replaced a genuine smile from just a minute before. This inability to do homework at home began in high school and returned when Harvard closed. Instead, she routinely did her assignments at her parents' restaurant. "My mom expects me to go to the restaurant and help them out." A little deflated, she continued, "I get it. I'm at home, help them." In the back of her mind, she knew how helping her family undercut her ability to work and study. As she said, her ability to focus on her classes was "not great at all. It was just stressful."

The expectation to help was always there. So was her hesitancy to comply. She didn't voice these thoughts to her family, though, for fear of hurting their feelings. Instead, she looked for workarounds. Trying to minimize disruptions and account for college being more demanding than high school, Amanda added another purpose to the restaurant's all-purpose storage room: an office. There wasn't much room. Bags of rice and stacks of woks stuck out the sides. And then there were all the things that couldn't fit on the shelves—prefolded red-and-white food containers stacked higher than her head and boxes of fortune cookies. Determined to have some space to do her assignments, she found a discarded rope and used it to tie together some "tiny chairs and a tiny little table" to form "a makeshift table to do my work."

If space was at a premium for Amanda, time was even more so. The most fluent in English in her family, Amanda handled "customer service and things like that," a phrase that she says as casually as it was all-encompassing. Sometimes that meant taking orders over the phone. Other times, that meant standing at the hostess station to help when people came in. If things got really busy, that also meant she had to "help them in the kitchen with making things, making eggrolls, or washing dishes." The problem she encountered all too often was that the busy times coincided with class and office hours. She explained, "It's hard to manage work and school classes. Every class, I have to go to the restaurant, and I probably can't stay in class. If we have office hours during the restaurant's busy times, like around 6:00 P.M. or 4:00 P.M., when a lot of my classes have office hours, if I need help with homework, I couldn't attend. I'll be in the restaurant helping them out. It's hard to attend these office hours with all this background noise, with the woks slamming, the phones ringing. I didn't want to show that on Zoom."

Amanda's work went beyond the physical. Yes, she pinched the dumplings the same way her grandmother had done; yes, she washed the dishes until they passed her mother's critical eye. But more exhausting was that she was the de facto manager of the restaurant—its representative to the outside world. These things could not wait and often took her away not only from office hours with professors but also from study sessions with classmates, club meetings, and hanging out with friends, even if they were all virtual. "Aside from household chores that I had to do," her duties at the restaurant ran the gamut. She helped her father "apply for a small business grant." She had "to help my dad call the landlord." Even though she and her father were both on the phone, Amanda negotiated with the landlord who "was actually nice enough to reduce the rent by like 50 percent. We still had to pay for it, but he reduced it by 50 percent, which I thought was pretty generous.... We didn't have income for two months" when the restaurant shut down during the pandemic. Adding to her list, she also had to "talk with the food supply company."

When things began opening back up and they started serving customers again, she handled logistics. Everything from small tasks like cleaning to big things like brokering deals with the food supply companies that sent them everything from twenty-five-pound bags of rice to the packets of soy and duck sauce customers always request. The salespeople, she noted with a rare smile, only knew her name and voice as she managed all the orders, stocking up on what they needed at the time and forecasting any changes. She wanted to be on Zoom with her professors but first needed to be on calls with suppliers.

Amanda believed what she did on behalf of her family was more akin to chores than work. When I commented on how much work she did at the restaurant, she said, "I don't know if it's a job; I was sort of helping out my parents' Chinese restaurant. I didn't really get paid; I was just helping out. But I did a lot of the aspects of what a job would incorporate, for example, talking to customers, putting in orders, doing all the responsibilities, but I'm not under a formal wage, pay, or job."

Like Amanda, Michelle (LI,L) shared how free time was persistently at a minimum and was in even shorter supply in those early days of the COVID-19 pandemic, and how most of what little she has she dedicates to her family. She sat quietly for a second before speaking; her demeanor seemed an amalgam of weariness and pride. Helping her father was her top priority. He is a hard man to love, but she respects him nonetheless for how he provides for the family.

This work began long ago. "I worked for my father as a secretary for his landscaping company. And I worked that job I think since I was 12." Not surprisingly, she said with a tired smile and something just short of anger, "I wasn't hired necessarily, and it wasn't paid either." What became clear, even to Michelle, was that the nonexistent pay was not necessarily the reward.

> Every work that I did would go towards feeding the family. I would register clients on QuickBooks. I would communicate with clients via calls, voice messages, voicemails, emails. I got really good at writing emails. I think that grew a lot of my writing skills, having to, at the age of 12, pretend I was someone older. I would essentially pretend I was either my father or a different secretary. I tried searching for better advertising methods. I studied and pretty much mastered a 3D architectural design software that my father downloaded on the computer because he would essentially just make sketches of the way he wants a patio to look like for his client. I'd make that into a 3D design and bring everything into reality.

Helping her family, in every way, was paramount. She lifted her head high, her tired smile displaying her pride as she chronicled the myriad ways she prioritized her family. Michelle was creative in her attempts to not only lower costs but also help her father be more professional. In doing so, Michelle began to move through the world differently. Yes, she learned how to use two computer programs, QuickBooks, for accounting, and another one, an industry standard for landscapers that was beyond her father's capabilities. But what became clearer is that communicating with clients on behalf of her father gave her not only confidence but also opportunities to develop her voice. As she noted, pretending to be an adult when she was a twelve-year-old was no small feat. Yet it was one that she mastered.

However, like Amanda (LI,A), Michele discounted all the work that she does. She doesn't think it should count. "I don't necessarily think that the job I had at first, which is working for my dad, which clearly was many, many years of actual office experience," was real; that work "feels invalid to me because it's my father." Because it was connected to her father, because she was working for and on behalf of her family, it is separate and different. Her accounting and 3D design skills were just part of her childhood days, long as those days were.

This work continued when she entered college. It was such an ever-present reality, it got in the way of her processing the closures in March. Amanda shared how she was unable to stop crying as she sat in the car; saying goodbye to her friends and to campus was too much. Her tears were laced with fear, not knowing when she would see them again. Her father had taken the day off to make the three-hour drive from New Jersey to pick her up. His presence on campus added additional weight on her heart; she knew that a day off is a day without pay. She knew that his time off could be the difference between making rent and screening calls to avoid their angry landlord.

So, before they even started down I-90 toward home, Amanda got to work. She knew her first priority was to reset his calendar. "He needed me to send texts to his clients," she says, her words slow and solemn. She started making arrangements, trying to compensate for the delay that she was causing. "I remember being in the car as we were coming back to New Jersey. He was like, 'Alright. Here's five clients that I postponed their meetings and stuff. Can you send them emails saying, 'This is what happened with my family.'" Michelle did, like she has always done, as her father asked.

Mona (LI,N), inquisitive and determined, was like Michelle and Amanda in that she too wore many different hats at home. To help her family, sometimes she wore many at the same time. And it was not easy. "I was having to navigate personal and family responsibilities with my academic life. And it definitely did not go well for me. I definitely struggled. It was not the ideal situation." She continued, "There were times, I think because of my first-generation and low-income background, I felt the need to sort of play it off as if I was doing okay to my parents. To this moment, they still don't know how much I struggled. I would just play it off and be like, 'No, it's OK. I can help you out with this and I can still do my homework. It's fine.'" It was not fine. Neither was Mona.

The pandemic laid waste to what little savings they had. The freeze that hit Texas in February 2021 made matters worse. A pipe burst in the kitchen, forcing them to "take the dishes that they would normally wash in the kitchen sink to the bathroom, which is obviously inconvenient." They couldn't afford to hire a professional. Her father, with help from YouTube alongside his knowledge from when he worked in construction, tackled the project head on.

Mona admires her father's work ethic. He has a motto, for himself and her: "Solamente Cien," which means "only 100 percent." Her father transitioned to landscaping from construction when she was younger. He tended to the pipes on those rare days that he made it home with more energy than was required to get out of his sweat-stained clothes and boots. Most days he made it to his favorite chair and nodded off. Knowing how hard he works and seeing him so drained after a long day, Mona, like Sofia, often accompanied her father, to lighten the load. "I would try and help him out with whatever I can." This sometimes meant going to the city dump together, to "get rid of the debris, like branches and leaves, from the week's work." But before they drove off, truck bed loaded up with black bags punctured by stiff branches that refused to bend, Mona arranged payment and scheduling with their current clients and kept an eye out for potential new clients in each neighborhood they passed through. She even introduced herself—and their service—to neighbors when they showed the slightest bit of interest. Like most lower-income students, she brushed off this work, saying these were just "the sort of everyday tasks that I was doing at the same time I was at school."

Those "everyday tasks" included "something as simple as going to a store" to things more involved like "going to the bank, trying to see a client, things like that." Mona's parents looked to her not only because she was more proficient in English than they were but also because she was more familiar with technology. That was one of the reasons she was tasked with helping them find and secure new inventory for the landscaping service as well as things needed at home. Their search often took them all over the city. Not surprisingly, it was not always possible to schedule these excursions during breaks in her academic schedule. "There would be times where I would be running errands or helping them out with something and be on my phone in class at the same time. It was definitely rough." She shared,

> I remember, this is where the low-income part comes in, my parents have this app that they go on quite often, I think it's called Offer Up. Yes, it's Offer Up. They would go on there to find deals. They're on there quite often, browsing, trying to find stuff. My dad, he finds tools or machines for yard work sometimes. My mom just looks for things for the house. I remember one time my mom wanted to pick something up or look at some item. And obviously she has limited English capacity. So, I was going with her and, at the same time, I was in the computer science section. I had it on my phone, trying to do both at once. We were driving, on the way to see the item, and I was in class at the same time. I didn't take much away from class because I was distracted. But I was trying to help my mom.

Offer Up was their marketplace, a veritable cornucopia for household and work-related needs. It was Mona's job to compare prices, assess quality, and determine quantity of the items needed, always keeping in mind the needs of her family and their limited resources. And she was keeping in mind the four classes she was currently enrolled in. On this particular trip, Mona was calling in to her computer science course, in which they had begun discussing the foundations of keyframe animation and interpolation. The voices of Google maps and her mother crowded out that of her professor. Mona admitted that she "didn't make it super clear" that she was in class. All her mother saw was that "I was on my phone and there was sound coming out of it. I think she just assumed it was fine."

Mona knew that things could not continue in this way. She was missing class. The possibility of staying involved in extracurriculars, which her parents did not understand or see the importance of, was almost nonexistent. She felt compelled to petition to return to campus after a year of being home. It was a hard choice with an even harder goodbye. "When I told my dad, he did seem sad and serious. I remember he said,

'Now there won't be anyone to help me.' That obviously hit me." He knew her going back to campus, to study without disruptions, errands, and distractions, was the family's best shot at future security. He also knew how much help he was losing at that moment.

Buying Companies vs. Buying from Them

Unpaid labor illuminates how students' time is differentially rewarded and differently taxed. Unpaid internships are seen as an investment in the future. Unpaid labor on behalf of families is seen—when it is seen at all—as paying down the present. Yet, for the latter, the tasks lower-income students took on were neither simple nor quick; in fact, many required skill sets that went well beyond typical, student, entry-level positions. Sometimes they even mapped on to a student's career interests. In their unpaid work, Denzel (UI,B) and Amanda (LI,A) both spent a lot of time talking to representatives from different companies. And they each wanted to enter the corporate world upon graduation. But Denzel was making connections with potential future employers, while Amanda was ordering supplies for the restaurant while she pinched dumplings. Yes, she became adept at negotiating and developed her voice, but it was different. These differences went beyond the nature of the calls. One of the biggest differences between Amanda's and Denzel's responsibilities, which generates inequality more than reduces it, is that only Denzel got credit for the work. The unpaid labor that lower-income students like Amanda do on behalf of their family all too often goes uncounted and, consequently, is undervalued. This dual effect undermines mobility.

That we celebrate some kinds of unpaid work like internships and ignore other kinds is most clearly seen in the experiences of Hannah (UI,W) and Sofia (LI,L). What was required of them both in carrying out their duties—assigned and inherited, respectively—was as similar as it was different. Both gained valuable skills and experiences that graduate admissions deans, and recruiters who flock to Harvard year after year, look for in candidates. But only Hannah's resume would ever tell that tale.[13]

Getting off the T and heading to the office was something that Hannah looked forward to every day, a semblance of normalcy. In addition to having a morning commute that did not involve running to catch the Harvard shuttle, Hannah enjoyed her time at the venture capital firm, although she admitted a little glumly that her hands-on experience was a little more removed than she wanted it to be. She recognized that "some of the work I was doing there was pretty menial. Interns get tasks that other people don't really want to do, which was what I would have expected, so that was fine. But I did like it a lot." Speaking about the "grunt work," she said,

> Well, a lot of the things I was working on would be pitch materials or buyer lists for who could sell a given company that we were working with. One example, we had 100 buyers that could potentially buy this company, whether that be private equity firms or strategic buyers. They would give me that list, then they would say, "Find the logo for each company." So I find 100 logos and then find a contact for each company. I would spend an hour just finding logos, reformatting, taking out the background, making it look good, sticking it on there. And that could get a little bit boring.

Nevertheless, for Hannah, exposure was everything, no matter how distant. Yes, she could talk to her brother for tips of the trade. Yes, she could call on her friends' parents for insights into the industry she wished to enter upon graduation. After all, if they could help her get the internship, they could probably help her secure an actual job in mergers and acquisitions, or maybe in investment banking, if she decided she was ready for a change. Seeing behind the scenes, however, is what she sought. And to some extent, secured. The research and collecting of contact information may have gotten a little "boring," but it provided insights into the career she wants. Familial support freed her of any other obligations, allowing her to focus on what she was assigned at work. And now, on her resume for as long as she needs it, is proof to a potential employee that she already knows how the world of mergers and acquisitions works.

Sofia rose just as early as Hannah—sometimes a bit earlier, so as not to delay her clients' pool-splashing. Sofia's job had plenty of grunt work, just like Hannah's. But hers was physical—scrubbing and scraping, patching and measuring. It is unlikely that a white collar employer will ever look at that work as anything beneficial. Sofia's job, however, also had a whole other element. Like with most jobs, the work Sofia did leading up to the cleaning was just as important and sometimes more time consuming. That work often included research too, but of a different sort. As Sofia noted, she "helped them figure out what equipment was the best and started buying little things here and there" to get the business started and also to help it grow. Sofia took product research seriously. Who had the best bleach, pH tests, and plaster? Whose prices were the best? Dolphin? HDX? She knew funds were limited. She also knew buying cheap meant buying more often. Cheap products tended not to last as long as the more established, albeit pricier, brands, which was something she learned from the bargain basement finds her family would buy.

So much was riding on the first clean going right. Sofia described how first impressions were everything. There were lots of other people just like her father willing to do the same work. Sofia knew that she had to choose the right products. If the first cleaning dazzled, then her dad had a good chance at keeping the person as a client. The choices she made determined so much.

Her imprint on the family finances was not limited to the purchasing and cleaning. She handled scheduling, which included ensuring that cleaning schedules aligned with taking care of her younger siblings. As Sofia said, with her head lifted a little higher, "I've done some kind of work with my parents since I was in high school, and even before that. It was a lot of writing up invoices, writing up emails or text messages, and sending them." When a new pool construction job was done, she would reach out to see if the homeowner "wanted us to do pool maintenance for their pool for a month or two." She continued, "It was a lot of contacting previous clients that we had done pool remodeling for and ask them if they were looking for a pool maintenance service. It was a lot of dialing up older customers and just talking through that with them. It was really just trial and error for us. My parents didn't really have much experience with pool maintenance, but it was a measure that we had to take."

Sofia was the jack-of-all-trades for her family. She helped them get the equipment they needed and helped them learn how to use it. And kept track of bills and payments. And completed invoices. And recruited new clients. And followed up with old ones. And did inventory, client relations, networking, recruitment, and aspects of accounting. She transformed her father's side hustle into a pool cleaning service. To this day, her Venmo picture is not of her, as so many of her peers have, but of a matte, white bucket with vibrant yellow mop and pink bottle cleaner peeking out of the top—yet another manifestation of "the tug between who I am back home and who I am here on campus."

A saying attributed to physicist Albert Einstein goes, "Not everything that can be counted counts and not everything that counts can be counted." This sums up the way work factors into students' lives. Not all work is paid. Not all work is counted. That is the problem. We need to count it, or at least account for it. Hannah spent her days researching which companies her firm's clients should buy. Sofia researched which companies to buy from. After eight weeks with her company, Hannah added a respected venture capital firm's name to her resume with a job title that any corporate recruiter would recognize. Sofia helped her family. But that wasn't all. In the language of business and finance, Sofia networked and sourced business. She coordinated outreach, cultivated contacts, and convinced people to hire them. Sofia grew her clientele. Hannah was handed hers, collecting logos and contact information. Sofia was on the porches of clients, on the calls with suppliers, and in the room when decisions were made. Hannah wasn't.

None of these duties, responsibilities, or skills were added to Sofia's resume. No well-known firm and no recognizable job title polished her resume credentials. "Helping out my dad" and "good daughter" don't quite make the cut on a resume. Yet, Sofia was instrumental in growing the family business and providing some financial stability along the way. One could say same skills, different backdrop. But, in many respects, that would, yet again, undervalue the work that Sofia did on behalf of her family.

Conclusion

In the context of the global pandemic, which brought some countries—not to mention millions of families—to the brink of financial collapse, many wealthy students took on unpaid internships. The hope was simple: to gain experience to help them secure the future they wanted. Hannah got her wish: an up-close look at a corner of the financial sector she wanted to enter upon graduation. During summer breaks and gap years, privileged students focused on maximizing present opportunities for future gains. They continued their march toward a career even as they delayed graduation. Low-income students, equally interested in curating that same future or at least one free from insecurity, were often pulled by current concerns—namely, the everyday needs of home—in directions that made such internships impossible. Sofia picked up her pencil along with her bucket of pool cleaning supplies and went to work with her dad. She, like other low-income students, felt compelled to help the family, even if doing so in the short term sometimes got in the way of accomplishing long-term goals.

Yet many of the tasks that lower-income students took on, home-grown though they might be, permitted them to develop skills similar to—and sometimes even more valuable than—their privileged peers. Sofia handled business, and so did Mona, Amanda, and Michelle. They liaised and negotiated and grew clientele. And, at each step, those efforts gave their family a little more breathing room, even as the world was coming down around them.

It is important to note that so much of this is not new. Lower-income students have long been taking on duties within their families, extending their parents' capacity to care for the family, nuclear and extended. These duties did not stop when they went off to college. Their time, like the money they earned in their campus jobs, was earmarked. The pandemic increased the tax on their time in ways that their more affluent peers did not have to worry about or even consider. While trying to keep up with coursework, often in spaces crowded or loud or otherwise not suited for studying, lower-income students took on responsibilities that often disrupted or took them away from class altogether. Mona tried to do both at the same time, but, as happened so often, class lost out to clients.

Lower-income students, however, discounted much of this work that they did on behalf of their families. These two worlds—home versus Harvard—were so utterly different there seemed to be no point comparing the two. There was no time spared for thinking about how the skills they developed at home could translate to campus, let alone to careers after college. As Michelle noted, it was just duty to family, despite learning two computer software programs in the process. The work that lower-income students do on behalf of their families, especially work done during the pandemic, is, for many, a continuation and amplification of what they were already doing for their families. The attempt to unpack this work is not some naïve way of simplistically equating life experience with work experience. It is about accounting for skills, especially those that employers say they want and that data show make good employees. Understanding how and under what conditions lower-income students developed these skills, which otherwise go unnoticed by conventional methods of hiring, provides greater insight into an individual's drive, ambition, and, perhaps most importantly, ability to work under difficult conditions.

But scholars and administrators must go beyond unpacking. We must take steps to help ensure that this double discounting of students' skills and experiences does not continue. There are steps that colleges and universities can take to better address the inequalities inherent in the world of work among undergraduates. How colleges and universities can take up these issues, and thereby better support students, is the subject of the next chapter.

6

Making Work Work

HOW DO we make work work better for students? In April 2022, Williams College, a small, liberal arts school in Massachusetts, announced that it would remove the work requirement from all students' financial aid packages. This change in policy makes it the first college in the nation to eliminate work (along with loans) from the ways it helps students pay for their time at Williams. This move is an important one. Work study is a staple element of student aid packages, mandating that students take on some form of work with upper limits being twenty hours per week. Freeing students from the contractual requirement of work permits them to integrate more into campus life in many different ways, from having more time to focus on their courses, to joining extracurricular organizations, or otherwise rounding out their undergraduate experience. Having an immersive college experience is valuable for whatever career or program of graduate study students enter upon graduation. But removing the mandate to work does not free students from the needs of their families. Students seek jobs not just because their financial aid letter says they have to; they do it because their families need them to. Working keeps the lights on back home and the fridge, if not full, at least not empty. Removal of the work mandate is one thing. Helping students secure positions that lead to opportunities, especially the often-promised unique opportunities that they come to college in order to have—and that also serve the dual function of filling in gaps back home—is another.[1]

The ways in which universities, especially elite ones, handle employment need to be rethought and reworked. Job fairs are necessary but insufficient. Moreover, they are not neutral ground. For many students, they are overwhelming. As Jacob (UI,B) outlines, you must not only be comfortable with the explicit intent of getting something from that person, whether it be an introduction to someone who is hiring or the job itself. Job fairs embody the presumptions that we make about our students—that they are comfortable marketing themselves and schmoozing with grownups—all things that are second nature to many wealthy kids and terrifying to many (albeit not all) low-income kids.

More hands-off approaches, like job fairs, let preexisting inequalities dictate behavior, creating more divergent experiences for students as they move through college. The way each student looks for jobs, just like the way they ask for help (or don't), is a reflection of where they come from. Gertrude (LI,W) was put off by the job fair and made even more uneasy at the thought of engaging faculty. She sought a job that was flexible and kept her away from having to network. While Gertrude distanced herself from faculty, students like Carmen (UI,B) wanted close contact. Carmen not only sought out one-on-one meetings but also reveled in the idea that it was her job to push faculty to be better teachers and mentors. Left to their own devices, the students had disparate approaches to finding work, just as we see in almost all other facets of campus life, from club involvement to office hour participation. And for lower-income students, especially those without exposure to elite places before college, that means many will shy away from positions that provide them access to institutional resources, from money to mentorship.[2]

Not everyone, to be clear, is interested in research or working with a professor. Those positions should not be held as the gold standard per se. But these positions and jobs like them do provide access to influential gatekeepers, those who can provide guidance on postgraduation plans as well as the letters of recommendations needed to secure those positions. Still, research is just one example of a position that engages the mind. Carmen worked at the Bok Center with members of staff who are equally important in opening doors for students. Not only did these positions withstand campus closures, but they provided students with a host of benefits beyond pay. They brought the possibility of deep and meaningful connections with faculty and staff. They even provided extra hours, pay, and support during a time of great uncertainty. Yet, the number of lower-income students who see those positions as "not for me" or "for those people" is troubling. It is made even more so when thinking about the number of privileged students and those educated in elite spaces who presume the opposite.[3]

And early support pays dividends later on. Letters of recommendation and references, for example, are the coins of the realm. Not everyone enters college knowing that fact. It is not in class alone that these key pieces of future success are secured. Your boss or supervisor writes them too. Carmen's bosses can provide such support. And they are administrators, with titles that are recognizable beyond the campus. Given how much they fought for her to stay on, one can imagine the letter would be a good one. Alice (UI,W) worked with a professor in multiple capacities, first as a student and then as both a research and course assistant, deepening their connection.

Gertrude's boss, in contrast, was her peer, someone she passed the salt and pepper to in the dining hall and sat next to in class. Betty (LI,B) had multiple side hustles, opting rather to take on gig positions in which contact with any supervisor beyond those short spans of time was nonexistent.[4]

There is stark contrast at elite universities between the culture of, resources for, and approach to campus jobs and those of internships. The two are more different than night and day. There is an entire industry around internships, fueled further by the entrepreneurial culture that has taken root from Harvard to Stanford and many campuses in between. Staff in the Office of Career Services at Harvard specialize in different industries so that students can get insider knowledge long before they even begin their careers. For campus jobs, the university relies on once-a-semester fairs; a host of disparate, disconnected websites; and a comparatively understaffed office of student employment.[5]

Why keep the two offices—student employment and student careers—separate? Harvard is not alone in this less efficient division of labor. Colleges, both public and private, also have multiple offices doing overlapping work. Yet this need not be the case. Universities can better coordinate support services to help students create plans that unite class content and career exposure throughout the year, not just during the summer months. Privileged students are doing it with the help and guidance of family and friends. The university can be that support for lower-income students.[6]

Northeastern University in Massachusetts combines on-campus work with future employment in one place—the Office of Student Employment, Graduate Assistantships & Fellowships—coordinating and centralizing their efforts. Students have a central and, importantly, single location for all work-related opportunities. This office, and the fact it coordinates many aspects of employment, also permits students to become familiar with staff over time, which education scholar Becca Bassett has shown helps build trust and rapport.[7] There is a real opportunity to help students gain insights into the many futures that college presidents and deans tell them that they have come to campus to pursue, while also helping them earn a little money in the present.

Universities must take a more active role in matching students with jobs. Doing so can break down hurdles, presumed and real, to on-campus positions that help students secure the resources they need and the mobility that they came for, both during the college years and upon graduation. Preterm immersion and pre-orientation programs help close this gap. These programs, which bring select groups of students in before the semester begins for exposure to academic and social life on campus, can also help plant seeds for employment as well. These programs can introduce students not just to offices that are hiring but to the individuals in those offices, labs, and institutes that they would be working for. Muhlenberg College in Pennsylvania provides an example. The college hosts the Emerging Leaders Program each August, a program that connects first-generation college students to peer, staff, and faculty mentors who help them select classes as well as assist them in securing on-campus employment before the term begins.[8]

Any focus on working in college, however, is incomplete without an examination of unpaid labor. Both paid and unpaid work direct so much of lower-income students' time in college. Both paid and unpaid work shape how students move through college. And students' testimonies about unpaid labor they do on behalf of their families shed light on both their responsibilities away from campus and the underexamined skills and experiences they bring to the table.[9]

Both to get into college and for whatever comes next, curating your resume is as important as your GPA or major. Sometimes it is more important, as it signals to gatekeepers—whether HR reps or admissions officers—something essential about you. Questions abound. Your resume is your chance to preemptively answer as many of them as possible, your first impression to someone you have yet to meet. So many things get overlooked on resumes, however, especially when reviewers only look for buzzwords and big names. But the bigger tragedy is what is absent from resumes altogether, especially those of lower-income students. Part of this absence is because so many people—those within the academy and even students themselves—don't consider the labor they do for their families as work. The other part is that there is no space for it.[10]

In 2010 the Common Application added a "family responsibility" section for applicants to explain why they may not be as involved in extracurricular activities like glee club, football, Rotary, or National Honor Society as their peers. These traditional activities take up much of students' time before or after school and weekends. But for many students that time is dedicated to taking care of siblings or working at McDonald's.

This section accounts for cumulative disadvantages and additional responsibilities that set students apart. It opens an avenue for colleges to better account for the time students dedicate to familial responsibilities and provides opportunities for students to share if their high schools lack such activities. In all, this accounting isn't about leveling the playing field. It can't. But it can provide insights into just how uneven and unequal it is. I think, however, we can do even more.[11]

While this change in the application—one additional open-ended question—focuses on helping students at the front end of college, it can serve as a model for a new application at the tail end. To truly promote diversity and lower barriers to entry, especially as considering race in admission and hiring is being questioned and banned, graduate and professional schools as well as businesses could add a section that asks students to share—not explain—why their list of extracurriculars, jobs, shadowing opportunities, and internships might not be as extensive as their peers. This additional section could also ask students to share skills and experiences that they bring to the position that might not show up on their resume. Indeed, some graduate programs have already done this. The Psychology Department at Harvard University offers this option to applicants. Some critics to this approach may say that the opportunity to share this information is in the interview, in a more personal face-to-face or one-on-one setting. This objection, however, ignores just how many applicants are lost using traditional screening measures.

If we adapt, or at least expand, our approach, corresponding growth is needed by those reviewing the applications. Training for those who screen applications to be more sensitive to cultural differences, which is where the conversation often stalls, is the first step. We must also sharpen our understanding of greater forms of inequality that fundamentally shape their applicant pools. These changes would not only account for the additional responsibilities that COVID-19 brought upon the most vulnerable but also provide insight into the everyday realities and unpaid labor that were present in students' lives long before the pandemic and that will surely remain for years to come.

Equally important, we must work with students to help them identify and frame the skills they have developed through the varied opportunities that life has provided them, whether formally through paid labor or the work they do on behalf of their family. These experiences are part of what education scholar Tara Yosso calls "community cultural wealth," those rich resources that lower-income students bring with them to college but that go unrecognized by college officials and recruiters.[12] Yes, we must recognize these competencies and skills, but we must also stop discounting them. Not all students will be willing to count this as work and many, like Charlotte (LI,L), who couldn't see a long interview process through, might balk at these conversations more generally. However, making it explicit that the conversation is an attempt to value and highlight *all* the different skill sets and experiences that they have could lower the barrier to entry. This training can take the form of coaching within student employment and career services offices. Of course, this means that the staff would need significant training to understand students' home lives and students' strategies for minimizing the toll poverty takes on their families.

This push to capture the dynamic nature of unpaid labor brings up a more fundamental question, especially for colleges. How should universities handle unpaid internships? Outside of a system-wide reset—abolishing unpaid internships entirely—what can be done? More specifically, should universities like Harvard, well aware of both companies' desire to hire their students and the inequalities that unpaid internships create, permit companies and firms, especially for-profit ones, to post job announcements for unpaid internships on their job search websites? As we know, students who can afford to take unpaid internships are disproportionately White and wealthy; they also have connections that lower-income students typically do not. Hannah (UI,W) checks both of those boxes and is most definitely connected. She had three inroads to her venture capital internships: her brother, father, and roommate's dad.[13]

If universities continue to host these companies, the university could tax these companies at a rate commensurate with a stipend that pays students a living wage during their time with the company to both push back against unpaid internships and to generate revenue to support students. This process can be facilitated by offices of career services, which spend years curating relationships with these companies and the head-hunters and recruiters who frequent campus. They know recruiters' likes and dislikes so intimately that staff often coach students on what colors to wear and what vacations to mention in their interviews. Instead of focusing career coaching sessions solely on privileged modes of presentation, universities can be students' true advocates long before the interview begins.[14]

Universities should take note of grassroots efforts to make companies more accessible for students from nontraditional backgrounds. Putting pressure on companies works. Take internships on Capitol Hill, for example. Arguably one of the most celebrated internships an undergraduate can get is an internship at the White House. These positions have historically been unpaid, leading to more privileged (and Whiter) classes of interns. As we know, not everyone can work for free, let alone pay rent and eat in a city as expensive as Washington, DC. Things, however, have changed. In March 2022, through lobbying efforts by organizations like Pay Our Interns, the White House announced that it would, for the first time, pay interns in its prestigious program, paving the way for a more diverse applicant and hopefully intern pool. Higher education institutions like Harvard should not sit idly by in this push for equity.[15]

Examining work is important because of the undue pressure it places on students, especially on lower-income students as they compete with their more affluent peers in their classes and on the job market. But some things render even money's protection insufficient. As students were dealing with exacerbated inequalities in the world, albeit differently, they also witnessed social unrest and racial violence. Amid the great upheavals of the last several years, some students felt even more isolated and even more aware of their precarious position in society, and other students just continued on. It is this uneven experience that we turn to next.

PART III

Fault Lines

7

But I See What You Do

SEND A TEXT. Leave a voice message. Organize a Zoom happy hour. As the COVID-19 pandemic raged on, experts implored us to check in on our friends—not just for their sake, but for ours as well. Before long, Zoom parties caught on—from nights of virtual Spades, full of trash talking, to big games of charades, in which friends roasted each other for their bad acting. These weren't substitutes for being in the same room as other people, but they were needed, albeit short, reprieves from reality. But, as we developed ways to manage the isolation of the pandemic, we were also inundated with the worst impulses of humanity. As the pandemic wore on, we learned with terrible regularity about more police killings of unarmed Black citizens and of attacks on Asian Americans. News outlets also began, albeit begrudgingly, to cover the tragic stories of missing Indigenous women and two-spirit people. As long days turned into longer weeks, experts offered the same plea. *Reach out.* In 2022 the *New York Times* highlighted the power of the eight-minute phone call. Even small check-ins, it seemed, carried a lot of weight. Every little connection, it seemed, was a balm.[1]

The advice is sound. The problem, however, is that reaching out is not always palliative.

Dawn (LI,B) needed to connect, or at least to feel connected. Campus closures robbed her of the community she had built. And now on top of worrying about COVID-19, she was scared of the hate shown toward people who looked like her. It was the summer of 2020, and she was living with her mom in their cramped Cincinnati apartment. Then she got an alert about a man dying on the street in Minneapolis. She clicked the link and endured the first seven minutes of the video showing Derek Chauvin extinguishing the life of George Floyd. She could not finish it. In the coming weeks, she stayed glued to the news and to Twitter; she saw marchers and witnessed buildings burn. With each update, her fear of what dangers may come increased.

Just remembering those days brings about a change in her. Sitting in her bedroom, almost a year and a half later, she goes from calm to fidgety. Dawn admitted that she still hadn't finished the video and had no plans to ever do so. For the second time in our conversation, she reached out for her pillow and held it against her chest, as if it were a safety blanket. Dawn came to see her phone as a bearer of bad news. From CNN to the Washington Post, any app she opened seemed to showcase pain and loss. Even ESPN and Buzzfeed, usually bearers of good tidings, brought more of the same. There was no escape from the coverage of killings. George Floyd. Breonna Taylor. Tony McDade. A host of others, all at the hands of police. She had seen up close how police killings affect communities. She told me about Sam DuBose, an unarmed Black man who was killed by University of Cincinnati officer Ray Tensing in 2015, when she was barely a teenager. She lived only a few neighborhoods away, near enough to feel the chilling effects of DuBose's death long after the local protests died down.[2]

Dawn had seen police officers hound people in her neighborhood, sitting in their patrol cars, waiting to pounce on the slightest infraction, real or imagined. She had also seen the backlash against those who supported activists lifting Black Lives Matter flags as they marched through the street. Her voice dropped to barely a whisper. "I was so terrified that people were going to start mobbing down people in the streets with machine guns. Anytime I saw a White person I was on edge. It didn't matter who it was or where it was. I was like, 'Is today the day we get got simply for being Black?'" Her only companions, besides her mother and the high-energy cousins she babysat, were Assata Shakur and Octavia Butler. She carried their books from room to room. But Shakur and Butler's words, rich as they were, weren't enough.

So Dawn returned to her phone, reaching out to Harvard classmates, especially her Black friends. "When I'm at home, there's no one in my family who's my age. . . . The peers I talk to about stuff like this would be friends at Harvard. We FaceTime, we text, but it's not the same as being in the space, feeling their energies, feeling the physical pulse of the room around these things." Their online conversations did offer a measure of solace. But few things could top sitting around a box of Insomnia Cookies with her friends, drowning their sorrows in still-warm, soft-baked treats.

As the dog days of summer came and went, and racial strife continued to dominate the headlines, Dawn's phone began to ring anew. The calls were from Harvard classmates. The names this time, however, were different. These messages, unlike the others, angered her. With an incredulous look, Dawn says that, in the wake of George Floyd's murder, it was "really strange" to have "my White friends texting me like, 'Oh, I'm so sorry. How are you doing with everything going on?'" It is not that they said anything wrong, it was the fact that it was "the first time you've ever asked me about things like this. . . . We've been friends for four years. This country been racist all those four years. Why are you just now reaching out to me, starting *this* conversation?"[3]

Dawn paused, sat back, and straightened herself to her full height. "It just felt very performative," she began, words heavy. "I was having a hard time thinking about how to feel about that." Instead of calming her, making her feel cared for, these check-ins added to her general unease. Their nascent show of concern set Dawn off. She shared how it "was hard to deal with, because again, I'm sitting in my small apartment with my mom, and I have all these people reaching out to me. You are very comfortable wherever you are. You're in Vermont. You're in Maine. You're chilling. You live nowhere near a city at all, just engaging for the sake of telling people you're in it." But the problem was deeper than just these clumsy texts, she explained. Dawn and her fellow students of color shared a history of uncomfortable and exclusionary racist encounters that could not be ignored. Dawn found it hard to be asked how she was doing by people who made her feel unsafe and unwelcome on campus, a place where they were all supposed to feel at home.[4]

The horrors of that COVID-19 summer and the loneliness of being away from school were tinged with and inseparable from the mundane pains long endured on campus. "I have seen a litany of microaggressions over the past four years that just accumulate and grow and change how people navigate spaces." Before campus closed, there were many moments, some overwhelming, in which Dawn found herself in a classroom or in the dining hall, bearing witness to things that prompted her to "start looking at the other Black people in the room." In the few times when she wasn't the only person of color, she caught herself more than once mouthing, "Are you hearing this?" Dawn says these moments spawned uncomfortable yet needed "camaraderie," bonds forged in the face of "needing to verify I'm not crazy. Like, no, this is racist."[5]

As the world was coming apart at the seams, Dawn's disparate worlds collided. She wanted, and even needed, to connect with friends. But the calls and texts from some classmates, specifically White ones, didn't cement her place in the Harvard community; rather, they reminded her of the many ways that she wasn't a full member of it. The racism she experienced on campus *before* closures—that "litany of microaggressions" enacted by many of those who were now showing concern—had been ignored. Their messages in the summer of 2020 thus felt hollow, devoid of substance and sincerity. They apologized for what was happening outside the gates. Yet all the while, they ignored what happened inside the gates—on the problems embedded in campus culture, and especially their own transgressions. Dawn, and many students like her, felt the weight of James Baldwin's words: "One is in the impossible position of being unable to believe a word one's countrymen say. 'I can't believe what you say,' the song goes, 'because I see what you do.'"[6]

For many Americans, most of them White, the protests that exploded in the summer of 2020 may have felt separate from the explosion of the coronavirus a few months earlier. But for so many people of color, these two events were equally seismic and inextricably linked. Both placed racial inequalities front and center. Both highlighted the racial fault lines that have long troubled our divided nation.

When campus closed, students faced more than just a health crisis. From protests to riots to insurrections, students had a front row seat to some of the most stunning moments of social upheaval in a generation.

For months, it seemed like we got constant reminders of just how fragile our democracy was. Most students endured this upheaval without the touchpoint of campus, their home base of sorts for discussions and debate, commiseration and companionship. As one student noted, "I'm tired of living through history," underscoring a wish to live in precedented times. For many, it was a time to come together. Presidents and deans at colleges across the country called for solidarity in the face of injustice. The Ivy League created an "8 Against Hate" campaign to communicate a commitment to condemning prejudice and embracing inclusion. Scores of clubs and organizations on campuses across the country published statements denouncing racism. Some even held fundraisers to support antiracist organizations. But Dawn, and many students of color like her, genuinely struggled with these calls for putting up a united front against racism.[7]

How are students like Dawn to respond to calls and texts saying, "We stand with you" from the very people—and institution—who made them feel uncomfortable, unsure, or downright unsafe? And worse, what are they to think when those same calls carried condolence-cloaked requests to teach the sender about racism?

Campuses are in the world even as they pretend to be set apart from it. As we have seen again and again, we want to believe that the campus gates create a bubble, a utopia that shields and protects, but they don't. At least, not fully, and definitely not equally for all. Moreover, it is not always outside entities that are the greatest threats. As communities of color have known for generations, there are homegrown horrors in these hallowed halls. Teachers and classmates, both intentionally and not, hurt and harm. This unprecedented moment in students' lives—both because of campus closure and widespread protests—forced a painful reckoning with the inequities of campus life.[8]

You're Doing It Wrong

Most of the White students I talked with, and to a similar degree, wealthier Asian students, found the racial climate on campus to be welcoming. More often than not, they were eager to tell me how they valued Harvard's diversity; Harvard presented opportunities to interact with more diverse groups of people than their high schools did. In fact, when asked to reflect on how racial inequality shaped their experiences on campus, many struggled to find answers. They stuttered and stammered their way through incomplete responses. When probed about racial strife on campus, Jade's (LI,W) words stand tall. Rocking her classic, aviator style glasses, she noted, "You can be blind to it if it doesn't affect you." Similarly, Jamie (LI,W) offered a parallel assessment. She noted, "I can't talk about it from my point of view because, you know, a lot of issues that affect them don't affect me." For both Jade and Jamie, it was almost as if they occupied a different space and time altogether. The *them* in their narrative is their Black and Latino classmates. (Native students rarely made it to White students' consciousness.[9])

Harvard was about meeting new people, or at least having that option. The thorn in White students' side was how segregated campus seemed to be. They portioned blame on their Black and Latino peers for making it so. Like generations before them, they questioned why Black and Latino students sat together in the dining hall. Affinity groups, to them, were particularly worrisome. Jack (UI,W) grew increasingly frustrated sharing his thoughts on the matter. Even though he called his rant a "half-baked thought," he was steadfast in his beliefs about how this clustering is holding Harvard back, both the students and the institution as a whole. In fact, he connected it to the real racial problems on campus.[10] He noted, "I'm frustrated by the way people self-segregate. Not to hold my hand up and say, 'Oh, I'm trying,' you know. 'I'm doing better than everyone else.' It's really hard; you're most comfortable around people who have the same experiences as you, right? My blocking group was four White guys, three of which all live in the same city. I'm not saying I'm perfect, but I'm frustrated by the way we seem to self-segregate. I'm frustrated by the way that race has become the only inequality issue when, in fact, there are many."

Jack knows Harvard to be a place where "everyone is friendly, which is very good. I don't feel there's any overt hostility." Yet Jack is upset that race is too central to conversations about belonging on campus and annoyed when classmates self-segregate by race on campus. At the same time, however, he disclosed that his three roommates are not only White, male, and from similar privileged backgrounds but also that all three of them come from the same city. In his friend group, he is the diversity. Still, he lifts himself up as an exemplar of a student who is trying to make connections across campus. His words betray him, however. Discussing how he has "been grappling with how to actively push back against" the self-segregation on campus, Jack noted, "I could do a better job making Black friends and Hispanic friends and Asian friends, absolutely. Or whatever. Pick your favorite ethnic group, right?"

Going further, Jack adopted what sociologist Eduardo Bonilla-Silva calls a color-blind racial ideology, in which a person believes race should not factor into how people move about society, while ignoring how their own race shapes so much of their daily life. "People who are campaigning against structural racism at Harvard are doing good work. But I think we might be better to focus on thinking about what the future ought to look like at Harvard, and then thinking about what the rest of the country looks like, instead of just projecting it all onto Harvard." Jack never said what looking to the future entails.[11]

Sociologists Carson Byrd and Victor Ray capture such sentiments in documenting how White students frame racism more as a historical feature of college campuses while ignoring how the legacy of slavery and racism is part and parcel of how universities have functioned and continue to function.[12] Moreover, White students liken diversity initiatives to intrusions upon campus life. Jack fits this mold. Indeed, there was a dismissive tone to his words. Every time he acknowledged the work or voices of other students, he immediately offered a corrective or posed a question to undermine their efforts. There was always a but. Yes, combatting racism is good, but is it the best goal for the future of Harvard, and for America? Even during a time of social unrest, there wasn't any real effort to understand his peers' experiences.

Jack was not alone in his convictions. White students had strong ideas about what was appropriate behavior for their Black, Latino, and Native classmates, where they can be, who they hang around with, what activities they should be doing. And they let those biases be known. Many Black, Latino, and Native students shared their own experiences engaging with students like Jack—those that admonish the purported self-segregation of others while they practice their own version of it.

More Moments Than Stories

The racism that permeates campus, students note, was often different from what they saw at home and saw on the news. Comparing Harvard to her small Midwest town, Meredith (UI,N) remarked on how home is "all White, a smattering of Natives too, right? We had one Black family, no Asians." She and her family make up a good part of the "smattering." Going further, Meredith noted, "There's an understanding, for the most part, that people aren't White supremacists at Harvard. That's much more common in my town." Thinking about community at Harvard, Jessie (LI,N), who is also Native, noted, "At face value, most people at Harvard don't seem racist. But when you get into a conversation with them, then the microaggressions come out." Dawn (LI,B) offered a similar assessment. She associated "ridiculous showings of racism that comes with places like Charlottesville or the people banging down the doors of Columbus being like, 'Open up the city; the pandemic is fake!' Those kinds of showings of White rage, I didn't associate those with Harvard." Although Jonathan (UI,B) said that campus had entered "a tolerance era" with respect to race, that did not mean that there were not racist incidents that soured students' experiences. It was more subtle, a smattering of moments that seeped into everyday life rather than a shocking event that grounded life to a halt. Or, as psychologist and education scholar Beverly Tatum put it, racism on campus was indeed "like smog in the air."[13]

There is a tenor to the racism on campus, or rather a central tenet. And it can be best expressed in the form of a question: whose campus is it? Or put more pointedly, to whom does Harvard belong? White students policed campus. They assumed, just as many before them had for centuries, that Harvard belonged to them, and so policing emerged as an almost unconscious instinct.[14]

Cassidy (UI,B) captured the experiences of students of color with racism at Harvard, and at universities across the country, when she said, "I have more moments than stories." For her, these moments were the off-color comments about her hair and peers' never-ending questioning about why her friend group was "so Black." Stories, for her, are those more dramatic, horrifying incidents. Like in December 2020 when Enrique Tarrio, founder of White supremacist group Proud Boys, stole a Black Lives Matter banner from a historic Black church in Washington, DC and then set it afire. Cassidy makes clear that those incendiary incidents hurt and were meant to shock, intimidate, and torment. Equally unsettling acts, she explained, are those that are the most ubiquitous—those fleeting exchanges that happen every day. They are quick yet send students reeling not just for hours later, but for weeks. They become part of campus lore, the making of communal trauma.

Some students, although they missed connecting with peers, were happy to be off campus when news broke about George Floyd's murder. Andrew (LI,B) was one of them. With his voice as chilly as his glacial stare, he said of being home, "I daresay that my peace is protected more. I'm able to grapple with how I feel, how I respond to these things within a safe environment. I don't know how I would have reacted, if I would have been calm enough, patient enough, to be surrounded by White peers, friends, colleagues, teachers, administration." Asking why, Andrew shared some of his first experiences on campus, literally. In fact, his distrust of Harvard, his peers and the institution, began during Visitas, the coveted "pre-frosh" weekend where Harvard invites recently admitted high school seniors to spend the weekend on campus.

The weird thing about Visitas is that during that weekend, students go from applicant to admittee, from courter to courtee. To convince students to enroll, Harvard, like all colleges, rolls out the red carpet. The lawns are mowed with extra care. Fresh mulch is laid out in the week or two prior, filling the air with barnyard odors. Colorful Adirondack chairs are placed strategically around campus, inviting passersby to stop and sit a spell. Even Crimson "H" shortbread cookies, delectably crumbly but always a little dry, make their appearance, matching the swag that fills goodie bags. But as Harvard polished its welcome mats, some-one Andrew would later share a house with showed him the door.

> I was a pre-frosh at Visitas. Me and a group of Black students went to a freshman dorm. All freshman dorms have a common room. They stay open all night. We didn't know that. So we're in this common room, and this White man, he's in the common room with us. We're playing games; we're getting to know each other. We're laughing. We're a little bit loud, because we're having a good time. He tells us to shut up. He's like, "Hey, hey, you guys need to quiet down. Our proctor called and said that you guys need to shut up." We're like, "What the hell?" It's already disrespectful. It's causing tension. And we're like, "OK, fine." So we're still talking, still laughing and joking, and we get loud again. He's like, "All right, everybody needs to get out. My proctor texted and said everyone needs to get out." So we get out.

Andrew was scared. That fear returned, with anger and disgust, as he recalled that evening and how quickly things turned. The night began with joking and trash talking as they lounged on stiff couches reminiscent of a scene from any 1990s high school movie. It devolved into confusion, hustling to grab sweaters and leave before any more harm was done. Andrew was away from home and in a new place. He was meeting new people but didn't yet have any friends. The student's threats sounded official and authoritative. "We don't know what a proctor is. We don't know who this guy is. So, we leave." Andrew didn't want to put his admission to Harvard in jeopardy, nor his and his family's dream school and shot at future financial security.

But there was no text. There was no order from a proctor declaring that anyone was being too loud or instructing anyone to shut up or leave. In fact, Andrew shared that, after they were forced to leave the common room, news spread of what happened rather quickly. "Proctors come up to us and they're like, 'We want you guys to know that that student was completely unauthorized to do that. No way would a proctor tell another student to tell students to shut up and get out. That wouldn't have happened.'"

The White student weaponized an imagined proctor in order to police a common space, a place that, should Andrew come, would be his
too. And one that students are encouraged to explore during Visitas. But
the real proctors' words offered little comfort because of what he saw
next. As the group made themselves scarce, they noticed something:
"There were some White students who came in, and they were like, 'Oh,
what's going on in here?' They joined the game." The White students
got to stay in the room, occupying the seats that they were just evicted
from. He and the Black pre-frosh looked on from afar. As prospective
students with no rooms on campus of their own, being barred from the
common room meant having to leave the dorm altogether.

As often happens, Andrew felt exposed and alone. It colored his
experiences on campus from then on. Even though Andrew admitted
that he hasn't had many other moments like this, the murders of Breonna Taylor and George Floyd forced memories of Visitas to the fore-
front of his mind. He wanted to have conversations about what was
happening, the analytical kind where you discuss facts and theories
about police brutality and also the more emotional, given equal space
to process complex emotions. But Harvard, for him, is not the space
for the latter.

Dakota (UI,N), like Andrew, found out early how inhospitable Harvard could be. First-year orientation is supposed to be fun, filled with
meeting new classmates as you partake in different programs, from hiking to community service. For Dakota, however, orientation was less
about making connections and more about learning new ways that she
did not belong.

For our interview, Dakota sat in her room, with a white wall as her
backdrop. It was simply decorated with a string of small white lights and
decorative green leaves. A single sheet of off-white paper containing a
handwritten note was taped beneath one cluster of leaves. The thick
cable-knit of her sweater matched the vines. She was quiet at first, a little
reserved, but became more animated as the conversation progressed,
especially when speaking about her first moments on campus, which
were both joyous and jolting. She had come to college—finally a taste
of independence, both academic and personal, was on the horizon. She

wanted to learn how the brain works and explore things that were not presented at her high school.

Like many Native students before her, however, she felt like her peers believed she was only admitted because she checked a rarely checked box for Harvard: Native American. Her classmates made such suspicions known early and often. On her very first day she was roped into a conversation she neither wanted to be a part of nor was prepared to partake in.[15] "I was eating lunch. One of the girls was talking about affirmative action. She was Asian. She was going on about how she thought it worked against her. I wasn't really listening. Then someone was like, 'Hey, Dakota, what are you?' I was like, 'Oh. I mean. I guess I'm Native.' She was like, 'I bet you're here because of affirmative action.' I was like, 'Oh, OK.' I've been here for 12 hours, and I've already had this weird encounter."

Dakota felt both devastated and annoyed. Her first encounter with the old trope—affirmative action equals lower standards—was beyond unsettling. She didn't know how to respond. Do I ignore her? Do I curse at her? Do I turn tail and just leave, food unfinished? Dakota was just trying to have lunch, not defend her admission. She wanted to escape. "I felt—" She took a deep breath, holding it in a second before slowly exhaling. "Just awkward. I felt like I couldn't make myself small enough."[16]

Common spaces—ones that students have to return to daily during their tenure at Harvard—can become sites of trauma. As Dakota put it plainly, "It was just very awkward for that to be one of the first student-on-student encounters I had." Some students were even more blunt and dismissive in their inquiries. One White student in particular stood out to Dakota. "I had a lot of people give me the whole, 'Oh, I didn't know you guys still existed' response. I just . . . I stopped responding to it." To make matters worse, there was no escape for Dakota. The student wasn't just a peer, she was a classmate and member of the assigned group she had to work with all semester. Biting her lip and looking off in the distance, Dakota said, "She was a roller coaster of a person to work with."

Like Dakota, Brandt (UI,N) enumerated moments that made them terribly uncomfortable. Raking their fingers though their close-cropped hair with frustration, they recall the many times classmates approached them "thinking that it was appropriate to interrogate me about my blood quantum, in other words, how much Native one is, and thinking it was appropriate to tell me I had benefited from Columbus whether I 'like it or not.'" Speaking specifically of the resentment aimed at them by White classmates, Brandt shared how "I remember being told, 'Oh, so you're Native and Jewish? You're every college's wet dream.' I was like, 'Thanks, Mikey.'"

Kelile (LI,B), not ever one to mince her words, shared with a depressing sigh, how it was "draining defending your existence"—not to mention correcting racist tropes, debunking stereotypes, and just generally justifying your place on campus.

Students of color shared how these moments happened with even greater frequency once the dust of orientation had settled. Amy (UI,B) is a ball of energy, from her smile to the way she perches on the edge of her seat, as if about to take flight. Harvard wasn't new to her. So many people from her ritzy West Coast prep school came to Harvard each year that she knew people in each class on campus. Social almost to a fault, Amy knew everybody, and everybody knew Amy. Sometimes being the social butterfly, however, left her exposed. She had had too many conversations that made her question not only her place on campus but her grasp on reality.

Amy's room was often the hangout spot. From pregaming to late night takeout from El Jefe's Taqueria, she and her roommates were good hosts. Classmates also stopped by to study or just chill. An exchange with Erica, a White student who lived a couple doors down and visited often, cut through the lightheartedness of their space, syphoning off the joy and substituting something more caustic. Amy, brow furrowed, recalled how Erica had treated Travis, a Black classmate. His crime was forgetting his Harvard ID when he came to their dorm to visit Monique, his girlfriend. Amy said, "Travis was waiting for Monique. She hadn't gotten back yet. He was literally in our year. He's on the football team. Erica sort of knew him. He asked, 'Oh, can you let me in? I'm just waiting for her.' She said, 'No.' Upstairs, in our room, I was like, 'Wait, what?' She's like, 'Yeah, I think he's at our school.' I was like, 'That's Monique's boyfriend. Why didn't you let him in?' She said, 'Harvard students can be thieves, too.'"

Amy looked heartbroken as the memories returned. Erica knew Travis, had seen him on campus, even in the dorm's narrow hallways when he visited Monique. For Amy, it wasn't just because Erica didn't let Travis in. It was Erica's rationale and the blasé manner in which she explained herself, making an inordinate amount of eye contact with Amy as she did so. Erica didn't see a classmate, a peer. In Travis, she saw a problem, or at least a potential one.

"Harvard students can be thieves, too," Amy repeated Erica's words for the third time. They weighed on her. "It's not like we watched her mysteriously not let him in. She said, 'Harvard students can be thieves.'" She was shocked by how brazen her reason was, "I was like, 'What? I'm out. I don't know what to say here.'" In that moment, Amy didn't feel comfortable being in her own room. She had no words.

As she recounted the incident, her anger boiled over, her voice shrill. Her sentences began to come in fits and starts. She abruptly stopped to find her words. Amy shared that she didn't let the moment pass completely unchecked. She told Erica, "I don't need to tell you the stereotypes of Black people right now. It's not my—I could tell you, but you already know these stereotypes exist. You hear yourself playing into them, right?" To Amy, there was little doubt about how race shaped Erica's actions. "That was the most textbook—it's admitting to their own racism."

Like so many moments of racism, so many discriminatory encounters, those on the receiving end are left to deal with the emotions that remain long after the incident, even as the perpetrator moves on with their day. Amy later sought support from friends that she was not overreacting, which only served to anger her further. "I told one of my friends. I'm glad that the friends, the close ones I relayed those things to, were also like, 'That is racist. That is crazy.'" They shared their own stories, or similar moments. Amy was comforted but not reassured by her friends' words. She still had to return to the same dorm that Travis was barred from and still live in the same hall with Erica, who would, before week's end, return to their room as if nothing happened.[17]

Each of these encounters lingered; each dampened their sense of belonging. It made them question just how open their classmates really were. Students offered scores of examples of their time at Harvard being policed, moments of othering and surveillance, nearly always enacted by White students. These moments, and the feelings they inspired, contrasted sharply with their White peers' declarations against racism. Students of color dealt with the disconcerting reality between everyday acts and public pronouncements.

At the time of my interviews there were no official reports of nooses or flag burning on campus—those classic examples of public intimidation. But there were updates to such techniques. It is unsettling to think about Andrew's first visit, Dakota's first trip to the dining hall, and Amy's time in her own dorm room alongside the recent rise in cases of "swatting," when police are called with false reports of armed assailants and respond in full force. Swatting takes on particular racial tones as it is almost always a person of color whom the police are called to investigate. On campus, it has been used to target Black students in particular. In fact, in April 2023, members of the Harvard University Police Department, armed in riot gear, descended on the room of four Black women after an anonymous, and false, report of an armed person in the room. The women opened the room to officers, guns drawn. They were scared to say the least. And their pain deepened as Harvard took hours to acknowledge the incident and more than a week to issue a statement. The community was equally dismayed at both the incident and delay. Swatting is not new, but rather both a return to and an escalation of age-old intimidation tactics.[18]

Black Squares and Empty Gestures

Not all students labeled the calls, texts, and messages from their peers as disingenuous. Alex (LI,A) described to me how his spirits lifted when his classmates reached out, even as their messages reminded him how much pain there was in the world. "With all the AAPI hate, I have had many friends checking on me—which is great, by the way. They're like, 'How are you feeling? How are you holding up?' I'm like,

'Honestly, I haven't had time to process any of this. I have midterms. I have papers. I have shit to do. I'm not able to worry about these things right now, because if I do, I'm not going to be able to complete my assignments in time.'"

Elena (UI,L), on the other hand, was more critical. And less forgiving. She sat tucked away in the corner of a Starbucks. A medley of Bad Bunny and Aventura emanated from the store's speakers. The early morning California sun poured through the wall of windows to her left. Her Zenni Aviator sunglasses sat on top of her head. Our conversation was as easy as the warm breeze she missed dearly when in Boston. "Even though it's winter," she began with a lighthearted smile, it is "75 degrees out—perfect for outdoor studying."

The conversation turned from weather to life at Harvard. There was an "I've been here before" feel to her words. Her prep school days helped her transition, both academically and socially. She had her eye on joining a final club, one of Harvard's elite undergraduate social clubs and knew she had an advantage in the punching process, Harvard's name for pledging. "Those private school experiences helped our names get out there." Between sports, clubs, and collaborative community service events with other independent schools (which also sent students to the Ivy League), Elena had friends long before classes started. In fact, Elena and Amy, who spent the first COVID-19 spring bouncing from one Airbnb to the next, attended the same ritzy, West Coast day school. Harvard was, if not a family affair, at least a familiar one.

She was upbeat, outlining her many connections across campus. But then I noticed a change, as if an unwanted memory resurfaced, cutting against the grain of her sunny disposition. Her gaze drifted to the right, and her voice developed an edge to it, more annoyed than uncomfortable. I asked her about the change. With little hesitation, Elena began to tell me about Leland, "the repeat offender."[19]

Leland, dirty blonde and blue-eyed with a look that screams *lacrosse*, was known around campus in that classic Harvard way. He went to a feeder high school just like Elena. He was also in a final club. But his washboard abs weren't his signature feature. It was his words. Elena described the first time they met, introduced by a mutual friend at a mixer. When he heard her name, he looked her straight in the face, and said, "Can I just call you Maria?" And, without so much a pause, proceeded to do so. It wouldn't be the last time either. They knew the same people and hung in the same circles. They had partied together (and would do so again). But he couldn't, or rather wouldn't, get over wanting to call her Maria.

Elena's story was a common one. Leland had a problem with boundaries, especially as it pertained to women, and especially women of color. As Elena noted, "I genuinely think Leland had no experience with women of color, or anyone of color in his life. He was known for approaching women of color . . . and his pickup lines were flat out racist. He would ask Black women, 'Is your hair real? Can I touch your hair?'" Peers weren't always silent about it; many students called Leland out on his behavior. As Elena noted, however, "He knew his behavior was problematic. Yet he'd continue on. . . . He would make really racist comments." Elena still grapples with the emotions that come up every time she thinks of her interactions with him. He wasn't sleazy, like the seedy men who catcall women. As she explained, it was something more disturbing. Maybe because he was a peer or maybe because she knew him. Either way, his actions undermined her sense of belonging and showcased his power to treat people however he saw fit to do so. After another pregnant pause, Elena said, "I don't know what to make of this as I share this story. He made many people really uncomfortable."

The unease that settled over Elena continued to grow. She scrunched her nose, as if wrestling with a lingering smell, and pulled her chin to her chest. Then she told me about how Leland posted a black square on his personal Instagram account on Blackout Tuesday, the day of collective online action in the summer of 2020 to protest racism and police brutality. She and her girlfriends texted each other screenshots of his account, as proof of his Dr. Jekyll/Mr. Hyde act. He wasn't alone. So did many of the members of his final club, people who Elena assured me were cookie-cutter copies of Leland in many ways. It was unsettling, she said. Like Dawn and so many students of color, group chats became a digital sanctuary to check in, debrief, and vent. Elena and her friends did a mix of all three when so many White classmates posted black squares.

> We would talk about people who posted black squares. Like, "This person is flat-out racist" or "This person is known for saying the n-word" and they're here posting a black square. That's what I'm getting at. A lot of people posted it to try to say, "Hey, I'm not racist." But at the end of the day, you're doing racist things. . . . What are you saying by this black square with no substance behind it? There were people where it's like, you have made me feel uncomfortable in a racial—like you've made a racist comment, prejudiced. Yet you're here, posting a black square.

The black square began as a sign of protest against police brutality and anti-Black racism. It quickly morphed into a sign of solidarity, used by people of color in general, and then became a signal for allies. It just as quickly became like a mask, at least in the eyes of many. Elena's words flew out like daggers as she recalled the parties where "all these White people are saying the n-word" with freedom and sometimes a little too much feeling.

Elena paused for a moment, thoughtful. She said, "People could learn. People could grow," giving space for an awakening of sorts. However, that grace was short-lived. After no more than a heartbeat she continued, "But the whole black square thing was overcompensating. People did it out of fear, not out of support. Like, fear of being canceled or tagged as racist."

A mischievous look came over Elena. "I wonder if his square is still up," she asked with a morbid curiosity. Elena picked up her phone, opened Instagram, punched his name in the search bar, and started scrolling, thumb flying from the bottom to the top of her screen as she found Leland's posts from June 2020. His black square was gone.

Switching to another profile—another White classmate with tendencies like Leland—she discovered the same result. She did this one more time. Despite her interactions with Leland and the other classmates she looked up, and she was still optimistic that there was some substance behind her peers' posts. What hope Elena had, fleeting and fickle as it was, vanished. She didn't look shocked, just irritated. And some of that irritation was at herself for holding on to that hope. "I obviously think a lot of people are overcompensating," she explained. The lines around her eyes seemed deeper, the downturned corners of her lips stood as opposites to the easy smile that usually graced her face. Elena sat in this vacuum, uncomfortable and sullen. The hollowness of their gestures set in as she raised her wrist to her forehead and took another pause. Words hard and tone harsher, Elena posed a series of questions of her own, each one underscoring her frustration: "How many people deleted that black square? What was their thought process in deleting the black square? Are you no longer in support of this? Which, again, it's all trivial stuff because a black square doesn't mean anything, but it meant enough for you to post it and then delete it. What does that mean?" Looking out the window yet again, she taunted, "The world may never know."

Deleting a black-square post may not be a clear-cut sign of a performative gesture. There was, of course, a very different interpretation. Some lamented how the posting of black squares by millions of individual users drowned out the targeted messaging that grassroots organizations hoped to share—about ongoing protests, demonstrations, and calls to action—through the campaign. But Elena did not make space for her White classmates to be aware of, let alone responsive to, such calls. There was too much history to overlook.

Students shared how decisions about what to do—or more often, what *not* to do—were shaped by these moments. Such incidents, again passed along via group chats and word of mouth, may have been small moments, but they had a big impact. They made students like Michael (LI,L) develop "a fear of white spaces." Feeling similarly, Carolina (UI,B) did not think things would get better. She resigned herself to the idea that Harvard was not some idyllic place to study, but rather a place full of "mice and racists"—the parts of Harvard that are not featured in the viewbooks but are part of the everyday reality of being a student of color. Emphasizing each syllable with a clap of the hand, Carolina discussed her "place-less-ness," the lack of connection and grounding she felt walking on campus.

The feeling of being surrounded by disingenuous peers was one that came up again and again. When it came to the racial climate of Harvard as a whole, LBJ (LI,A) noted that her grasp of the racial climate on campus is "very much centered around what I'm seeing on Instagram, what I'm seeing people post." And LBJ had seen what she needed to see. What was posted did not reflect the campus she knew. As she noted, "It's very hard for me to separate, especially for *some* of my peers, what is performative versus what is genuine."

Similarly, Yasmine (LI,W), whose family is Middle Eastern and community is Black, talked about whiplash. She sat propped up on a single white pillow. Her bulky, over-the-ear Beats headphones sat on top of her mountain of curls. There was a frenetic energy about her. Used to being on the go, she has a passion for community organizing, especially for efforts that bring about racial and economic justice. Coming to Harvard was both blessing and burden. She could learn more about the social justice issues she was passionate about, but she would be forced to do so alongside people who, she believes, only pretended to care. In fact, Yasmine scoffed at the perception that "everyone on campus is an activist." She explained, "Everyone has read *White Rage*, or *The New Jim Crow*, or *How to Be an Anti-Racist*, et cetera. They use all these big terms about how they're not racist. I'm specifically talking about White people on campus. Everyone is an anti racist. But I don't think they realize how the things they do are really harmful to actual people of color. We're at Harvard right, where a lot of us are definitely outspoken. We can definitely speak for ourselves, on our own experiences. Why are you interrupting and speaking about us instead, right?"

Yasmine said that her classmates could talk the talk but, for her, it ended there. There was no follow through. Instead, her classmates "overpower and take over the voices, coopting them for their self-aggrandizement." Yasmine abhorred her classmates for using Black Out Tuesday to feign allyship, and she despised how they were capitalizing on the moment, on someone's death.

She immediately recalled forced conversations with classmates who pretend to be concerned about the state of Black America, yet all the while silence their Black and Latino peers and propagate stereotypes. She remembered being grilled by White peers about drug use in Detroit, forcing her to defend herself and her city from racist tropes. One set of questions hurt more than others. "People at Harvard were really out here sniffing white powder, but then they would ask me, 'What's the gang violence like in Detroit?' . . . People are really out here talking shit about people who are selling weed and selling crack, but they do cocaine." She found herself in a tough position. She knew her community struggled. But she also knew that there was a lot of good being done. Still, the question blindsided her. As with Brandt, the question came from over her shoulder, looping her into a conversation that others were having. She quickly realized who the question was coming from, the same White classmate who bragged about her own community service work in Detroit and even wrote about her time in the city in her college admissions essay. Yasmine's words came stumbling out as we spoke, "You can pop Adderalls all you want to concentrate, and you can look cute while you're sniffing your cocaine."

Jerome (LI,A) was equally frustrated with his friends' privilege. Black and Asian solidarity was part of his childhood. He lived in the shadow of race riots that scarred his city, commuting past streets still hollowed out from disruptions that happened a generation ago. He knew of the shared pain in both communities. Moreover, he knew firsthand that to address the inequities you must first listen in order to learn. Sharing stories can often lead to shared strategies. In his characteristic softspoken manner, Jerome discussed the silencing that happens at the hands of the "activist climate" on campus. He explained,

> Something that I've been uncomfortable with is a lot of students at Harvard are activists. Racial justice is something worth fighting for, but I think—I don't know how to phrase this well, but the White savior mentality complex of like, "I am so guilty, and therefore, I'm going to fight, be an activist, call out injustices, and use the privilege I have to do this"—I mean, it's a good intention, but one needs to recognize that—along with being active—one needs to take time to listen, to hear the stories of communities of color, of people who have gone through, or at least the ones suffering from racism and White supremacy. There should be an emphasis on that. I haven't seen that.

Like Yasmine, Jerome feels like his voice and that of students like him get crowded out. He is spoken for but not allowed to speak for himself.

Each One Teach Many

Of course, not all White students purported themselves to be experts on matters of race. Some admitted their ignorance of race relations in America, especially the inequalities that undergird so much of the tension. Here, however, a different but still painful problem arose. These White students asked and expected their Black peers to educate them about racism, even as they ignored their own transgressions against the very peers they were now asking for help. Angelica (UI,B), like Amy, was questioned by her White peers about whom she associated with. For Angelica, these inquiries came from her teammates. "You say hi to a lot of Black people," Angelica remembered Erica, her White teammate, saying as they walked home from practice. "Why do you know so many Black people? Why don't you have other friends?" Did Erica also count how many White or Asian or Jewish students Angelica said hi to or how few non-White peers Erica spoke to? Angelica did not say. But it went deeper. One day, Erica asked Angelica similar questions about a party that was happening that night. Angelica decided to invite her, thinking that Erica's barrage was rooted in F.O.M.O., fear of missing out. Alas no. Angelica recited Erica's words. Voice harsh, she said, "Those parties are too aggressive." Angelica recalled being paralyzed in that moment; Erica's brazen dismissal was one thing, but calling the parties aggressive was another.

These exchanges, routine as they had become, stood out in Angelica's mind as news about George Floyd and Breonna Taylor surfaced. Because months later, sitting at home, one of the only Black members of her varsity team, she was now bombarded with a new set of questions. "How are you feeling?" "What can we do to help?" Then the conversation took an unexpected turn: "Can you teach us about racism?" "What should we read?"

And teach she did. Like her professors in her classes, she curated a makeshift syllabus. Her role as team educator, however, came at a cost.

"I had periods where I literally could not look at my phone." Like many students in her position, she was worn out and felt drained by everything going on. But she couldn't turn her back on the moment and felt that she couldn't let down her team, despite previous exchanges that sullied her relationship with some of her teammates. As Angelica noted, looking tired and angry, "I didn't have the motivation, but I was so invested." She wanted time away from the onslaught of bad news. It all was "too recent." And yet she couldn't let her teammates remain ignorant of the reality that caused her so much pain. She had to process and teach teammates who "didn't really know anything at all" on top of classes. As she noted, her words fighting each other to come out, "It didn't really resonate with them. It wasn't really emotional for them. They just saw a sad story and it was just moving on." Angelica stayed glued to the television, computer, phone, and tablet, each bringing different batches of bad news.

And still, she felt like she wasn't doing enough. Looking tired, slumping a little in her seat, Angelica described being pulled in so many different directions. She wanted to disconnect but felt obligated not to. "If I was truly in tune to what is going on, that would heavily impact the work I'm doing with my team and my friendships. But you should be doing it. But it's almost, like I said, you don't want to be doing it. You don't want to tune into what's going on." The same classmates who counted her hellos, tallying them up by race, the same teammates who called her parties too aggressive, now needed her help to understand animus toward Black people off campus as if their actions didn't cause harm, pain, and scars on campus.

Involvement in clubs and sports is usually associated with a boost in belonging for students. Clubs and teams provide ready-made families, built-in communities that also provide routine and support. But at colleges across the country, and especially elite colleges, as education researcher Jeffrey Selingo notes, teams are disproportionately wealthy and White. Harvard is no different. And this demographic fact shapes much of what kind of community is built.[20]

Rufus (UI,B) loves being outside. His eyes crinkled and a smile spread across his dimpled face as soon as he started talking about what it means to be in nature. He organized his time at Harvard balancing research on climate policy and nature hikes, the latter informing the former and vice versa. He also joined clubs that exposed him to the elements, making what he thought were deep connections with people who also aspired to protect the environment. To round out his schedule, he also joined one of Harvard's most competitive club sports teams. The field, just like the nearby forest, called his name and he answered. He began to question some of those connections, however, when he was unceremoniously asked to pen statements of solidarity for not one but three groups that he was involved with on campus. Rufus explained,

> I had to write a statement for two different clubs, about solidarity with the Black Lives Matter movement. It ended up being a lot of us being pulled into groups' and organizations' efforts to denounce things that happened over the summer. It was definitely weird. Most of them came from people that I love, and was well-intentioned. One of them definitely got under my skin. . . . One request I got from the team, it was essentially to the tone of "Hey, Black members of the team—would you guys be willing to each individually post a video of yourselves denouncing White supremacy, and explaining what diversity means to our team?"

The work, Rufus noted, wasn't just in penning the statement. It was the emotional labor that went into grappling with the requests, the intention behind them, and ultimately the futility of the gesture, as well the actual time it took to come up with statements. Moreover, Rufus saw a clear difference in the requests he received. "When things came from places like love and vulnerability, and wanting to learn, it felt fine. When it came from a place of 'we want to do this public show of solidarity that we think you'd be the right face of,' it felt wrong." The team's request became the straw that broke the camel's back. He felt pushed to the boundaries, seeing more clearly how his friends saw him. Or at least, how they came to see him in the wake of such social unrest. Rufus, looking like he lost a longtime friend, said that there was "a general lack of community among the team over the summer. I feel very distant from the team now, despite being an involved member, and being the captain. I feel pretty distant from them now."

There were real consequences to how students of color dealt with calls and requests. It caused many to question friendships and their membership in different teams and clubs. Angelica was exhausted by old questions and new responsibilities. Rufus felt like a pawn, something to be sacrificed for the greater good.

Not Just Peers

Almost none of the students of color I spoke with expected the university to support efforts to address racial inequality. It would go against what they had seen before campus closed. As Ryann (UI,B) noted, "the racial climate on campus is not one that lets Black students, or BIPOC (Black, Indigenous, People of Color) students more generally, really thrive, feel included, heard, comfortable, and all of the things that you would hope your institution, your home for four years, makes you feel." In many ways, students felt like for the university to offer any statement in support of Black lives was just as incongruous as those shared by their disingenuous White friends.

Dawn (LI,B) was adamant about this fact when we spoke in March 2021. She felt like she was being gaslit by her arts and humanities professors, especially inside her department.[21] When their statement of support came across her email, she was immediately skeptical. Discovering that they were setting up a fundraiser to support grassroots organizations did not inspire hope or joy, but rather annoyance. She stammered and repeated herself, every word dripping with indignation. Taking a second to compose herself and look around the room, she continued,

> There was this wave of initiatives across campus from all these spaces I've seen harm, talking about how they're in support of Black Lives Matter. It was just sad to see. Y'all are patting yourselves on the back, you're going to feel great about this, knowing damn well you're going to go back to the ways that you disenfranchise students on this campus. My department was very much like, "We stand with Black Lives

Matter." But you've had students of color tell you for years that you're teaching colonial rhetoric, we only studied White men in our classes, and we don't want that anymore. And you giving us hell over trying to change that. How, as an institution, can you promote a zeitgeist that has really real consequences for a lot of your students, but then continue to perpetuate teaching styles or content that is actively harmful. It felt hypocritical.

Dawn felt like it wasn't just her friends who offered empty gestures in the wake of harmful acts. It was as if her professors, her department, and Harvard as a whole were cut from the same cloth. Their words did not align with her experience. In fact, their words contradicted them. And, just like with her White classmates who are "just engaging for the sake of telling people you're in it," the effect these acts had on her were the same. Dawn loves the arts and chooses her courses according to her passion and interest. But her department is one of the "spaces I've seen harm." Faculty inaction made her feel as much of an outsider as their actions. She encountered silence when trying to engage them on being more inclusive in what plays and playwrights they teach, what art they engage with. For Dawn, it wasn't just the quashing of conversations about updates to the curriculum that made her feel invisible. It was how the faculty permitted conversations to unfold in class that rendered her mute. And in one particular class, a required course for all majors, she encountered the most roadblocks. "Every single week, for fourteen weeks, someone brought up the question, and we would discuss it ad nauseam, 'Why is blackface bad?'"[22]

I spoke to Dawn again a few months later. Her grievance with Harvard had increased. Dawn noted how "everyone was doing this grandstand on what they thought Black Lives Matter meant," when campus was closed and racial strife was headline news, but once campus gates reopened, "we've not heard anything about it again. September was back to normal, like Harvard stuff minus race."

Many students of color lamented Harvard's "inaction." However, it was less inaction and more action that either felt performative or hollow or that didn't push the needle in the direction that students thought it should go. And they did not limit their criticism to a single department. Kelile (LI,B) said Harvard is "not a healthy place" and that many of the programs and initiatives are "just for show." Aisha (LI,B) concurred, saying it was hard "not being able to have a space to address anti-Black racism on campus."

Harper (LI,B), too, was highly critical. "What stands out to me are the emails about caring about Black Lives Matter." Here, Harper referenced an email then-President Lawrence Bacow penned on May 30, 2020, with the subject line, "What I Believe." It was reflective and deeply personal, sharing his own experiences from adolescence that included the assassination of Dr. Martin Luther King, Jr., in 1968. Bacow was not alone in offering such a statement of solidarity. Race scholars Ishara Casellas Connors and Henrika McCoy examined presidential statements following the murder of George Floyd. These statements, though they underscored a call to action, located the problem of racial hostility beyond the college gates and paid little to no attention to the harm being done to their own students by their peers and the institution itself.[23]

This omission of what was happening in their own backyards did not escape students' eyes. Students of color scoffed at such statements from administrators. Harper saw them as "constantly invoking George Floyd and Breonna Taylor's name with no real action." Harper cared less about Bacow's words, about what he, as president, believed, and more about how Bacow was going to put those words and beliefs into action.

Aisha (LI,B), near tears, shared an email she sent to the deans at Harvard. She held nothing back: "You have us out here surviving and we should be thriving. You're failing your responsibility to a significant portion of your community." She felt that so much of what the university was doing was "symbolic," just like her peers who chose black squares instead of real action. She explained, "In terms of Harvard as administrative response: useless. They always have a task force. What do they do? Beyond me. They're like, 'We're adding paintings to the dining halls.' You're not doing anything that's actually going to help me. Half the time, I'm looking down, I'm stressed about schoolwork. I'm not looking at the walls. I don't even know who's on there right now."

The loss of Black and Latino faculty—compounding the near non-existence of Native and Indigenous faculty—to other universities in the years immediately prior to and during campus closures hit students especially hard. Faculty of color, and especially women of color, do a disproportionate amount of unrecognized and uncompensated service and care work, particularly mentoring and supporting students from underrepresented groups. Education scholar Amado Padilla calls this "cultural taxation," additional duties and requests on professionals' time and energy because of their race or ethnicity.[24]

Students look for faculty with shared experiences, especially in times of trouble or distress, putting faculty on the front lines of campus upheavals. This "Black Tax," as it is commonly known, is caustic because it undermines scholars' productivity. Yet, at the same time, the work being done, as research shows, provides a social safety net for students of color. And yet while many peer institutions established hiring clusters, where departments across the university were prompted to identify and recruit scholars of color whose work focused on racial inequality, roughly a dozen Black and Latino faculty members left Harvard in quick succession. Some left of their own volition. Others felt forced out. Still the number of faculty of color dropped. And no departures were more public than cultural critic Lorgia García Peña and philosopher Cornel West. These departures, which meant fewer faculty of color as well as classes that centered race and inequality, were further highlighted with the perceived protection of David Kane, a White adjunct professor who promoted increased policing of Black communities. Moreover, Kane extended an invitation to campus to Charles Murray, conservative political scientist who the Southern Poverty Law Center listed as a White nationalist for championing Black inferiority through "racist pseudoscience."[25]

Speaking on Harvard losing faculty of color, Ryann (UI,B) said, "There is no world in which that makes sense." But it agreed with what she came to know about Harvard. She was particularly upset at the departure of West. She explained, "To me, Harvard is terrible at dealing with issues of race. But even, if we accept that, which I do, and we say Harvard is just an institution that wants to put jewels in its crown, that wants to build up its prestige, even that's an argument for why this brilliant man should be given tenure. That's what I'm saying, there's no world in which I can make this make sense other than a world in which racism is at every single part of the decision making that institutional leaders have to employ."

Ryann was incredulous. She saw the departures of not only West but the dozen faculty of color who left as a signal of university priorities. She saw official statements about the university wanting to support students, and especially students of color, but not actually supporting faculty of color as Harvard showing its true colors. To Ryann, one of the best ways to support Black students was to actually support the few people on campus with whom she felt comfortable speaking about these issues.

Rahel (UI,B), thoughtful and critical, was not surprised. If anything, she was annoyed, something that became like a steady state for a Black student seeing so many Black faculty leave. There was nothing that happened that didn't agree with what she came to expect from Harvard. In fact, Harvard's action aligned with one of the greatest lessons being on campus has taught her: how to do the bare minimum. She noted, "Harvard's really good at giving lip service. Harvard taught me how to give lip service and get away with that. There's just too many things for me to be convinced of that this school cares. The list is too long. I'm not convinced that they care, but I've never expected them to care. I'm not surprised; it's just not an expectation that I have." But it goes beyond just what's happening on campus. Rahel sees Harvard as a "force of capitalism and what promotes White supremacy in this country, and what keeps the oppression of people of color and a lot of low-income people." Similarly, even Nathaniel (LI,W) joked that the university is good at setting up "task force after task force," with nothing coming of it.

The void left by what students saw as both inaction and disregard for what matters to them was filled by student groups, putting additional burdens on those who were already doing so much. Like Angelica (UI,B), who played the dual role of teammate and teacher, even after racist comments were volleyed at her, many affinity groups organized virtual meetups, check-ins, discussions, and other activities to promote community well-being, taking up the mantle to be the voice of and for students of color on campus.[26]

Angelica's experience was not an isolated one. Many members of the community discussed widespread burnout. The pandemic taxed everyone, albeit unequally. The animus toward Black and Asian communities took its toll, again unevenly. The silence on issues facing Native and Indigenous women and two-spirit people reverberated in the vacuum. The performative actions from Harvard—perfunctory calls from friends and empty statements by the university—became too much. Ryann said that, after time, she became "emotionally divested" from not only the larger Harvard community but from those pockets of campus that once provided protection. Regina (UI,B) noted how, for the first time since she has been on campus, there was no energy around elections for leadership positions in clubs. "I think it's just a symptom of being burnt out."[27]

The exhaustion students felt was palpable. And it was just the beginning. Lower levels of club involvement had ramifications for student well-being going forward; affinity groups served as "counterspaces," locales where students from underrepresented groups feel valued and seen. Moreover, these groups and organizations provide "counterstructures," identity-affirming services that the college should provide but doesn't. Gaps in these resources mean gaps in the socioemotional safety net for current and potentially future students.[28]

But such is the nature of racism. It always launches a multipronged attack. Taking on roles of club president or outreach coordinator is not just filling your schedule or helping your peers. They also fill out students' resumes, helping secure a desired future. Some employers and graduate school selection committees look at involvement in different clubs and societies to get a sense of who a student was and, more important, an applicant is. Consequently, this burnout can undermine mobility in addition to morale. Everyone is tired. The thought of taking on additional work that students feel the university should be doing is too much to ask. As Harper noted, "It's draining and demoralizing because I just want to focus on learning." That simply was not a luxury afforded to him.[29]

Conclusion

Poet Maya Angelou wrote, "People will forget what you said. People will forget what you did. But people will never forget how you made them feel." Students of color, spirits raw like an exposed nerve, remembered all three. The racial unrest that gripped the nation, and the world for that matter, served as a backdrop to ongoing problems of inclusion that plagued campus. As Elliot (LI,B) succinctly stated, "There's a difference between being diverse and being inclusive." Harvard, like many colleges that have adopted progressive admissions policies to diversify their campuses, remains what sociologist Elijah Anderson calls a "white space," an organization where people of color are marked—both physically and emotionally—for being different. Students of color lived in that no man's land, vulnerable. And when they looked to the institution, instead of false statements, they got something worse than silence: empty promises.[30]

While some students appreciated check-ins, many more hated fielding the calls from White classmates, especially as those calls put them in conversations with people who seemed to have just discovered that racism exists. It was a marathon in emotional management. Even their professors and departments didn't make it any better. Dawn felt silenced in her attempts to democratize the curriculum by the same people who were now purporting to dedicate themselves to causes that uplifted Black voices.

Students saw their friends' calls and posts as performative, lacking intention or substance. Their evidence was the callers' and posters' own track record. These were the same people who turned a blind eye to racism on campus, or worse, were the usual suspects in harassing moments that went viral in group chats and email threads. The same was said for how they read the university's response. One consequence of this was, rather than giving them a roadmap for the future, it grounded them in the past. As Elliot noted, "We know this university wasn't made for people like us." And despite generations of progress, diversifying the campus in unprecedented ways, he felt like the university couldn't shake its stubborn roots.[31]

Importantly, this experience is one that students of color have navigated and endured for generations. But it is equally important to underscore how this dynamic undermines in new ways the image of the college as a bubble. We have seen how the bubble metaphor falls apart: how family and community dynamics shape campus life for students as well as how responsibilities at home take a toll on how students move through college. The same is true with respect to national issues like racial injustice. It seeps in through the gates, effortlessly, like a low-hanging fog. And yet again, some students feel the damp chill more than others.

8

Between Struggling
and Surviving

FIVE MINUTES without traffic. Just over three miles. That was the distance between where Kelile (LI,B) grew up and the site of George
Floyd's murder. Kelile, with her big family in tow, had walked down
Chicago Avenue countless times and shopped at local stores. It was familiar. The intimate knowledge, of people and place, is what made "it
hurt a lot more; this person was suffocated to death." But there was
another dimension that made the connection special. "I understand
that life is precious, having six brothers that are Black, one of them being
a very large Black guy who is super—he has the biggest heart. He's the
miskiin, the loveable, unfortunate, quiet one of the family. He's probably
just as tall as George Floyd if not taller." She stopped, stumbling a little
over her words. "I know that if someone saw him, they would perceive
him as a threat." When she saw Floyd's body, she shared, many thoughts
ran through her mind. But, she admitted, one thought dominated her
thinking: "This could be my brother in a traffic stop. This could be *any*
of them because this is happening in the same location."

Kelile loves all her brothers, but the shy one has a special place in her
heart. When she watched the video, she saw Floyd on the ground, on
pavement her feet have traversed, and she struggled to make sense of it
all. The image of Floyd, large and splayed, was burned into her mind's eye,
hyperlocal and hyperreal. But the image in her mind sometimes switched;
sometimes there was a substitute lying on the ground, one of her brothers,

her *miskiin*, in Floyd's place. Like many Black students I spoke with, she and her brothers had long had experiences with the police that left them shaken, feeling less than human. But after the video circulated, the usual low-level discrimination became something entirely different. As the police became "extra hostile," she and her brothers became "extra cautious," especially when they came to North Minneapolis.

The thing is, Kelile loved the neighborhood like family. Seeing it struggle was especially difficult. Watching her brothers move around like they were walking on eggshells made her angry. North Minneapolis was one of the few places where faces looked familiar. "You'd see a lot of Black people, probably the only place in Minnesota where you'll see a lot of Black people just walking around." Pushing back in her seat, she talked about how this dynamic made them all targets during the summer of 2020. Power was cut off in the city during protests, shrouding the Blackest parts of the city in darkness. When Kelile thought she was getting a handle on things, Daniel Michelson, a medical student, defaced a public mural by using spray paint to blackout Floyd's eyes, an act of vandalism that sent Kelile spiraling once again.[1]

> If a person is willing to ruin someone's memorial, if they can do that, if they can try to harm him while he's dead, that highlighted just how deep racism was. They were going after a Black man while he was dead, and they couldn't physically harm him anymore. The person going after him was not just a regular person. It was a medical student. Someone who was very educated. Someone who, in the near future, would be at Fairview Hospital or hospitals near us. He would be actually servicing Black people.

The disregard for Black life weighed on Kelile. Doctors are supposed to heal, not make the pain worse. Yet from experimentation on Black bodies to discrimination in everyday care, time and time again, history has shown us otherwise. Kelile witnessed history unfold anew with the desecration of Floyd's memorial by someone training for a career in which they vow to do no harm.

Kelile didn't just see Floyd's body go limp on the ground. She saw years of bullying and intimidation. She saw domestic terror. She saw backlash against a community naming their pain. It was all around her, down the street and at her doorstep. There was no escape. And she was not alone.

We saw how students' acute awareness of off-campus events heightened their attention to fault lines on campus, deepening their distrust of their peers and increasing their angst navigating Harvard. Here we see a different manifestation of that same problem: students' disparate experiences with racism and animus toward people of color during campus closures underscored just how differently burdened students are. Violence against Asian, Black, Latino, and Native people during campus closures, particularly during the height of the pandemic, and community responses to those incidents were not something to simply be consumed via the news and social media by members of the community. At almost every turn, violence shaped how students moved about the world. Sometimes danger came knocking, direct and in their faces. Other times, it seeped in through the crevasses, quietly disrupting every aspect of social life. The unraveling of the social fabric was on full display, in their communities and in their homes. What happened during COVID-19 was, in many ways, a *further* unraveling. So much of what we saw during the height of the pandemic was not new, but an amplification of an ever-present background noise, an exacerbation of long-simmering tensions. These deep-set problems are nearly impossible to escape from; they followed students of color as they made the enormous transition to college life, and then again as campus closed. Universities cannot always shield students from the ugliness of life. But we can learn from these spasms of violence, and our collective reaction to them, in order to develop a greater understanding of ingrained inequities and the ways they permeate campus boundaries.

Looking On from Afar

It was pretty hard to be alive in the summer of 2020 and not be impacted, in one way or another, by the social unrest that gripped the nation and the world. But for the White students I spoke with, especially the wealthy ones, that tumult, like the COVID-19 pandemic, was often defined by a degree or two of separation. One White student summed it up best: "I can only imagine." Hannah (UI,W) was in Jamaica with her college roommates, looking on from abroad. She explained, "It was me and three other members of my blocking (rooming) group in Jamaica—and we talked a lot about that. We also talked about how it's interesting that social media's become such a big part of this conversation." There is an almost academic way in which Hannah spoke about social unrest, almost as if she were presenting an argument in class. It wasn't that she was disinterested or lacked concern for others' well-being. She cared. But it was not her experience, not her burden to bear. Moreover, it was something that she could turn off when it was time to return to the beach. And even when she returned from her vacation, one of many she took during lockdown and the months after, she was unbothered. Ever the one to connect with friends, she would drive to nearby cities, skirting rules of curfew in the same way she ignored the closure signs of Muir Woods. "To be honest, I was definitely out driving past curfew once or twice; it wasn't super heavily enforced. For me, it wasn't that much of an inconvenience."

A telling conversation captured the uneven toll exacted from students of color compared to their White classmates. Jade (LI,W) and her best friend Alicia, who is Black, had been close for a good long while and shared many happy memories. Closures forced them to share even more and be there for each other through some darker moments. Jade even had candid conversations with Alicia about why Alicia "always drove very, very carefully." Alicia obsessively followed the rules. Hands at ten and two. Full stops at stop signs. Approach the speed limit but don't go over. Alicia was earnest in her response: "I don't ever want to be even pulled over." When news of police brutality flooded their newsfeeds, Alicia returned to this conversation and asked Jade a question: "If I'm pulled over with you, would you get nervous?" Jade's answer left them both speechless. "I would get nervous, but not for me."[2]

Jade's answer was honest, brutally so. After a pause, Jade noted, "When I said that, I didn't even realize—I said that and we both were like, 'Oh.'" A wounded expression crossed her face. She loves her friend; that much was clear by the hurt in her words. But as she put words to how different their lives were, Jade had to grapple with both her own privilege and her friend's pain. "It was very sad; it was a very sad thing to realize."

The majority of White students talked about reading reports of police brutality and acts of racism. They reflected on it. Many were saddened by what they saw. But it was so often talked about as if it were from a distance. Even when speaking to a friend, sharing in a hypothetical that was not just possible, but probable, given the way Black drivers are pulled over more than White ones, some White students admitted having revelations about the crippling fear doing even the most mundane activities can inspire for their Black peers.

Up Close and Personal

Venturing out into the world came with its own set of risks. And not just because of the COVID-19 pathogen. There were unique dangers for people of color due to the callous disregard for their well-being and their lives. Going outside brought them closer to danger, increased the risk of being accosted and harassed for nothing more than being who they are. For Jane (LI,A), the danger came while shopping at Wal-Mart in her small town of West Virginia. Standing a little over five feet tall with a wiry frame, she does not present an imposing figure. Even when her face is hidden behind a mask, she often wears a Cheshire cat smile, eyes crinkling all the while. But the shape of her eyes, the creases and folds, made others see her as a threat. "I remember in Walmart, someone came up to me and was like, 'You and your kind need to get out,' and started yelling at me." He was belligerent. She was frightened. Her instinct was to run as fast and as far away as she could, but the latter felt too risky. A quick move on her part might startle him, giving him license to do more than yell and scream. "I'm not saying anything. I'm just walking away. You know, it's like, what do you even do?" She read, not just the room, but the community. The Confederate flags she passed on the way to Wal-Mart and her state's open-carry laws made the moment particularly scary.

For people of color, it wasn't just when they went out that they experienced such animosity and hate. Delaina Ashley Yaun, Soon Chung

Park, and the other Asian women at Young's Asian Massage and Aromatherapy Spa in Atlanta were at work, simply trying to earn a living, before Robert Aaron Long came in on March 16, 2021, opened fire, and killed eight people and wounded another. As students shared with me, sometimes trouble came knocking. Loud and hard.[3]

For many people around the world, the United States is the land of opportunity. People leave language and loved ones to strive for a better life in the United States. Amanda's (LI,A) parents, who came from China, were but two out of millions of immigrants who uprooted their lives in the hopes of giving their children a better life than what they had growing up and what they could have provided had they stayed there. But it wasn't a total loss of culture. Amanda's parents, like many, brought a little bit of home. They worked multiple jobs each, saving every penny. They left Amanda and her brother with relatives who saw them more than her parents did. It all paid off. The family was able to open a Chinese restaurant in Florida, where the menu is dominated by Americanized dishes but still had a few unaltered staples.

They were living the American dream. Amanda had become a naturalized U.S. citizen. Her mother got her green card. The restaurant had regulars and traffic was fairly constant. Things were looking up. As news of Wuhan and the spread of COVID-19 across Eastern and European borders in January and February 2020 ran with greater frequency, the calls began. By March, they were disrupting business; for every few orders for food, there were expletive-laden directives for them and "their kind" to leave the country. So as not to rattle Amanda, her father tried to keep things from her, but every once in a while, he would slip and "offhandedly mention, 'Oh, just a prank call today. People saying, 'Chinese virus.' 'Is there virus in your food?' Which is unfortunate." The sad thing, Amanda said with a shrug, was how familiar it felt. "I'm not surprised. It's been happening even before COVID. In terms of maybe frequency, it's kind of similar. It's just the jokes have changed to more COVID-related things. . . . It makes me mad, but I've grown up with it. I've dealt with it." Tellingly, Amanda noted, "I'll be more surprised if it stopped." By the time she arrived home in March, however, she couldn't ignore the impact the taunts were having on her parents, on her. Again,

as Amanda explains, the jibes weren't new. But then the torment esca-
lated beyond the calls.

On one random day, Amanda said, "This guy just came in, and he's
like, 'Why don't you just go back to China? Talk to your relatives and tell
them to stop eating bats? They're bringing all this here and they're killing
all of us.' And then says some not great words that I don't want to repeat.
My parents felt really threatened." Amanda was afraid that things would
devolve even further. She explained that her parents "didn't have the vo-
cabulary to communicate with him to say, 'This is not OK.' They're really
frustrated. They're understanding that this is a verbal attack, My dad also
gets pretty flustered at times. When he gets flustered, he screams back.
We just don't want the situation to escalate."

Her family's response to these incidents, especially as they grew in
frequency and intensity, was categorically American. "I'm going to get
a gun," her father told her one night in the early days of the pandemic.
Amanda was in shock. Even as we spoke, months later, she started fidgeting in her seat and blinking quickly as she speaks about the moment.
All she could say to her dad was, "What?! We never talked about getting
guns in our house. We had no interest in guns at all, ever." But her father
was tired of being scared. He read the news. He heard the stories. He
had already shut down the store for two months, hoping hostilities
would cool down. They didn't. The racist rhetoric blaming China, and
Asians in general, for the COVID-19 pandemic continued and intensified. The fear of another heated exchange with another racist antago-
nizer was too much to bear. Amanda still looked uncomfortable as she
talked about it. She was not emotional but was recalling the things that
were said to her parents that she couldn't bring herself to repeat, which
unsettled her. And as she began to share about the "family trip" to the
gun store, the source of her unease became clearer. She said,

> My dad's like, "When you get home, I want you to take me to a gun
> store and talk to the guy. Get something that can protect us." That's
> how COVID impacted my family. . . . It was scary. I never thought
> about getting a gun. My family, we do everything together. So, I'm
> sure the guy there thought we were going insane because it was four

people, mom, dad, a daughter, and a son, walking in the gun store. My dad is like, "OK, go talk to him." I'm like, 'I don't know anything about guns." And then I'm like, "OK, so we're thinking about buying a gun for home protection." And he's like, "OK, what kind do you want?" I was like, "I don't know. One that works?"

Amanda felt completely put on the spot. She didn't have time to research what type of gun or test out different ones. She was juggling classes, cooking, and accounting. Doing so would have made it all too real, especially as she hoped that her father's desire to purchase a gun was a fleeting one. She just rambled through questions that came to mind. Amanda explained,

> Can you just show me what you have? The price range? How it works? He's like, "OK." And then pulls down so many different guns. I felt really scared. Oh my gosh, guns are scary to me. He's like, "We have this model. This is how it works. This is how you put in the bullet. We have gun training lessons that you can attend." I was very overwhelmed. I'm like, "OK, Dad, just pick one. Which one do you want?" He didn't know. Then the guy was telling me, "OK, these bullets, they're pretty fatal or with these bullets, you can shoot the person, and you probably won't kill them. You'll probably just injure them, slow them down." I'm like, "Oh my God. I don't want to think about this."

Of racist calls and bullet calibers, American dreams met new immigrant realities. From the very beginning of the pandemic, Amanda was tasked with dealing with threats to personhood and prosperity. The answer to managing both was an old, used Glock. It was all they could afford. Economist Justin T. Huang found that Chinese restaurants lost an estimated $7.42 billion in revenue due to anti-Asian hate in 2020. Amanda and her family experienced their share. What these loss estimates don't show is how families like Amanda's dipped into their limited reserves for protection.[4]

And it goes deeper than lost earnings. Amanda was the spokesperson for her family. She wanted to be strong as she stood in the gun shop,

translating for her parents, just like she had done in countless government and medical offices. But this time was different. She was afraid of
guns. And now, she found herself surrounded by them. Even worse, she
was searching for one to take home. Sure, no one in her family really
knew how to use it; the seller's quick demonstration did nothing to aug-
ment their understanding. But the Glock fit both their tight budget and
their imagination of what one needs to be safe in the United States.
Despite reports that gun owners more often hurt themselves than in-
truders, it gave them a sense that safety was in their hands. Although, in
truth, they were as afraid of the gun as they were of who they would
have to use it on. "It's my family," Amanda began with an eerie calmness,
eyes once again shifting upward as she searched for words, "I'm really
fearful for their safety. You start with someone saying mean things, verbal attacks, what's next? Physical attacks? I'm really afraid that they
would get. . . . What's going to happen to them?"

Worries about family were commonplace for students of color. Even
though separated from her family, they were always on Mia's (LI,M)
mind. As we talked, Mia sat in her boyfriend's house. It is where she held
up for a couple of months after campus closed in March. Her family
lived just a few miles away, finally moving from their car to the studio
apartment she helped them secure. She wore huge over-the-ear headphones to drown out the general din of the comings and goings behind
her. The room was dim, but her computer screen made her face shine
brightly; her eyes, almond shaped and deep brown, stood out. They
began to shine as she spoke about attacks on people of Asian descent
during the COVID-19 pandemic. Being half-Asian herself, the rise in
animus toward communities of color was top of mind. "It's made me
glad that both of my grandparents, my Asian—they're Filipino—
grandparents have passed away." She caught herself with a start: "Not
that I'm like, 'Oh, I'm glad they're dead.' But I'm glad they don't have to
witness any of that."

Her words came out before she fully understood their weight.
Waves of emotion washed over her as she batted her eyes faster and
faster. She sighed audibly. "It's a sad thing to say, but . . ." The shock on
her face, followed by fresh tears, deepened as she talked about her

dark-skinned father. Mia feared that his brown skin and his Asian features would place him squarely in society's crosshairs. The fact that the family was living in the car for the past year and half left them even more exposed to the outside world. Her voice trailed off as she dabbed her eyes with a piece of tissue. The shooting in Atlanta hit particularly close to home for Mia. "I know what immigrating to the United States and working every day to support your family looks like. I see my dad, I see my grandparents. It's upsetting. . . . I just want everyone to be safe and be able to live."

As Amanda and Mia pondered their families' safety, Jessie's (LI,N) family worried about theirs for being Native, for being two-spirit, for a host of other things that made Jessie the target of hate. I could tell Jessie was tired. We sat in my office in November 2022, one of the few instances I got to meet a student in person. Their face, hidden behind a mask that they tugged on when speaking, had taken on a weathered look, an exhaustion that wasn't there when they were last on campus. So many responsibilities weighed them down. They had sent money home almost since the day they arrived at Harvard, but then, like many in March 2020, they lost all three of their jobs on campus. Back at home, with no Wi-Fi and no privacy, even applying for remote work was a struggle. Home on the reservation meant dealing with two sisters, four and twelve, and two small dogs always vying for their attention. Still, knowing they needed money, they looked for work back home. After weeks of searching, they became a contact tracer. This job provided money, for a while, but it brought them face to face with the brutally uneven death rates that Native communities faced. As they made calls, they came across familiar numbers and names. It wasn't just at work that they faced loss, either. "My grandpa—he actually passed from COVID-19. He was on a ventilator. I remember feeling like he was on a ventilator so long, and the medical staff were like, 'Oh, he's doing better, he's getting better.' And then, out of nowhere, I get a call at 2:00 A.M. It was my aunt, and she was just crying hysterically."

They came back on campus in January 2022, gearing up for their last year after a more circuitous route to graduation that Native students tend to follow more than their peers. Time off, as they note, was something they had been considering; then the pandemic made it their only option.[5]

Life had always been a struggle for Jessie. The reservation was full of love but low on just about everything else. Sometimes help from outside the community was how they survived; a reality that became starker once the COVID-19 pandemic hit. In fact, Jessie said that another Native student at Harvard was so worried about them that "she created a GoFundMe. And I was surprised, because I had never used GoFundMe before. Within two days, I reached my goal. I just was so grateful, and my family was able to buy the supplies we needed. We bought two loads of firewood. We paid off the utility bill. I was able to get the things that my sister needed."

Jessie rarely thought of themself first. At almost every turn they mentioned their grandparents, an aunt or an uncle. Family was so important; they call their grandmother "Ma" because she is the only mother they've ever known. Their grandmother's hands tucked them in at night and those same hands got them ready the next day. Jessie pays that caring forward, knowing the sting of having an absent parent. So much is about their little sisters. They have a true bond. It is a multifaceted one, because they are at once sister and surrogate. Jessie worked tirelessly to make sure their family had what they needed.

One night during the summer of 2021, Jessie told me, they needed a break. They wanted to take more breaks, but between their sisters, Ma, and the dogs, they couldn't carve out much for themselves. There isn't much to do either; home is "barely even a town—nine miles of just rural area." But the stars shine so bright in the darkness of the wide-open desert. Jessie was able to escape home for just a few hours; it was such a reprieve, short as it was. They could unwind and just be a childless twenty-year-old sitting outside under the stars with friends. But the joy they got from seeing people their own age was not meant to last. When Jessie got back home, their sister Nayla "opens the door, and she was holding a knife." Jessie imitated Nayla's lighter voice but was unable to keep it free of their own anger: "I heard there are people going around killing people. They're killing Navajos. I thought you were one of those people.'" Jessie paused and took a deep breath and sighed, their mask ballooning. "I felt sad. It made me feel really sad, because my sister is twelve."

In recent years, after endless silence, there has been increased reporting on the killing of Black citizens. Sometimes, there is even video footage, horrific but incontrovertible evidence. Many news outlets have also covered the depressing rise of attacks on Asians in recent years, aided by the base cruelty of then-President Donald Trump. But there has been shockingly little coverage of the attacks on Native and Indigenous people across the nation, let alone of those that have been missing for months and even years. And this is especially true for Native women and two-spirit individuals, who have been reported missing or murdered at alarming rates.[6]

According to the U.S. Department of Justice, although they constitute the smallest ethnic group within the U.S. population, the second-highest number of reported missing persons identify as Native or Indigenous. Blythe George, a sociologist and member of the Yurok Tribe, spent two years compiling data on and narrative histories of missing or murdered Indigenous persons (MMIP) in California to shine light on this epidemic. The groundbreaking report, "To' Kee Skuy 'Soo Ney-wo-chek'"—Yurok for "I will see you again in a good way"—shows that 62 percent of all missing Indigenous women, girls, and two-spirit people in California are not present in any state or federal data repository.[7]

Jessie and their family, living just a few states away, saw this unfold on their streets even if it didn't make headline news. In fact, just days before Jessie's short-lived reprieve they witnessed more than a few White Lives Matter rallies and heard tales of White militia roaming around the neighborhood. Community members shared sightings on Facebook. There was "a picture of these White people in a van, and they were wearing masks, like cartoon mascot heads. . . . People said that they had weapons. I remember they were all in the van, and it was like a picture taken of them going down the highway. People were saying they were going around terrorizing people."[8]

Depressing as it was, Jessie was not surprised. "Those border towns around the reservation are very racist, very right-wing." They were not

beyond physical threats either. Calling it "a terrifying time," Jessie recalled how "there were some folks going around threatening to hurt
people, specifically Biden supporters, and lefties, or just people of
color. And there were many posts on Facebook going around, nearby
here, that told people they had to be careful in the border towns,
because there are White supremacists going around hunting Native
people and people of color." Looking straight at me, Jessie said, "They
wanted to hunt Navajo people specifically." Their sister heard these
same updates, often at the same time Jessie did. They were inundated
with reports from within the reservation, even if the news didn't report
the incidents.

On the night Jessie finally took a break, their return home was more
eventful than they could have ever imagined, making them wish they
never left in the first place. Jessie climbed the three steps to the porch,
the door opened, and there was Nayla. The porchlight was off, but the
lights were on in the house. Jessie noticed Nayla's Nike flip-flops and
mismatched pajamas. Nothing new there. But her hair was a different
story. It was pulled tight in a ponytail. Nayla almost always wears her
hair down; she is proud that her dark auburn hair hangs low on her back.
Jessie then noticed a glint near their sister's hip. Jessie was stunned; all
they could do was ask their baby sister, "Why are you holding a knife?"
From questioning to pleading, Jessie exclaimed, "Put that knife down.
You almost poked me. Please put it down." Jessie, feeling what peace
they got from their night out evaporate in the space between them,
could only ask Nayla one thing: "Why?"

Standing on the porch, Jessie was in a near face-off with someone they
care for and love. It almost broke Jessie. "I know that knife because I
hated that knife," they said blankly. They remembered the day they pur-
chased it from Family Dollar. The blade was silver, the handle, black. "It
was the biggest knife in the kitchen." But it was terribly dull. Jessie
avoided using it as much as possible. They never thought it would be
used as a weapon, let alone against them. And yet their sister, all of twelve
years old, armed herself with what she could find. Nayla wanted to defend her home, her sister. She even took time to pull her hair back, knowing that it would be harder to grab hold of if it were already pulled back.

But it was the sign of the times, one that ate at them daily, changing their desire to go out, changing how they interacted with their sister. Describing the "cloud that has been hovering over us," Jessie noted, "It just seems like we've been taking blow after blow after blow after blow. You would think that the pandemic will be the only thing you would have to worry about. But no, there's also just the added layer of racism, added layer of poverty and anti-indigeneity, and just having to really struggle through that." In that moment, on a random summer night, Jessie knew that there was a larger history to Nayla's concern. The names of the missing and the murdered from her own community played through their mind. The effect was chilling. "Afraid, I was very afraid."[9]

Native students shared how living on the reservation, even with its own problems, was a pocket of protection from the surrounding areas that were White, conservative, and littered with examples of animosity toward and attacks against Native people. For Dakota (UI,N), this was a reality she had known since childhood. How much worse things got during the pandemic left her near speechless. She noted how her "town's very racist to anybody who's not White, period. And they always have been, but they definitely made it heard this summer. That was a shock, because I was like, 'OK, I knew that you weren't that good of people, but you're being terrible.'"

There was little to no distance from the upheaval that gripped the nation. Reflecting on the deaths of George Floyd and Breonna Taylor, Dakota noted, "We've also seen this happen at home with deaths of rez citizens by the town cops. It was reigniting that type of fight." Sitting in her room, she adjusted her round tortoiseshell frames. Initially her answers were a little shorter, more measured. The longer the interview lasted, the more she relaxed. When speaking about the silence around what is happening in and to Native communities, she became more expressive and determined. She wasn't talking about a long ago story, or something that happened to a friend of a friend; she was talking about her own family and the all-too-recent past. "He was found dead." Dakota said of her cousin, her voice somewhere between pain and longing. "He was one of my closest friends. The last time I talked to him was the summer" of 2020, mere weeks after she returned home when campus closed. Dakota knew he wasn't perfect. But she also knew that his faults didn't refute his humanity. What happened next was even worse and left her feeling angry and helpless:

> The community believes he was murdered in a violent way by some-one purposefully causing him harm. The medical examiner said that no foul play was detected. That's the big conflict that's occurring right now; this just happened last weekend. And he was found, actu-ally, not even that far from where they reported him missing. It al-most felt like they were never looking for him. He was literally found near the casino, which is the most heavily populated part of the rez. So that turned into a thing. He was there for four days and the cop's search party didn't find him.

Dakota felt failed by the system. In her eyes, the search party barely looked, and the medical examiner ignored clear signs of trauma. No one cared because he was just another Native. Dakota is saddened by how common her cousin's story is. "It's hard to see someone that you care about go through that," she began, "but then to see it end so badly is just jarring. People are going through things like that every day."

Even in these dark times, we try to hold on to some hope. In the wake of police violence, many communities waited for the reports of coroners and medical examiners, hoping that science would cut through the poli-tics and emotions of the moment. Maybe the report would bring some vindication of their feelings. But there again, bias can show its face. Ex-perimental data show that knowledge of a deceased individual's race influenced forensic pathologists' classification of the death as either a homicide or accident. Dakota was sure that the same thing played out with her cousin.[10]

With so much going on in the world, many students searched for what few safe spaces were allowed to them. But as we have seen, home wasn't always that place. Neither was just outside their houses. For Nancy (LI,M) and Eleanor (LI,M), both women who were proud amal-gams of two rich cultures, the entire world had become inhospitable. Ni-cole is "not a completely white-passing person," reveling in retaining features from her mother's side of the family. While her Asian physical characteristics have always been a source of pride, the targeting of Asian women made daily activities more fraught. "My concern is always like, do I look Asian? If somebody is trying to target an Asian person today, are they going to come for me? And so that's been a concern that I've had." She constantly checked out her surroundings. "I've always been hyper-aware walking down the street. Somebody who is planning on attacking an Asian person that day will probably not target me. And then on the other side of it, especially wearing a mask, I look more Asian if you're looking at my eyes. Especially with the rise in violence I've thought a lot more about." Completing the most mundane tasks, if they involved going outside, and especially if she wore a mask, became a calculated risk. "I am uncomfortable in the T station," she said flatly. It is truly disturbing how wearing protection from one pathogen put her at greater risk of that other, far older, one in our society—hate.

Eleanor had similar thoughts and feelings. She was scared all the time. And it showed; just talking about social unrest brought about a change in her: from talkative and excited to someone more pensive, as if the words themselves could exact punishment against her. She talked about the shooting in El Paso that targeted Mexicans and Mexican Americans. She talked about the shooting in Colorado. She choked up when speaking about Atlanta and shared how it felt that America had become a place where it's "let's kill all people who are not White Americans." The chilling effect is strong. "Every time a shooting happens," she said, "I remember my hyphenated Americanness and am scared." One day it all became too much. In front of her roommate, who was White, she broke down crying. Sitting on the couch, in her roommate's arms, she said, "Sometimes I wish I could just wipe the color off my skin because it's a reason why I get targeted."

Students faced the consequences of social unrest in many ways. Sometimes it was direct, head on. From folks moving away from them as they passed on the street to other people walking closer to harass and spit on them. Some students, like Amanda (LI,A) and Jessie (LI,N) and their families, girded themselves from attacks they were sure were coming, arming themselves with new purchases and old household items. For other students I spoke with, the manner in which the pressure of the pandemic and unrest got to them was more circuitous, but its effect was just as debilitating, underscoring their vulnerability. While some students were forced to tackle challenges head on, other students felt blindsided by how things snuck up on them even as they tried to stay vigilant.

Gabrielle (LI,M) sat in an overfurnished room, couches and chairs making the space look more like a labyrinth than a living room. A window overlooking the street framed her. Plants lining the sill basked in the light as short bursts peeked through the bouncy curls that sometimes hid her eyes. Only one of the plants is hers, a basil plant. "I realized how lucky I was to have, like, fresh herbs in my living room," she started. With a rare smile, she continued, "Basil is not cheap." The countless succulents and vines crowding the windowsill, like the furniture, came with the sublet, her first of many. Her sunny backdrop stood in contrast to her demeanor, subdued and timid.

Since middle school, she has been trying to get as far away from home as possible. The pandemic has been a brutal reminder that home is inescapable. For Gabrielle, COVID-19 closures represented an unexpected intermission, sandwiched between the perils of yesterday and the promise of tomorrow. When campus closed in March 2020, she had no choice but to go back to her mother's house, where "things progressed from belts and hangers to using her fists." She loved being near her brothers again; leaving for college had left her siblings emotionally and physically vulnerable. But at home, she always found herself in a fog, never knowing when a jolt of pain across her face would wake her up. Sometimes Gabrielle would be making dinner. Other times she would be finishing a calculus assignment. Her mother's hand would suddenly be in her peripheral vision. Shock would give way to blinding pain. Pain succumbed to panic. Sadly, time with her father, whom she saw less frequently after her parents' divorce, proved no easier or safer. His temper often got the best of him; stalled mobility and limited prospects made him feel inadequate. And he took his frustration out on his family. "He would yell, 'I'm going to kill you' with veins popping out of his neck." She took him at his word, seeing him lose control time and time again throughout her life.

College was a gift, a reprieve. No more pain. No more abuse. And then the COVID-19 pandemic came. Campus closed. Her security disappeared. She tried her best to avoid any place she was forced to call home, both her mother's and father's houses. Gabrielle moved six times between March 2020 and when we first spoke, almost thirteen months later. With a shrug, she shared that she is preparing for her seventh. A holdover from her days of switching between her parents' houses after the divorce, she noted, "I only had two suitcases and a small box, I always made it a point to travel light and not keep much stuff." Sadly, Gabrielle fared no better with the sublets and the roommates she had to have to make rent work. The apartments she secured were in different parts of the city, and she only had a bike to get around with. There was one commonality: living with "cockroaches and centipedes." Infested apartments were all she could afford. In addition to battling bugs, however, she has also had to contend with a stranger's demons, those of her newly found roommate.

Unbeknownst to Gabrielle, Nicole, her first roommate, was struggling with more than just the pandemic. She had a broken heart and an empty wallet; both caused by a manipulative, older man whose intentions were never good. Gabrielle was forced to call the police for help. It wasn't her first time calling the police; her parents' fights spurred her to do so many years before. But this time, it was different. She was older now, and after the murders of George Floyd and Breonna Taylor, making the call was so much harder. These calls to the police came at a "time when there was a lot of protests against police brutality, and that made me a lot more upset too. You know, police brutality and response to police brutality, and just lots of BS was breaking her down." The murder of George Floyd eroded what little trust Nicole and Gabrielle had in the police. To make matters worse, when officers came, Gabrielle felt that they were dismissive, giving little care to two young women of color in need of help.

With all avenues for help exhausted, they felt especially vulnerable. And then came the protests of Floyd's murder. They had front row seats to the thousands of people congregating in the streets, flooding their Chicago neighborhood. Most of the demonstrations were peaceful, no loss of life or damage to property. Gabrielle talked about the power of the people on the streets below, how beautiful it was to see them speak out against injustice. Rather than being inspired by disciplined approaches to protest, however, the protests eventually broke Nicole and sent Gabrielle spiraling. "She started crying and having a panic attack. And my focus, at the moment, was to comfort her, and not try to make her feel like I was ignoring what she was saying. But, at the time, I didn't realize that was as big of an issue as it was." Things worsened, for both of them. Nicole felt closed in, like she was being encircled by strangers who wished to do her harm. The arrival of the National Guard to keep the peace did not help. Gabrielle felt compelled to take care of someone while she struggled to take care of herself. The tumult outside "was constantly on my mind. She was constantly on my mind. It made me super angry. . . . So angry; I preoccupied myself with trying to make sure that she had care or was getting better." Going further, Gabrielle noted, "I was probably trying to suppress any feelings about myself or my own feelings. I was just mad at the world at that point, to see this effect, and then trying to make sure she was OK. And the next morning she kind of acted like nothing happened; I think that worried me a lot more."[11]

Nicole was eventually committed to a mental hospital, leaving Gabrielle worried about both her roommate and paying the rent. With so much on her plate, she did what she always did when things went sideways at home; she buried her feelings. Gabrielle repeated herself, outlining her coping strategy. "Yeah, I was trying to ignore or suppress it, not focus on it, because there's so much going on." This strategy proved to bring about more harm than good. Gabrielle started drinking and looking to others almost in the same way that Nicole looked to her. She was vulnerable and turned to alcohol to numb the loneliness and pain of abandonment. Unfortunately, she found herself at the mercy of others, and some of the very people she turned to took advantage of her trust.

As we were finishing our conversation, she made what therapists call a "doorknob confession." Despite doing everything in her power to take care for herself—and be there for her friend who broke as she saw their city engulfed in unrest—Gabrielle was sexually assaulted, yet another victim in the "shadow pandemic" of violence against women. "It was early June still; was just an upsetting time and that led me to turn to alcohol." Her admission is sobering. "Maybe without COVID, I would have had more social support." The thing is, she felt like she could let her guard down. She wasn't out and about. Her world became her apartment and that of just a few friends. She was inside with people she knew.[12]

But as the old saying goes, no one can hurt you like your kin. And often women know this reality most acutely. It was not a stranger who hurt Gabrielle, but rather someone she considers family. With great disdain for mental health services and a true discomfort with asking for help—exactly what had left her in academic trouble while on campus—she had not yet sought help. Underscoring the precarious nature of her life, she noted, voice hollow with sadness and anger, "I felt that COVID was supposed to protect me from stuff like this."[13]

Six weeks later, she was starting to be able to talk more openly about these horrible events. The silver lining that fueled her as she moved from apartment to apartment, neighborhood to neighborhood, at least for a while, was that she'd been able to keep her basil plant alive. But even then, it was not meant to last. She discovered little red and brown spheres that moved ever so slightly on the plant. And then the tiny holes in the leaves began. Alas, her constant companion began failing, tormented by spider mites. Tired and weary, Gabrielle looked away from the place the plant once soaked in the sun's rays, slowly turning her attention back to me. "I'm going to have to find consistency in other things now."

Conclusion

Millions around the world watched the constant stream of videos of racist attacks and social unrest. Universities, like politicians and public figures, put out statements condemning such acts, to mixed reviews. It is important to understand, however, how students didn't just consume these encounters as they do viral TikTok videos; many lived the very experiences themselves.

White students talked about acts of racism and the resulting social unrest that came about in response to it from a distance. The incidents were definitely happening in the world. Just not in their corners of it. As Jade (LI,W) noted, "It's just an aura; you can just sense it." But many of the most debilitating events were not necessarily in their immediate orbit.

For students of color, however, their own experiences during campus closures matched what the rest of their classmates saw on the news. The social unrest and animosity shown toward communities of color hit home, literally. It was all consuming, viewed on screens and out the front window. Even as they tried to shelter in place and have a sem-blance of continuity in their lives, whether in their houses or while at work, the pandemic's sequela left scars that must be understood. The troubling accounts of being followed, accosted, and spat upon were chronicled in their journals, forever etched in their memories. Eleanor (LI,M), near tears, shared the paradoxical space she occupied as she grappled with the growing racist attacks in the news, in her community, and in her own family. "In that moment, I remember just sitting down and writing in my journal, 'I've never felt so invisible in America than today.'" The next sentence underscores the liminal space she and her family occupy: "Never have been as scared to be Latina than today." To be seen is possibly to be targeted.

As Jessie's (LI,N) and Dakota's (LI,N) testimonies underscore, there were so many stories left untold, not deemed worthy of the front page. Asian students talked about how animosity and racist attacks against Asians existed long before people blamed them for the "China Virus." Native students felt this erasure most severely. Their stories, past and present, remained ignored and unremarked upon. Yet the incidents, passed on through word of mouth and on social media as well as dis-tressing calls from family members, shaped their every interaction, not only with the outside world but even within their homes. Jessie's sister pulled a knife on the very person she grabbed the knife to protect. And, as Gabrielle's (LI,M) story underscores, sometimes the most debilitat-ing instances happen in private; there's no bodycam footage or by-stander video that goes viral. And even then, footage is no guarantee that justice will be served.

So many students suffered in silence, left reeling from the punctured sanctity of spaces they called their own. It is these moments, the ones that we all witnessed but that only a few bore, that universities must be ready to help students through. Yes, these incidents happen off campus, but they fundamentally shape the socioemotional well-being of our students when they walk through our gates. As their testimonies reveal, the summer of 2020 was when the rest of the world found out about what they had been dealing with for a long time. And while many students were able to tread water before, the compounding effects of the pandemic proved too much for some. Attending to this inequality in students' lives—helping them deal with the pains of the past that the present has deepened—would ensure that fewer students fall through the cracks.

9

You Betta Recognize

THESE DAYS, few words are voiced around the college campus more than *diversity, equity,* and *inclusion.* But the very existence of efforts to openly discuss a more just educational system has, of course, sparked a backlash. Republican elected officials across the United States are enacting legislation to ban any efforts or programs that fall under the umbrella of DEI (the common shorthand used for such initiatives) from their state universities. In January 2023 Florida Governor Ronald DeSantis introduced a bill "prohibiting higher education institutions from using any funding, regardless of source, to support DEI" and other "discriminatory initiatives." Despite these absurd objections, many colleges are continuing efforts to make their campuses spaces for all students to feel like they have an equal stake in the life of the university. We are reminded daily that our campuses, like our nation, are divided. That is no surprise. But if we look closer, we also see that the weight of our divisions falls unevenly on the shoulders of those whom colleges spend millions to recruit.[1]

How do we deal with the fault lines on and off campus, the wear and tear that racism and exclusion exact upon our students? Racial microaggressions, those everyday slights that undermine one's dignity, and racial macroaggressions, like the murder of George Floyd, are not relegated to two distinct worlds. We cannot fool ourselves into thinking that the former occur on curated campuses, in dorm rooms and lecture halls, and the latter occur far away, in front of convenience stores in impoverished neighborhoods. No. Racism runs the gamut. These experiences—enormous and small, brutal and banal—interact with and reinforce each other, a steady undercurrent of daily life for students of color, a state of constant tension. This dynamic is crucial for understanding how students engage with the university and with their peers as well as for how much energy students of color expend in even the most mundane encounters. Moreover, students' acute awareness of off-campus events heightens their attention to fault lines on campus, deepening their distrust of their peers and their angst navigating Harvard.[2] That acute awareness—the impossibility of separating what happens on and off campus—has always existed for the students of color who enter the ivory tower of academia, but it has become even more palpable, and even more painful, since March 2020.[3]

How do we respond to students' needs in a way that makes them feel seen and heard? Because as Dawn (LI,B), Elena (LI,L), and many other students testified, university responses—individual and institutional—were not absent, just woefully insufficient in the eyes of students.[4]

We have explored the necessity of building mental health services on college campuses. It is heartening that some colleges and universities, like Virginia Tech, have worked to place mental health services front and center in undergraduate life by locating counselors and therapists in dorms. But proximity and preparedness are not the same. It remains imperative to diversify not only the skill sets of mental health counselors on college campuses but also the staff members who occupy those offices. The injury inflicted upon students spawns from entrenched inequalities in America and the racial tensions that exacerbate them. Counselors must be keenly aware of these inequities and best practices for working with students through them. For Hannah (UI,W), the pain that gripped the country was something that she could watch from her phone and then walk away from. When the news got too intense, she put down her phone and strolled to the beach, listening to the calming sounds of waves hitting the beach, erasing her footprints from the sand. Physical distance matched emotional distance. For others, like Gabrielle (LI,M), there was no such retreat. No escape. The weight of the pandemic and social unrest slowed her progress as she made her way across the city, moving from sublet to sublet because home was too toxic, leaving her searching for answers in all the wrong places. And the calls from those who watched from afar only served to deepen the isolation. This is not to say that only Gabrielle was negatively affected by George Floyd's death. No, Hannah and Gabrielle both were, just in fundamentally different ways. One looked on from afar. The other was so close she could see the tears of protestors. When students enter the offices of various support services, or any office for that matter, colleges must be both aware of this difference and prepared to help students equally.[5]

Yet so often when universities focus on diversity work, it boils down to photographable gestures. From ribbon-cutting ceremonies to cultural celebrations, the current strategy seems to be a recycled one: putting Black and Brown students in photos often standing beside a White president. The renaming of old buildings and diversifying the portraits that hang on the college walls are two popular strategies. Harvard has organized a committee for naming of buildings to shepherd it forward; it has rebranded the shields and crest of a residential college and the law school because of their ties to slavery and the American confederacy. These initiatives are important; breaking ties with racist people, families, and institutions is an important first step. And yet, to students, such grand gestures can feel empty, especially in the face of such racial and social unrest. The gestures feel somewhat removed from student life, especially in how undergraduates move through campus. As one student noted, highlighting deep-seated feelings of invisibility, "I'm struggling and you're putting up portraits."[6]

In addition to (and more important than) such efforts, students need help navigating everyday moments of disrespect that remind them that they are a part of but nevertheless apart from the college. This sentiment is magnified when similar dismissals of their citizenship and rights come from outside the college gates. It is not just the major stories that make the news that are the most debilitating. As Jessie (LI,N) noted, so much that happens in and to their community is not deemed worthy of news, whether national or local. Or, as Amy (UI,B) shared, often it is the fleeting moments that pass you by that you return to that hurt the most.

Students are frustrated with universities' responses to the animus shown to communities of color, both on campus and off. Understanding the source of this frustration is key. The experiences of Native students give a clear example of our selective and uneven responses. In the last four years, colleges have taken to reciting land acknowledgments, statements that recognize the ancestral lands of Native and Indigenous communities where universities reside. There is an inherent contradiction in naming the local history of settler colonialism that has been ignored for generations, but ignoring the far messier reality facing Native students today. How can we name past processes of disenfranchisement and exclusion, but not acknowledge present pain? Addressing the reality of students' lives is far harder for it requires individual responses to very specific, ongoing, and ever-evolving problems.[7]

Students' present-day outcries are part of a long tradition of speaking out. We have seen, again and again, an outpouring from students—sometimes of grief, sometimes of rage—when they feel they have been rendered silent and invisible. Listening to these students took me back to 2014; "I, too, am Harvard," a campaign organized by students to document racism on campus, reverberated across time in students' words. This campaign, as the slogan makes plain, centered on students' search to be seen as full members of the community, and revealed the microaggressions they faced, the many ways that their White peers declared the opposite. It quickly went viral; students at the University of Michigan, Oxford University, and a host of other colleges from around the world took up the call and created similar campaigns.[8]

Speaking with students in 2021, the reverberations were clear, and yet there was added pain to their words, as the heartless disregard for Asian, Black, Latino, and Native life felt even more omnipresent since COVID-19's explosion. Sociologist Michele Lamont gives us a lens to think about this dynamic. Lamont discusses "recognition gaps," which she defines as "disparities in worth and cultural membership between groups."[9] This framework is helpful because the central criticism that students had, especially students of color, was that their peers, and the university as a whole, did not recognize them or their experiences; that gap in recognition only deepened during campus closures. Of course, these months were harrowing for everyone, navigating enormous social upheaval alongside a vicious virus. But when members of the community—peers and professors alike—acknowledged the moment, students of color felt that their actions were perfunctory and performative, making them feel even more invisible than they already were. Dawn (LI,B) felt this acutely. Her friends' tone-deaf check-ins cut just as deep as the faculty who silenced her, even as they shouted their solidarity to Black Lives Matter. So many students of color found themselves searching for anyone to validate their experiences. Some still are.

Universities do a delicate dance when it comes to issues of race. They want to acknowledge it, especially when touting diversity statistics and crafting their newest campus brochure. At the same time, they don't want to be too preachy about promoting racial equality or addressing racism so as not to offend. In doing that dance, they do the entire campus a disservice. It leads, at best, to half-hearted attempts to foster community. At worst, it leads to face-saving measures with no intent to change the status quo. Yet, it is not as if universities have not had direct roles in shaping conversations around race and even state and national policy. Historian Eddie Cole, examining university leaders between 1948 and 1968, shows us how not only were university presidents active in national and state level policy debates surrounding Civil Rights, but they also forcefully used their offices as bully pulpits to segregate communities, defund Black institutions, and a host of other atrocities in the name of the university that rendered vulnerable communities even more disenfranchised. From a historical perspective, solidarity statements pale in comparison. The knee-jerk responses of many universities in the wake of the killing of George Floyd, Breonna Taylor, and others underscore university officials' lack of foresight in defending diversity today compared to actions taken to dismantle it just a generation ago.[10]

Moreover, these solidarity statements place the problem outside of the university's domain. This thinking permits universities to pass the buck, shifting responsibilities for addressing such brutalities on to an unnamed other. Yet when colleges recruit students from communities disproportionately haunted by such acts of violence and the resulting trauma, it becomes their responsibility.[11]

How do we meet students where they need us to meet them? The answer will forever be evolving. Times change. Demographics do too.

There will never be a one-size-fits-all solution. University officials need to sit with this fact. Like the Greek heroes who faced the many-headed hydra, universities must be flexible and adapt to the ever-changing problems in front of them. Dealing with the gauntlets of social and racial inequality requires not only improvisation and change but also a much broader understanding of human life.

Some universities have created different programs to investigate the legacy of slavery at their institutions, a major undertaking to examine how race shapes campus life. The College of William & Mary, Georgetown University, and Harvard have all created such initiatives. It is important that, when crafting such initiatives, the present-day experiences of undergraduates are not left out.[12]

Universities that opt for this path must champion student voice, centering those voices as they develop policies that will directly shape almost every facet of those students' lives. Students, and especially affinity groups, are already filling the voids created by colleges' blind spots about and ignorance of the undergraduate experience, especially the everyday reality faced by students of color. Year after year, students create identity-affirming spaces and programming, or what sociologists Elizabeth Lee and Jacob Harris call "counterstructures," to meet their needs and those of their peers. This current arrangement places the onus of responsibility on students. Regina (UI,B) spoke about this labor of love and how it came at a cost. She shared how Black affinity groups made space for Black student voices during protests and riots and advocated for changes on campus to better support students during such times. It was emotionally tiring work, which she believes led to burnout and a subsequent leadership vacuum in these crucial affinity groups.[13]

Yet, it is not students' job to do the work of the university. I do not argue that the work of affinity groups should be co-opted by university offices, but rather affinity groups should not be the first, last, and only line of defense against prejudice on campus. This means supporting such efforts, both administratively and financially. Instead of housing this work solely within student groups, we should create pathways to support this work through offices on campus that are empowered to enact change, especially the dean of students offices, which coordinate so much of student life, from academic support to student activities. We should work with a delegation of students, elected by their peers and hired as campus ambassadors, to serve on an advisory committee to provide input into not only identifying the barriers to fostering an inclusive community but also providing their insights into what is needed to minimize the recognition gaps on campus. This committee would be different from the task forces that students already dismiss as ineffective in that they are reactive, created after an incident has occurred. Rather, it is about being proactive, always taking the pulse of the community so as to be nimble in the university's support and engagement. Students' testimonies will carry hard lessons because they will expose the fallacy of "one campus," the notion of unity that has become the hallmark of many presidential campaigns and promises. Yet it is precisely these hard conversations that will best inform the policies that are most necessary.[14]

But helping students through the pain does not do anything to address the causes of that pain. We cannot treat the symptoms while ignoring the root cause. The anger surrounding Black Out Tuesday, and specifically the responses by peers and universities, was not just because students were tired from pouring what little energy they had into standing up for so many struck down by police brutality. Their grievance was that moments like Black Out Tuesday, or more specifically, seeing peers feign support for racial justice, reminded them of the unprovoked and uninterrogated animus they felt on their own campus. It is critical that we examine anti-Blackness and other forms of exclusion in higher education and respond to the ways it tears away at the social fabric of campus life. Many universities, like SUNY Brockport and Colorado State University, have adopted bias-reporting systems to alert administrators to events on campus. Understanding the frequency and nature of these events is incredibly important, and more universities should consider adopting similar protocols.[15]

But again, this move is a defensive one, a response after the fact, rather than proactive teaching and engagement that roots out such behavior. It is possible to promote a more inclusive community. Here, the University of Michigan offers an example. Centering student voice and active engagement, the Program on Intergroup Relations provides space for students to grapple with complex issues like identity, social inequality, and race relations, both on and off campus. For this program, work begins in the classroom but extends far beyond it. Professors and Student Life staff members are central to the conversation, learning from and alongside the students, and using what they learned to inform research and practice.

Any such move to address these issues head on is sure to receive pushback. Claims of liberal indoctrination are imminent. But that should not deter universities from helping students deepen their knowledge about the world around them. We can adopt curricula that deepen students' understanding of entrenched inequalities in society, and especially on campus. And we can implement antiracist approaches to social life. Doing so can help students develop the tools to recognize, understand, and respond to structural and interpersonal racism on campus as well as to respond more sensitively to moments that happen outside the college gates. Universities typically have shied away from such initiatives. This continued distancing is a mistake.[16]

Conclusion

BYE, BYE BUBBLE

Havens are high-priced. The price exacted of the haven-dweller is that
he contrive to delude himself into believing he has found a haven.

—JAMES BALDWIN, *NOBODY KNOWS MY NAME*

AS I REFLECT on students' experiences at the onset of the pandemic
and in the months that followed, it is impossible to ignore the very different reality today. Today, Harvard is humming. Campuses across the
country are fully open. Students are flooding the halls, decorating their
dorm rooms, debating in classrooms, making up for lost time. Some of
the new students are again members of classes making headline news
for their "unprecedented diversity." Colleges are offering the promise of
a return: both to traditions forged generations ago and to a sense of
present-day peace. I think we are all eager, students and faculty and staff
alike, to embrace these assurances of a "return to normal," like a security
blanket protecting us from the atrocities and horrors that marked the
early days of the pandemic. Who can blame us? Aren't we all clinging to
the hope of better days to come after enduring so many dark ones?

It is easy to think of the college campus as a bubble, a space both
protected and protective. The metaphor conjures a community where
only a select few go in or out, where the outside world ceases to have
influence on the world inside. Pictures of college campuses in those

glossy viewbooks and on admissions websites reinforce this thinking. From ornate iron fences set between obelisk gates to modern electronic pads with blue lights drawing your eye and mandating your ID, the boundaries between campus and the outside world are repeatedly drawn, bright and bold.[1]

Yet essayist James Baldwin cautions us against believing we have found such havens.[2] He is not alone. A few students I spoke with, like Dawn (LI,B), articulated this hesitation directly, voicing conflicted feelings about whether to consider Harvard a haven. With more than a few others, this suspicion was a lingering undercurrent. There is a price, Baldwin asserts, one that so many students have learned all too well in recent years, attached to believing that you are in fact safe and sound. But it is not just the haven seeker who is naïve in their thinking. The one promising sanctuary is equally deluded.

When colleges extend those sought-after invitations to students, especially in their efforts to admit and enroll classes that more reflect the diversity of the world and not just the top 1 percent, they are inviting more than students to campus. They are inviting families. They are inviting communities. They are inviting a long, tangled history of exclusion that shapes so much of students' everyday lives, both en route to college and each day after that. Yet at many colleges, especially elite colleges, the focus has mainly been on expanding who they admit and the financial aid needed to accomplish that goal. It is as if these colleges are repeating a mantra: "If we pay for it, we've done enough." To be clear: it is not enough. Not by a long shot.

Hard Lessons Learned

In this book, we have examined students' changing relationships with their families, finances, and fault lines, both on campus and in the country as a whole. My aim is to explore the inequalities in students' lives that universities are only just beginning to acknowledge, let alone address. The COVID-19 pandemic was so disruptive, so traumatic, on a scale very few of us had experienced in our lives, that it is easy to make it the centerpiece of the last several years. It is easy to feel like every story is a COVID-19 story. But this story is different. Because the COVID-19 pandemic didn't make our world unequal. It exposed more people to just how unequal it is. It made so many aspects of life much worse, especially for those already struggling. It laid bare the entrenched problems that litter students' paths to and through college.[3]

Harvard, like most institutions of higher education, closed its campus in mid-March and remained closed for a year. Some places were closed for even longer. Closures permitted us all a front row seat to just how different students' lives already were, and allowed us to see—in real time—these gaps grow wider. Closures permitted us all a front row seat to just how different students' lives really were and gave insight into how much worse things got. It became a story of freedom and restraint. Privileged students were free to focus on destinations, with parents providing both money and permission to gallivant around the world or study in exotic locales. And for those who wanted to stay closer to home, they could without much compromising on their part. Lower-income students grappled with the distractions of home, especially as recently laid-off parents, aunts, and uncles needed them to fill gaps in care, in compensation, and in capacity to meet the unyielding demands of life.

All families have their fair share of problems. For some students going home was an annoyance, and for others an enduring test of fortitude. For still others, going home was downright dangerous. Spurred by economic decline and already scarce resources, as well as deep-set family dynamics, rising tempers and incidents of domestic violence made home even more untenable. For these students, there was no escape, and without the protections of campus, many were forced to return to places where they felt their lives were in very real danger, and not just because of a raging pandemic.

Yet family is so much more than the people we share a bloodline with or who invite us to join their family trees. Communities matter. And yet all too often college administrators don't think about communities when considering students' lives back home, a reality that rural and urban scholars alike lament. Students of color from all class backgrounds, as well as lower-income White students, saw the debilitating effects of the pandemic—from the economic to the public health dimensions—up close and personal, unable to escape it. Their neighborhoods and towns bore the brunt of not only contracted cases but also deaths. Even before the pandemic, some local dangers made their way to campus through phone calls, texts, and, as technology advanced, through apps like Citizen, that wake students up in the middle of the night or stop them in their tracks during the midday rush from the cafeteria to class. For August (LI,L) and many other lower-income students, such disruptions are as regular as a professor's office hours. Then, when campus closed, they were forced to return to the site of these dangers and face them head on. Other students—particularly the wealthy and White—watched the COVID-19 pandemic from afar, their communities bastions of relative calm, their lives unnervingly uninterrupted.[4]

Money matters too, and not just for getting off campus and booking Italian villas. Even in the ivory tower, work matters. Both paid and unpaid labor shapes undergraduate life and exacerbates the inequalities in it. Privileged students held jobs like research and course assistants, deemed integral to the life of the college and protected by university officials, that not only gave them access to institutional resources but also aligned more with their professional aspirations. They were at ease both connecting with faculty and advocating for themselves. Lower-income students generally sought work that helped them and their families make ends meet. Future benefits took the backseat to present needs. Many students like Kevin (LI,W) thought academic work and paid labor should be held separate from one another, holding the opinion that it would be disingenuous to combine the two. Pandemic closures revealed unforeseen consequences of a class-segregated labor market: when campus closed, privileged students generally kept working, while lower-income students did not.

Paid labor, of course, is only part of the story, one side of the coin. The work students did on behalf of their families, especially lower-income students, remains discounted, or worse, completely unremarked upon, even when it required a higher skill set than the unpaid positions of their wealthy peers. We saw how Michelle (LI,L) learned two different computer programs, one for accounting and one for landscaping, to help her family. But even she saw this labor and her learned skills as just helping out her mom and dad. Alternatively, privileged students were able to secure positions that signal to future recruiters that they are good candidates even if their assigned work was, as both Hannah (UI,W) and Amy (UI,B) described, boring and requiring low-level skills. And yet, fueled by their ability to take on unpaid internships during the pandemic, they continued, crafting the right resume to secure the right position after graduation. While the unpaid labor done by students like Hannah and Amy is seen as a long-term investment to be rewarded and applauded, students like Michelle work invisibly and in silence with no avenue to reap rewards, beyond lightening the load of her injured dad and ensuring that her family could keep the lights on.

In addition to the uneven protective power of privilege and wealth, we see the menacing ways racism taxed students of color of all backgrounds. This taxing was happening long before 2020, of course, but again, COVID-19 compounded matters. Campus closures and mounting racial unrest not only opened old wounds inflicted on students of color by White peers but it exacted new ones. Students of color were asked to teach White peers about racial tension and hostility enacted upon communities of color, often by the very peers who ignored their own racist transgressions. Some White students even tried to make up for it with donations and public displays of solidarity, temporary as they were. The divisions laid bare in students' words push us to think critically about campus climate and the initiatives we create to foster community. Emotion-laden interactions with White peers in the wake of George Floyd and Breonna Taylor's murders in particular left students of color distracted from learning and ate away at their socioemotional well-being. But the stress didn't just come from the turmoil of that summer. The concerns stood in contradiction to what students had come to expect from their peers, not from hearsay or word of mouth, but from actual encounters where they were rendered invisible or silenced. Students of color need more than half-hearted nods to racial justice.

Applying Those Lessons

The contours of the problem are undoubtedly complex. Yet our possible responses are numerous. I offer actionable steps that colleges and universities can take to usher in inclusive and equitable policies and, consequently, to better support undergraduates. From rethinking leave of absence policies to diversifying mental health support services to making explicit the job search process for on-campus employment, colleges can take affirmative steps to better support students, helping them access experiences and resources that colleges offer instead of punishing those students who do not come from privilege. If anything, armed with the hard knowledge learned during the pandemic, I believe that we can indeed meet students where they are instead of where university administrators wish they were.

While I believe that these steps and others outlined previously are important and will push universities to be not just accessible but inclusive, I implore university administrators, especially those who set campus policy, to grapple with the legacy of slavery and settler colonialism that pervades our society and system of higher education. Accounting for this history undergirds the solutions offered in these pages. Again, leave of absence policies are a case in point.

It should be painfully clear by now that neighborhoods are more than a collection of homes and shops, more than uneven sidewalks or winding roads. Some communities protect their residents from hurt, harm, and danger. Others place them in the thick of them. The pandemic put these inequalities in sharper relief. Who had access to parks and space? Clean air? Clean water? Who felt safe? Secure? Communities of color, and especially lower-income communities, were hardest hit and slowest to recover on just about every public health and employment metric. This process is not random but rather is the consequence of historical patterns of exclusion. An honest accounting means understanding the lingering consequences of Jim Crow-era policies, sanctioned practices like redlining and block busting, discrimination in GI benefits and FHA loan programs, land theft, and attacks on Native sovereignty—policies that kept and keep the United States a separate and unequal nation.[5]

By ignoring the entrenched inequities that students must contend with while in school, as well as what they would return to if forced to leave, our supposedly therapeutic supports become distinctively punitive. Mandating students to return to communities with limited employment opportunities, and with little to no support from the university, yet also requiring them to secure full-time work, is not just counterproductive—it is assigning them a near-impossible task when they are already struggling.

If we can acknowledge the painful blind spots of our policies, we can reframe the conversation about what it means to open one's campus. Colleges, in their quest for racial justice, slow and uneven as it is, must move beyond paying lip service through building renaming and land acknowledgements. Universities must contend with the present-day manifestations of land theft and the intentional segregating of neighborhoods. These are not just dark episodes of American history. The policies set forth in previous eras have a cumulative effect on life chances today. These exclusionary practices shaped where students lived and what schools they attended. But it goes beyond that. It shapes what air they breathe, what water they drink, and what streets they traverse. Moreover still, it continues to shape the places their families remain after students leave for college, and what resources they have—and more often, don't have—available to them. Where we are from shapes so much of who we are. It is not destiny, but it does influence so much of our present and future. We need to fully acknowledge both the pain and the resilience in our students' origin stories, if we want to build a college community that honestly honors all its members.

Upon Graduation

Sociologists liken how higher education operates to a hub in a wheel; it is a relatively small part of our society but connects so many different parts of that society. It is important to remember that college is but one step on the path to adulthood; those connections to the rest of the wheel are arguably as important as the hub itself. As we look at the current experiences of students, we are also looking at the past experiences of future employees. When students graduate from college, even if they get their dream job, all of their worries do not magically go away. A bachelor's degree and a job offer are no panacea for the pains of the past, especially when current events open old wounds. As students' testimonies show, the insecurities of home and the inequities of society follow them on their path, wherever that path leads. And no matter how upwardly mobile that path is, this process is compounded by race.[6]

Companies and firms play the diversity game just like colleges do. They boast and broadcast their diversity numbers too. They build out diversity, equity, and inclusion teams and hire specific recruiters to make sure that their company brochures have just enough smiling Black and Brown faces to invite applicants to see them as possible employers. They give lip service support to identity-based employee resource groups to build community among employees from similar backgrounds or orientations. New first-generation interest groups are also popping up, which are only going to increase given continued attacks on race-based affirmative action measures and rulings from the Supreme Court. All of this is especially true for corporate America, where so many students from elite colleges go upon graduation. But here we have the same dilemma. These firms believe that a generous salary is enough, just like colleges believe that generous financial aid is sufficient. That simply is not the case.

———

The collective yearning in society for normalcy is deep and strong. But simply following the impulse to get "back to normal" will only be a setback. If we return to normal, we will return to what was; we will, once again, be held hostage to the inequities that plague higher education and society alike. We will, once again, hold ourselves and our institutions back from being what we could be, what we should be. Let us not yearn for normalcy.

Armed with a more nuanced understanding of how inequality shapes students' lives, on and off campus, in normal times and unprecedented ones, let us think bigger, let us act bolder. Actor LeVar Burton teaches us, "That which we can imagine, we can make manifest." Let our actions match the aspirations—as varied as they are fabulous—of each class of students who we invite in. As students make college their home, let us listen to them, let us work with them, let us learn from them. Let us move beyond soundbites and curated photographs. We don't need to extol the virtues of diversity. We need to manifest those virtues, day in and day out. Let's do the hard work of cultivating the potential of all the students who walk through the wrought iron gates, who lay out on the grounds, who sit in the lecture halls, and who lounge in the common rooms. Let us make manifest a campus community that is both accessible and inclusive in its practices, both affirming and equitable in its policies. For what is at stake is not just the vitality of our campuses, but the lives of students themselves—those beautiful, fragile, powerful beings that we invite into our world, and if all goes well, then usher forth to make a better world. Let us do all that we can to help them build that better world. Let us build that which we have yet to see.

APPENDIX

HERE I DISCUSS the methodological journey of this project, from the initial invitation to the last interview to writing what grew into this book. I also describe the emotional journey of this project and how it pushed me to grow as a scholar and person.

The Site: Harvard College

I am still not sure whether I chose Harvard University as my research site or Harvard chose me. I received an email, in November 2020, from sociologist William Julius Wilson. Bill was my advisor and had chaired my doctoral dissertation. He reached out, not as my former advisor, but in his role as member of the Presidential Committee on Harvard & the Legacy of Slavery. His subcommittee was tasked to examine how race—and specifically, anti-Black racism—affects and undermines undergraduate life. Given my research on how poverty and inequality shape everyday experiences among undergraduates at elite colleges, the committee asked me to consult. That initial consultation kick-started this project.

This invitation—to craft a project from the ground up at Harvard— fit my abilities and piqued my interests. I am keenly interested in how universities, especially those that serve lower-income and first-generation college students and see themselves as launchpads for upward mobility, proclaim to value diversifying their student body yet struggle to serve the students they so actively recruit. I had devoted a decade of my life to researching the topic and invested the previous five years in writing my first book, *The Privileged Poor: How Elite Colleges Are Failing Disadvantaged Students*. Since the book was published in

2019, I traveled around the country (with a few stops abroad), working with colleges on implementing policies that could make them more inclusive.

I was gearing up for a second major project. The study was to examine how working in college shapes undergraduate life. I wanted to break out of my comfort zone and embark upon a comparative study of three universities—one public, one private, and one community college—to examine how students approached work across different types of institutions. I wanted to explore the meaning students attributed to work and how they made sense of social mobility in the United States. And then the COVID-19 pandemic hit. Making new connections at new universities during such a tumultuous period would have proved daunting. So many campuses were closed, and so many administrators and staff at colleges around the country were being spread pretty thin with the transition online and taking on new administrative duties to facilitate online learning. I felt that my request, especially as someone from an outside university, would be delayed at best, but more likely ignored. I shelved the book idea, but the heart of the project lived on. In fact, the chapters on finances in this book—which investigate paid and unpaid labor as well as campus policies around student employment—stem directly from the preliminary research I conducted for that project. Months later, Bill invited me to submit a proposal for a research project that would eventually become this book.

I was excited to jump back into the field, and doing so at Harvard made practical sense. I was at Harvard as a faculty member. I knew faculty and staff members in the community and could begin to make inroads into getting permission from the appropriate deans. These connections made it easier to gain access, but everything was delayed, from responses to emails to final approval to begin the study. Like many universities, Harvard is very protective of its students and makes you jump through a number of hoops to interview them. And this goes double when speaking about sensitive issues or any topic in which the university could be painted in a bad light. But I knew some of the administrators who were protecting these students and could assuage their concerns or have them vouch for me with others who were more reticent.

Additionally, I was at Harvard for nearly fifteen years, first as a graduate student and resident tutor in Mather House, one of the undergraduate dorms, and then as a faculty member. I worked with thousands of Harvard students. I also worked with several student groups and even served as faculty sponsor for two undergraduate clubs. All this made calling on old connections, and establishing some new ones, more straightforward.

The pandemic also brought a new level of risk into research. I also was not about to risk my life going out into the world to try and start this process anew. I am the financial crutch for my family. I was often the first and last line of defense against the lights being turned off and my family going hungry. Alongside my brother, who serves as a janitor at my old elementary school and the local hospital, I was the only one working during lockdown and the long months that followed. My check was spread across three households. I was afraid that if anything happened to me, that safety net would be gone forever. I had to be safe and productive, which sums up so much of the never-ending struggle of first-generation college students.

The problem was that this project began before vaccines were widely available. People were debating if vaccines would be safe and if they would even take the vaccine. Universities were debating if they would mandate taking it. It was too much.

Harvard as a research site was, from the outset, not a bad thing. It fulfilled the conditions of theoretical sampling, choosing a site based on certain criteria that permit speaking beyond a single case, and allowed me to explore how poverty and inequality shape how students move through college and how the COVID-19 pandemic exacerbated those inequities. I am interested in colleges that adopt no-loan financial aid policies, and the present-day experiences of students at those schools in particular. Harvard's student body diversity, residential campus model, and plethora of institutional resources make it an ideal site to study how students who are from different socioeconomic backgrounds but are immersed in the same privileged milieu and attached to the same resource-rich institution fared before and during COVID-19 closures. Very few places in the world have students from both the very top and bottom of the income distribution, let alone from a host of racial and ethnic groups along this class spectrum. So Harvard it was.[1]

The People: Harvard Undergraduates

The committee that Bill led as part of Harvard and the Legacy of Slavery initially wanted someone to create and administer a survey of Black students at Harvard. I was happy that the committee, which was focused on Harvard's relationship with enslaved peoples and the institution of slavery more generally, was making space to understand the present-day experiences of Black students. But I don't do surveys. I'm an interviewer. My heart is in sitting with students, talking with them, creating a safe space to share their stories—our stories—and then grappling with what it all means. I also shared with the committee that if we are to more fully understand the undergraduate experience, and especially those of Black students, we need to include students from different class backgrounds across more racial and ethnic groups. This would allow for comparative analyses that give insights to how and when race matters on campus and how social class exacerbates or ameliorates racial differences. I pushed to include not only White and Latino students, but also Asian and Native undergraduates. Additionally, I wanted to invite students who identified as biracial, multiracial, or mixed as their experiences deepen our understanding of how inequality unevenly shapes students' pathways to and through higher education.

While I was keenly interested in class differences, the inclusion of additional racial and ethnic groups was important as well. While interviewing for *The Privileged Poor,* I did not seek to interview Asian students and ultimately only formally interviewed three Asian students. The study had a particular set of interview parameters: to interview native-born Black, Latino, and White students. But there were more than theoretical reasons for my targeted recruitment. I did not have the money to interview everyone I wanted. I was funding my dissertation out of pocket, and my funds were low from the beginning. As I traveled the country since the publication of *The Privileged Poor,* students shared how they saw themselves in my work. But invariably I would get a question from an Asian student, who would ask, "What about me?" I was never satisfied with my answer: that I did speak to three Asian students but didn't have enough money to continue building that number up and amplify their voices and experiences. I felt equally unsatisfied in not speaking to Native and Indigenous students. To be honest, Native students are so few at elite colleges, I did not think to include them. I was not going to make that decision again. With funding from the Harvard Radcliffe Institute and the Harvard & the Legacy of Slavery Initiative behind me, I sought to invite as many students as possible to tell their stories on their own terms.

I worked with the Office of Institutional Research to identify students to participate in the study, permitting me to sample for range and representation. My goal was to construct a class-stratified sample of Asian, Black, Latino, Mixed, Native, and White undergraduates, with a focus on lower-income students. Students who received full financial aid under the Harvard Financial Aid Initiative, those who come from families that make less than $65,000, were considered lower income. And those whose families made greater than $65,000 were considered upper income. Roughly 66 percent of lower-income students in our sample identified as first in their families to go to college, with neither parent earning a college degree in the United States, and 10 percent reported being the first people in their families to graduate from high school. In contrast, the vast majority of upper-income students interviewed came from families that made much more than $65,000. Despite initiatives like no-loan financial aid policies to diversify campus racially and socioeconomically, nearly one out of every eight students at Harvard comes from a family that makes more than $630,000 annually. Upper-income students were far more likely not only to be continuing-generation college students but also to have parents with advanced degrees. They were also more likely to report being a "legacy" at Harvard, meaning that at least one of their parents attended Harvard as an undergraduate and/or for their advanced degree(s).

For the first time, I worked as part of a team to collect data for a project. And the graduate students I hired to help me conduct interviews as well as the undergraduates who assisted with literature reviews and chronicling current events were amazing. Working with a team inspired a lot of growing pains and required a lot of growth. I was used to being the only one collecting stories, getting to know each and every student on an individual basis. But I knew to generate a larger sample of students in a confined amount of time, I needed help. I recruited four students from the Harvard Graduate School of Education who were interested in higher education and racial inequality to help me. One student was White, two were Black, and one was biracial Native. One came from an upper-income household and three from lower-income households. This racial and class breakdown of advisees proved useful as we were able to match some students to interviewers who shared similar backgrounds, either racially or socioeconomically. For some students, we were able to accomplish matching along both dimensions of identity. This matching along race/ethnicity, of course, was not possible for all students, but when I reached out to students to partner with me on this project, I had not yet developed a working relationship with an Asian or Latino student interested in qualitative methods. Class matching helped when racial matching was not possible. I was fortunate enough to serve on the dissertation committee of three of my research assistants, and the fourth was a student whom I trusted. Graduate research assistants were paid a rate commensurate with those set forth by the Harvard Graduate Student Union UAW-5118.

The team and I met just about every week for check-ins about how interviews were going. I was teaching C.R.E.A.M. (Cash Rules Everything Around Me): Class and Culture in American Higher Education at the Harvard Graduate School of Education, and three of the four researchers served as my teaching fellows, and the fourth was a student in the class. Our meetings served the dual purpose of preparation for classes and progress reports. In addition to these meetings, I also checked in with my graduate student researchers individually via Zoom and phone calls. In both the meetings and the phone calls, we discussed everything from best practices in sending invitations to how to get the best data out of conversations with undergraduates who signed up for the study. For example, one graduate researcher had an MBA and shared best practices for outreach based on her professional school training and other tips for using mail merge tools. I read interview transcripts after the first interviews to assess quality across researchers and provide any suggestions on how best to improve on the interviews. In general, my main advice to the team was to let students talk in their interviews. I advised one researcher not to begin by asking students if they had a "hard stop"; doing so prompts students to speak in shorter clips. With this adjustment, interviews began to go on longer, and students seemed to offer even more details and do so even more freely. I also coached the research team on probing for details that flesh out the moment, getting to them to think of the examples that students shared as the foundation for a short story. I pushed them not to let key moments of interviews pass without getting a cast of characters and a sense—from the student's perspective—of the beginning, middle, and end of the story.

In the end, we interviewed 125 Asian, Black, Latino, Mixed, Native, and White undergraduates. Fifty-eight students came from families that received some or no financial aid, and sixty-seven came from families that received full financial aid. Because of the initial motivation of the project, we did more targeted outreach of Black students and lower-income students. More generally, one unique dimension of these data is that we interviewed nearly all the students at Harvard who identified as Native. The goal was to interview as many students as possible to get a sense of how a diverse group of undergraduates were faring during campus closures brought on by the global pandemic. I interviewed forty-eight students, and the team split the rest of the sample in roughly equal portions.

A note on ethnic and racial classification and terminology is needed. Although I worked with the Office of Institutional Research to recruit students, the racial and ethnic classifications used in this book are those chosen by students. I use the term Latino instead of "Latino/a," "Latinx," or "Latiné," as there was neither consensus among students nor the field as to the best and most inclusive convention at the time of the study. Similarly, I use "Native" and "Indigenous" interchangeably, as the students themselves did and as is common in the literature. Harvard uses "Mixed" for students who identified as more than one race or ethnicity. This term is also used by students on campus; in 2018 students formed a club dedicated to Mixed students, Harvard Undergraduate Union of Mixed Students. Where students use a specific or different term, I stay true to their words.[2]

TABLE 1. Socioeconomic and Racial/Ethnic Classification of Students

Race/Ethnicity	Upper Income	Lower Income	Total
Black	31 (24.8%)	13 (10.4%)	44 (35.2%)
White	9 (7.2%)	13 (10.4%)	22 (17.6%)
Latino	2 (1.6%)	15 (12%)	17 (13.6%)
Asian	4 (3.2%)	11 (8.8%)	15 (12%)
Mixed	2 (1.6%)	10 (8%)	12 (9.6%)
Native/Indigenous	10 (8%)	5 (4%)	15 (12%)
Total	58 (46.4%)	67 (53.6%)	125

For context and to supplement interviews, we read and shared news from the *Harvard Crimson* and other colleges' newspapers and followed statements from the university and student groups. We also paid attention to social media posts from students, both at Harvard and at other universities across the country. This supplemental information provided additional context to what was happening on campus with students we could not interview as well as in higher education writ large.

Interviews took place via Zoom between January and October 2021. At the start, the virtual location of our interviews worried me. All of my previous research experience had been done face-to-face. I was more than a little scared that the online format would make the interview feel restrained or compromised in some way, transforming them from guided conversation into some sort of transactional exchange, indistinguishable from a survey. Those fears were soon laid to rest. Students were open, most from the first moments of the interview to the last minute. In fact, as we were wrapping up, and I was collecting their information for payment, it was very common that students returned to something they had said earlier, providing more details as something they wanted to say returned to them, or started a new conversation because something struck them. Some of these conversations, begun after the formal interview ended, continued for an additional hour and offered even more rich details about students' experiences at home and at Harvard. After graduate researchers noticed how often these conversations continued, we devised a plan to do something that I had just started to experiment with: rather than stopping the video recording after a student had answered the last question of the interview, waiting until the student had logged off of Zoom, in order to give space and value to those final moments of our time together.

I did conduct follow-up interviews with students in November and December 2022 as I began writing the manuscript. The purpose of these conversations was to gather additional information about a moment in their lives. For example, I asked Elena (UI,L) for details about her work history and her experiences with expressions of solidarity around Black Lives Matter in the wake of George Floyd's murder. My conversation with Jessie (LI,N), which happened in my office, focused on their relationship with their sister and the incident of coming home and having a knife being pulled on them.

I believe the loneliness of the pandemic and perhaps the separation from campus inspired students to open up earlier or sooner than they otherwise might have. I also think it helped that I had become a known entity on campus for my research, working with student groups like FYRE, the first-generation college students preorientation program, and continued engagement in policy conversations at the university and in higher education. I also remained vocal about being a first-generation college student myself in national outlets like the *New York Times* and CNN, and have tried to work with the *Harvard Crimson* and other student organizations whenever they have asked, whether giving interviews or participating in conversations about issues facing underrepresented groups. Students mentioned to members of my team that they were eager to talk because they saw that I was the principal investigator.

In the end, interviews ranged from 1 to 7.5 hours, and lasted, on average, 2.5 hours. For students who gave very detailed answers from the beginning of the interview, we asked if they would be open to completing their interviews over one or two additional sittings, to be scheduled according to their time and availability. We would ask students about their openness to complete their interviews across multiple sittings about halfway through the interview, where there was a natural break in the transition between discussing students' lives at home and then at Harvard. We didn't want to pressure students into giving shorter answers in the second half of the interview; rather we wanted to create an environment that promoted deeper conversations. So many students apologized for speaking too long or rambling, when, in truth, they were giving beautiful, full answers that let us into their worlds. Long, detailed answers trump short, truncated ones almost any day of the week. Having a natural halfway point in the interview helped us take stock. In all, forty students completed their interviews across two or three sittings, which were scheduled at students' convenience.

I secured funding to offer students $40 per interview sitting. If a student completed their interview over two sessions, they were compensated $80. For so many students, their time was not their own before and certainly not during the height of the pandemic. They were being pulled in many directions and had additional demands thrust upon them by the pandemic. I wanted to offer an incentive that seemed appropriate, something that would invite but not compel them to take part in the study, a balancing act that I consider in every project I conduct. It is important for students to be able to say no. I looked around campus and the community for guides. In 2021 the Massachusetts minimum wage was $13.50, and the Harvard federal work-study average wage was $17.00 at the time of the study. Therefore, a rate of roughly $20 an hour was neither exploitatively low nor exorbitantly high, and thus I hoped would not exert undue influence on a student's decision to participate or not.

It was also important to ensure that payment would be easy and immediate. While this is easy when interviews are conducted in person, the virtual environment required the use of outside services. Except for two students, participants were paid using Venmo at the end of the interview. Importantly, I turned off public notifications of payments on Venmo to help preserve students' anonymity. The two students who did not have Venmo were mailed a paper check at the address of their choosing. Using Venmo and checks did have an additional bonus: receipts. It became easier to track payments.

The Interviews

My team and I conducted the interview in generally the same way each time. To get students talking, we borrowed tricks from the toolkits of both interviewers and ethnographers. First, from the interviewer's toolkit, we began each interview by asking students to choose their pseudonym. I did this in *The Privileged Poor* and found it to be a great icebreaker. I will never forget one student choosing Beyoncé, because she loved the artist, and another choosing her sibling's middle name because, as she described, everything she did is for her little brother, and all she wants is for him to have it easier than she and her older siblings did growing up. Asking about students' pseudonyms worked just as well for this project. As education scholar Maria Lahman reminds us, for people who participate in qualitative research, choosing a name is more than just picking something at random.[3] The stories students offer provide a peek into their role models, their advisors, and their connections with loved ones back home. We also got a sense of their humor and creativity—especially for the student who chose LBJ, and another who chose Anonymous-Kitten, which was subsequently shortened to just Kitten. Pseudonyms also help students feel comfortable to share stories, knowing that there will be some distance between their identity and the project.

From the ethnographer's toolkit, we borrowed a practice from sociologist Annette Lareau, and found something in the background of the Zoom, or asked about an article of clothing the student was wearing—anything to get the student to focus on the details of their own lives instead of the fact that they were participating in a research project. With Dawn, for example, she and I talked specifically about hair and the benefits of locking one's hair. Such a personal focus helps people relax. And there's a bonus: you get a story, one often filled with meaning. Moreover, I opened myself to conversations about what students saw behind me and also brought some connections to their attention, if they mentioned something that linked with an item or book that I had behind me or nearby. Similarly, we sometimes shared a laugh about playing sports in high school as my sophomore year football (and prom) picture was on the bookshelf behind me. I also offered myself up in these specific ways to make connections and put students at ease, especially because we were far apart, both geographically and in terms of our roles on campus.[4]

Generally speaking, I treat interviews as ethnographic moments. When I am with a student, the space we share is the world that I am interested in inhabiting and examining. I want to know about the puppies, the artwork, the dreamcatchers, and anything else in their space that they want to tell me about. As mentioned previously, I would often ask about whatever caught my eye in their camera screen as we were getting started. And, unlike the mandatory camera-on policies of most classes, which I found made students less willing to open up about the world they were inhabiting, students were generally happy to share stories about the things around them. It was also neat to get a sense of their interests outside of school, whether photography or film noire, things that might not have come up in an interview. I was happy to learn more about students through these side conversations that then deepened the connections between us and made students feel more at ease.[5]

It also helped to literally say these details out loud during the interview because the transcription service we used captured all spoken words, including these observations; the result was an integration of field notes and interview transcript. I would frame my questions by first recapping the moment and saying something specific about what I saw or heard. For example, if I noticed that the interviewee was smiling or laughing or looking puzzled, I would say, "You seem to be smiling now. Why the change?" This helped me mark the time of the interview in which they smiled and also got them to reflect on that moment. I did the same for a full range of emotional moments as well. Once interviews were transcribed, I often searched for different variations of smile, cry, distraught, bounce, or other descriptions of moments, emotions, or actions, and had both a sense of what we were talking about and a reminder of how they talked about that thing.

In addition to the written transcripts, for those interviews I did not conduct myself, I either listened to the audio recording while away from the computer (like on walks) or watched the video recordings when at my desk, to get a sense of the demeanor, mannerism, and style of these students, as well as their emotions and temperament. Having both audio and visual recordings proved particularly helpful for this study.

After introductions, there were four parts to the interview, with, again, a natural pivot or break in between sections two and three. We asked students to return to the morning of March 10, 2020, when all students were notified that campus was going to close five days later. We wanted to understand how the news landed, where they were, and what they did upon reading the emails from administrators, and then what it meant to transition away from campus. Second, we asked about life after campus closed, with respect to their families and communities. Third, we explored their employment history before and during campus closures. Last, we talked to students about the racial climate on campus, as they had experienced it during their time at Harvard, and in the nation during the summer and fall of 2020. At each turn, we began with open-ended questions to allow students to identify the most salient experiences and memorable moments that shaped how they move through campus, and then followed with more specific questions that probed for context, background, and details.[6]

The primary questions for understanding students' relationship with home focused on their families and communities. For their families, we asked, "How has your family been affected by COVID?" before probing the myriad ways the pandemic shaped life at home. We asked students to describe their living arrangements when campus closed in March. We also asked if anyone in their family had lost employment or had died due to COVID-19. The probing questions provided opportunities to explore differences in resources and restraints.

To get a sense of neighborhood dynamics and how they affected students, we asked how safe they felt in their neighborhood generally and then probed about how safe they felt while they were at home. We then asked specifically about how people in their neighborhood fared during lockdown. After students' initial answers, we followed up with specific questions about their social, physical, and economic well-being.

To explore differences in experiences related to work and employment, we asked students to describe the first job they ever had. This got students talking about life not only before the COVID-19 pandemic but also before coming to Harvard, which provided context for many of their decisions about how to navigate college. We heard of positions as different as babysitting to working in a biology lab. Having students reflect on their work histories also opened up conversations about how much labor students did on behalf of their families, often that they didn't count as work. With respect to paid work, the data primarily came from answers to two prompts: "Tell me about working on campus" and "What did COVID-19 mean for working?" We also examined general reports about being employed while in college. These questions prompted students to outline their job-seeking strategies and important experiences working in college.

To examine racial tension and the resulting fault lines on campus, we asked students for their assessment of the campus racial climate and to take us back to the moment they learned of the death of George Floyd. These prompts got students talking about undergraduate life before and during campus closures, often speaking about how they inform each other. Some students talked about racial animus they experienced at Harvard that began as early as their visiting weekends and orientation, underscoring how those moments stayed with them even if they were now juniors or seniors. Students connected those moments to their read of campus today. We added questions about their thoughts on solidarity statements, like black squares on Instagram, after many students brought them up in interviews.

Interview audio was professionally transcribed by 3Play Media, a company specializing in captioning and transcription. Once we had transcripts completed, data were coded iteratively, grouping key discussions—family, finances, and fault lines—across transcripts by race/ethnicity and income group. I read interview transcripts and took analytical memos that summarized key emergent themes for each subgroup around the central themes of the book, everything from relationships with family, to work history, to experiences with racism on and off campus, and then I compared the results across groups.[7]

The interviews themselves were never boring; despite asking mostly the same questions each time, they never felt like stale question-and-answer sessions. Instead, these interviews seemed defined by emotion and commotion. Sometimes students needed a moment to compose themselves. I will never forget Dawn (LI,B) reaching for her pillow and squeezing it as her whole mood changed. I can't shake Michael (LI,L) recalling driving his undocumented mother to the hospital with a fever and pain shooting through her body; his fear, for her and her health, was palpable. Sometimes interviews were interrupted by pets and siblings.

Ambulances passed by, drowning out what a student was saying. Students themselves became animated in different ways, recalling the good, bad, and ugly sides of living through campus closures. All of these little (and not so little) moments gave us additional insights into students' daily lives. An additional bonus of using 3Play Media is that they put timestamps every fifteen seconds or so on all the interview transcripts. This permitted me to return to specific sections of the interview with ease. I relistened to and rewatched parts of interviews that I intended to highlight in the book after choosing the most representative and illustrative quotes for the writing.

Additional Perspectives

I also spoke with a small, diverse group of undergraduate researchers in 2021 and 2022 on this book project. Their primary role was to help me conduct literature reviews and compile information on college practices across the country during lockdown. For example, they researched what public and private universities require of students who are placed on mandated leave. I worked with four Harvard undergraduates who served as Radcliffe Research Fellows as well as a team who participated in Summer Research Opportunities at Harvard (SROH), a program for students from underrepresented groups outside of Harvard to do research with a faculty member during the summer. Of my Harvard research team, whom I worked with for a more sustained period of time, two were White, and from different classes. One student was biracial, Black and Latina, and received significant financial aid. Another student was Black and working class. Like with my graduate student researchers, our meetings were part catchup and part research. These conversations allowed me to ask their thoughts about emerging themes from an undergraduate perspective and get a sense of what was happening in student groups and organizations, both during closures and after returning to campus. I also shared early drafts of chapters with my research team for specific comments about my argument and also stage setting. They were living it, and continued conversations with them helped me keep my finger on the pulse of the community. They pointed me in directions of social media posts, blog submissions, forums, and other online conversations happening at Harvard. They also began sending me their own version of ethnographic field notes about what happened in class and in the undergraduate houses.

My SROH team came during the summer and from a number of colleges and universities around the country. I invited students from Amherst College and Emerson College in Massachusetts and Pitzer and California State University, Fullerton in California, as well as Emory University and Morehouse College in Georgia. Three students were Latino, two were Black, and one was Asian American. It was insightful to hear the experiences of students from very different campuses. Learning about the commonality in petitions, for example, underscored how the struggle to be seen in this particular way and in this particular moment was not something unique to Harvard, but rather the norm at many colleges across the nation.

Last, I held meetings with different offices on campus, like the Office of Career Services and the Office of Undergraduate Education, and gave presentations on campus, both at the Harvard Radcliffe Institute and the Research-Informed Teaching & Learning (RITL) Affinity Group. My lecture at Radcliffe as part of the Radcliffe Fellows program, which was based on an earlier draft of "But I See What You Do," was attended by Harvard faculty, members of the Dean of Students Office, and the Athletics Department. I was able to engage them on changes to academic leave policies, pushing them to revisit their decision on work requirements and the need for letters of recommendation. The RITL talk brought together administrators from across the university to discuss how to lower barriers to jobs on campus that improve retention, promote connection to faculty, and extend learning outside of formal instruction. I shared an early version of "Pink Slips for Some" and discussed lessons learned and potential best practices to facilitate greater connection between students and the different administrative offices around campus. Sharing findings in this way has not only led to fruitful conversations about the blind spots and biases of administrators but also started the process of changing policies to make the campus more accessible.

When Worlds Collide

I mentioned that the length of the interviews came as a bit of a shock, albeit a welcome one. In truth, it wasn't the length of the interviews that truly surprised me. It was how quickly students opened up to us. I'll never forget speaking to Jamie (LI,W) and the way her pain, anger, and angst blended together into a murky mélange. It was the first time our paths crossed. And she didn't hold back. She talked about the insecurity of home always being on her mind. She spoke about her long history of sexual assault with the two men whom she called dad. She shared with me how yet another man, her assigned peer advisor at Harvard, picked up where they left off. She unexpectedly sent me an email a few days after our interview. In it were excerpts and screenshots from her Title 9 report filing. Her first line, "Just attaching some information below." She wanted someone to bear witness to her pain, that inflicted by her assailant and by the university. In that moment, I was her somebody.[8]

There was so much in her words and in what she shared. Her email carried the full exchange she had with the Office of Dispute Resolution (ODR), the office on campus that handles instances of sexual assault. It was an intense back and forth. Jamie highlighted quotes from their decision, places where she felt "very misrepresented by you and your office," the most painful of which being when they felt "certain" that her body language opened the door to her peer's sexual advances. The case was dismissed. She sent an email asking for an explanation. Jamie never got a response back from ODR. She never got the closure she sought.

I was not ready for stories of domestic abuse and sexual assault, if I am being honest. And I was not prepared for so many. This was supposed to be a book about entrenched racial inequalities and about the gap between access to elite colleges and being welcomed by them. And, alongside all of this, there were *also* these heinous acts, carried out by family and by friends. Yes, it was the silent pandemic. But so many of the acts began before COVID-19 closed campus. Most students who reported experiencing it were women, but not all. Jerome (LI,A) cowered before a gun. But Jamie's interview was the first time I hated being a researcher—probing for more information made me feel horrible. I didn't want to be seen as nosy or voyeuristic about what happened to her; Jamie had already received such questions from her biological father. And yet I also needed to probe in order to convey what happened in the lives of Jamie and others, what made home and Harvard such hard places to be, and how increased economic vulnerability and insecurity made matters worse.

I hope I showed caring in the conversations I had with students who shared such unspeakable experiences. When possible, I checked in with students at the end of the interview to see how they were feeling emotionally. No one complained. In fact, some thanked me for caring enough to ask and to listen. Some students shared things with me that they had never shared before with their families or friends. But I didn't take that as a given. Some students didn't know they had started crying until I asked if they needed a minute to compose themselves. No student stopped an interview, even after divulging a secret or touching on a particularly painful memory or subject with me or a member of my team. I take solace in this fact and in students being willing to have follow-up interviews with me and my team, and with those follow-up interviews often lasting longer than the first. I also take Jamie sending over emails as a sign that our time together was affirming and did not lead to further scarring.

I had to take a long walk after so many interviews, especially those sessions where physical and sexual abuse were so much a part of the story. I did not rush to take notes after. I did not quickly move on to the next interview. I just left my house and walked, regardless of weather. I forced myself to limit interviews to just two a day, no matter the pressure to do as many interviews as possible before the school year ended. Listening to students' tribulations since campus closed began to weigh on me. I'm thankful to have had already been in therapy for two years at that point with someone who understands trauma and has helped me recognize when I am feeling overwhelmed. And thankful my therapist offered strategies to deal with stress as I remained in my apartment alone.

But as so many of us experienced, the added stressors of the pandemic just amplified all of the pre-existing issues we were already dealing with. Because of the COVID-19 pandemic, I was separated from my family. I had not seen my mom in over a year. I missed us together peeling ten pounds of potatoes to make potato salad. In that year, we had seen and experienced so much. The nation was witnessing and dealing with an unending barrage of loss, both from COVID-19 and other debilitating illnesses, and from gun violence. I lost people—friends and family—to all three. And I was hearing about students experiencing the same in what felt like every other interview. In fact, while speaking with Jamie in March 2021 I searched Google for details about a medical issue she mentioned struggling with that made COVID-19 even scarier. I wanted to return to it later. As I looked, I happened to see a Facebook notification. My cousin posted a just-taken picture of my Uncle Winston cutting the neighbor's tree. It made me smile because I had seen this so many times growing up. He would come over to get mangoes from the tree in our backyard and we'd eat them. The caption, however, made my breath catch: it was an announcement about him entering hospice with cancer. Even at his weakest, he couldn't sit still. It was the day before his seventy-third birthday. My walk that day was the longest I took during the pandemic.

There is so much to unpack about doing work during the pandemic, let alone doing research related to the very inequalities exacerbated by it. I feel that we will be attempting this unpacking for years to come. I am indebted to sociologists Karina Santellano and Asad L. Asad for inviting us to not shy away from such difficult conversations and give ourselves grace, put work aside, and lean on our community. Many more scholars will fill their own pages documenting the added toll of conducting such studies in similar ways as I have done, and probably with more detail. I am still processing it all. The aspects of the research I surface here are those that caused me the most pause as I was conducting the study. They returned as I listened and watched the interviews for a second or third time. It hurt to go back to the Zoom video recordings to search for how students expressed emotions, trying to capture the fullness of the moments. Rewatching their tears, the flashes of anger across their faces, and their fidgeting when talking about something sensitive all brought me back to the exhausting emotions of the day that the interview was conducted.[9]

I still don't know how I made it through, although I think I needed my time with students as much as they wanted to be part of the project. Investing myself into this project kept me sane. I came to rely on the interviews to fill my days. Therapy was key, and so were walks in the evenings, but my conversations with students helped me stay busy and helped to remind me of some essential part of myself until the weeks started to blur by, and I was finally able to make it to Miami to see my family, to surprise my nephew when I picked him up from school, after thirteen months of being all on my own.

ABBREVIATIONS

Social Classification

LI   Lower income

UI   Upper income

Racial/Ethnic Classification

A   Asian

B   Black

L   Latino

M   Mixed (two or more racial/ethnic groups)

N   Native

W   White

ACKNOWLEDGMENTS

LIFE'S JOURNEY MAY BE LONG, but I am fortunate that mine is not lonely. At every turn, I have had people in my corner. They spoke for me when I wasn't in the room. They spoke up for me when I was in the room and couldn't speak for myself. They championed me in ways I was unaware of, ways that I am still learning about to this day. They told me when to keep pushing and when to rest. They looked after me when I was knocked down, ensuring that I would not be knocked out. So, I offer up my best prayer to my best people: Thank you.

Bill Wilson, this book doesn't come to be without you. Your invitation to take on such a project is what started this whole thing. Our conversation that random day in November reminded me of graduate school. Not because it reminded me of being a student, but because it was a yet another instance of you treating me as an equal. You instructed me to take lead, offering detailed comments that helped me think through framing and then, just as you did when I was sitting in your office all those years ago, you told me, "Go for it." I hope these pages live up to the trust you put in me.

Tomiko Brown Nagin, your leadership matches your brilliance. Thank you for supporting me as a young scholar and researcher. And as a person. You made space for me, allowing me to share my work and my story with the communities of the Harvard Radcliffe Institute and the Harvard & the Legacy of Slavery Initiative. I'm thankful you gave me the chance to share my policy recommendations with top brass at the university. I have learned so much from you. You showed me how I can be an even more effective advocate on behalf of the next generation.

I have had the great fortune of having truly amazing people in my life. They saw me through the growing pains of diving into a second book.

But more importantly, they saw me through a trying period of life, sprinkling beauty into the swirling tumult. They have left a mark on this book, and especially on me.

Ameerah Phillips, if there is a person who personifies the notion of family being chosen, it is you. You love deeply and wholly. We leaned on each other, through good times and bad. And it is funny, as we talk about in our Sunday conversations, how sometimes believing the good is harder than dealing with the bad. You having my back during both has helped in ways that I can't quite put into words. And to have known your love and friendship for nearly twenty years is mind-blowing.

Robin Mitchell, you are a true gift from the heavens. I never thought that I could meet someone who, with a knowing look, could make a place that I've lived for fifteen years truly feel like home. And then I met you, Robin. Your smile, quick wit, honesty, and impeccable taste in fashion helped me see through the haze. You reminded me to carve out time for myself. Our outings to Pyara were more than just facials and manicures, they were invitations to recharge and connect with what matters. And then, if that wasn't enough, you were my voice when I could not speak. When I was weak and was left unprotected, you were my sword and shield. I thank you and love you for that and more.

Dawn Ling, to know you is to be in awe of you. You never saw me as another fellow at Radcliffe; you saw me. I learned from you. I even got to see *Hamilton* because of and with you. But more importantly, we shared outings around town that filled the tank.

Francesca Purcell, you rock. That pretty much sums it up. From that chance encounter at the American Academy of Arts and Sciences to being neighbors on Appian Way, from professional connections to friends, we have come a mighty long way. And with each step my love and appreciation for you grows. Your energy, your smile, your New York bravado on these quiet Cambridge streets—all this and more make me smile each time I see you.

Derek Bradshaw and Jeffrey Wiggins, from Mather to now, y'all have been there. Connecting with both of you kept me sane, and in near tears from laughing whenever we link up. Thank you for welcoming me in more than a decade ago and for holding it down ever since.

Becca Burke Miller, you are forever that calming force that motivates us all to be better. Thank you for our walks; they always seem to happen right when I need to do more than stretch my legs. They were good for the heart in more ways than one. I love sharing my current knitting projects with you, always hoping that my skill level inches ever closer to yours.

Erika Prahl, the homie. Watching you work is a masterclass. Your support of students is something that we should all aspire to do. Thank you for inviting me in, for those lunches on the deck that fed my mind and body.

Cherise Kenner, my ace in the hole. There is so much to say. Professional. Check. Personable. Check. Loving. Check. Kind. Check. Engaging. Check. Caring. Check. Funny. Check. The list could continue, but even Webster's dictionary would eventually fail me. My admiration of you knows no bounds. Thank you for everything and then some.

Lauren Pyes, what can I say but that you are amazing. The words *generous, kind*, and *loving* only begin to scratch the surface of who you are. Your support means more than you will ever know.

Kristin Bumiller, Jack Begleiter, and Gabe Rosenthal (and Ami!): My family away from home. What did I do to deserve you in my life? I may not know the answer to that question, but I know that I am loved. Your love envelops me, protects me from the loneliness of being away from home and the wildness of the world. Your love encourages me to be kinder, both to myself and to the people who come into my life. Your love inspires.

Amjad Asad, Asad L. Asad, Matthew Clair: I never take having you in my life for granted. From memes sent online to memories made in real life, you three are so very special. I miss you and I love you.

The Jackson Four: Vera, Ernie, Lavenia, and Michelle, my Coffee and Conversation crew. Joining the calls in the morning is a staple part of my day. The belly laughs and tough conversations are the best way to start the day.

Denise Orrell, my buddy. You are awesome, stubborn in your support of family and friends. From our $5 movie outings back in Amherst to screaming our heads off in support of the Connecticut Sun, thank you for being my friend.

The Frys: Nathan, Michele, Parker, Kendall, Annabelle, and Addison. My friends. From Pokémon battles to backyard BBQs to basketball games, thank you for making Cambridge and Harvard warm and friendly. The waves from your kitchen window and your front door flying open to say hello made Linnaean Street special.

The Savenor's Butcher Shop Gang: Y'all hold me down in so many ways. Stopping by the shop is often the highlight of my week. You've introduced new worlds to me through food. Special shout-out to Grace Mortenson, Michelle Samuels, Margaret Sargent, and Christopher Walker for your patience, kindness, professionalism, and support.

Angela Brown, Natashia Hines, Cyndy Jean, Ashley Payne, William Henry Pruitt III, and Mekka Smith, thank y'all for our honest conversation and pep talks. Sharon Bromberg-Lin, Caitlin Daniel, Jonathan Hampton, LeShae Henderson, Rebecca Horwitz-Willis, Garry Mitchell, Christopher Muller, Monique Roy, Lumumba Seegars, Megan Segoshi, Brandon Terry, Adriana Umana-Taylor, Sha Wade, and Whitney Wade, thank you for the calls and texts that filled my tank when I was running on E.

Katherine Albutt, you saw me when others didn't. Without your skilled hands and dedication to your craft, I'm not sure I would have made it. You and your amazing team saved me. You gave me a new lease on life.

I am thankful to have received funding from the Harvard Radcliffe Institute and the Harvard & the Legacy of Slavery Initiative. I wrote part of this book during a fellowship leave as the Shutzer Assistant Professor at Radcliffe and a 2021–2022 Radcliffe fellow. I hired the best team a researcher can have: Becca Bassett, D'Wayne Bell, Shandra Jones, Kemeyawi Wahpepah. You all were tremendous, dedicating time to this project as if it were your own. As I say in the pages of this book and in conversations with anyone who will listen, our check-ins were one part research, one part reunion. Each of you are brilliant and kind, creative and generous. You are shaping the future of scholarship. But I also see your imprint on me. You made me a better researcher and teacher. Having you as part of my team has been an honor.

Through the Harvard Radcliffe Institute and Summer Research Opportunities at Harvard, I had the unique honor of working with undergraduates who blew my socks off, as intellectually curious as they were fearless. For your candor and your jokes, thank you Galadriel Coury, Nadia Douglas, Zoree Jones, and Ellie Taylor, as well as Calvin Bell III, Virginia Cano, Quentin Jenkins, Leslie Luqueño, Cristina Santos, Diana Tiburcio, and Jenna Maree Wong.

I also got support to bring Carson Byrd, Elizabeth Lee, and Jasmine Whiteside to campus for a writer's workshop. Thank you not only for being brilliant sociologists but also for offering your time and energy to provide comments on early drafts of this work. Exchanging ideas with you in Cambridge was a true highlight. You pushed me to be clearer in my argument and sharper in my critiques.

For your time and critical eye during different parts of the writing process, thank you Jane Choi, Eddie Cole, Ranae Jabri, Melina Melgoza, Meaghan Mingo, Christine Mitchell, Malia Montalvo, Mitsuki Nishimoto, Kelle Parsons, Kate Penner, and Saron Tesfalul.

I have been extremely fortunate to work with Meagan Levinson at Princeton University Press, who was instrumental in seeing this project through. You knew what this book was before I did. For your sincerity and support, I am thankful.

I am forever thankful to David Lobenstine, and not just for your edits. Thank you for your patience. You pushed me to be clearer, be bolder. On each page you wanted to make sure my voice was present. You helped me honor students' narratives in a way that didn't render me silent. You also made time for me when I was sidelined, and never—not once— made me feel bad for taking time away to deal with life's blows.

A special thanks goes to LeVar Burton for introducing me to new worlds, near and far, past and future, big and small. You narrated my childhood. Whatever we were looking for, you invited us all to "Take a look, it's in a book." And now, as I'm nearing forty, the same is true. I have dedicated an entire bookcase in my house just to authors I've been introduced to from your podcast. I took your word for it and have been forever thankful.

Some words are put to paper. Others are put to music. JP Cooper transports me back to first crushes and old loves but always with an eye toward what tomorrow may bring. Beyoncé offered an anthem and prayer that sustained me. Adele reminded me to grow through pain. Vijay Iyer gave us musical combinations that brought new life into old favorites. Shirley Caesar, my perennial favorite, blessed me with a hug, both physical and spiritual. Each were on repeat as I walked and worked, wrote and walked. Thank you for being my soundtrack along this unexpected journey.

As always, my family is my rock, steadfast and unmovable. Always abounding in love and joy, even in the darkest and wildest of times.

To my mommy, Marilyn, love you. I will never forget sitting on the porch at the old house. It was like so many others passed under Miami's blue skies. You looked at me and smiled, eyes crinkling just a little. "You're weird." And then paused. "No, no that's not what I meant. You've always been different." I cracked up. You cracked up. I knew what you meant then as I know it now. I've always been bookish, wanting to play spades rather than play football. Ceramics over running around with the other guys. And instead of admonishing me, you supported me every step of the way, never making me second guess myself. I owe you for the nurturing environment that gave me space to be me, in all my nerdy weirdness.

To my big brother, Greg: I forever want to be like you when I grow up. And every day I'm learning more about how to do just that. You came when I needed you. You stayed when I couldn't even formulate the ask. By my side is where you have always been, my biggest and loudest champion.

To my sister, Aleshia, I am indebted to you. For your dedication of time and sacrifice of the same, thank you for being home when I couldn't be, for helping in ways that I am ill-equipped to do. For taking care of Daisy's baby as only you can, there are no words.

To my nieces, nephew, and great nephew, Shakia, Makayla, Amari, and Tareem Jr.: I love you. Y'all are glimpses of the future that I hope to see, that I work to build.

What can I say to those students—brilliant and bold, kind and considerate—who let me in to their lives? Thank you. You will never know how much logging on to Zoom to speak with you was my lifeline, my connection to a world that I missed dearly. Our conversations were not always easy; some were quite trying. They left my heart full and aching. In each interview you were present, offering yourself fully. Your words make this book possible. I am sorry that you have had to shoulder the burden of our desperately unequal status quo. I hope that your words help to disrupt that status quo, especially at institutions that preach inclusion yet too often practice everything but. I hope your words push us toward a brighter world, taking us places we can't yet imagine.

NOTES

Frontmatter epigraph: Lucille Clifton, *The Book of Light* (Port Townsend, WA: Copper Canyon Press, 1993).

Introduction

1. Colleges are indeed diversifying their campuses through different class- and race-based affirmative action measures, especially no-loan financial aid policies that replace loans with scholarships and grants. See Anthony Abraham Jack, *The Privileged Poor: How Elite Colleges Are Failing Disadvantaged Students* (Cambridge, MA: Harvard University Press, 2019); Nicholas Hillman, "Economic Diversity in Elite Higher Education: Do No-Loan Programs Impact Pell Enrollments?," *Journal of Higher Education* 84, no. 6 (2013): 806–33; Karen W. Arenson, "Princeton to Replace Loans with Student Scholarships," *New York Times*, January 28, 2001, sec. New York, https://www.nytimes.com/2001/01/28/nyregion/princeton-to-replace-loans-with -student-scholarships.html. For statements for universities regarding their landmark classes, see Emma Swislow, "College Admits 'Most Diverse Pool' Ever to Class of 2022," *Amherst Student*, April 3, 2018, https://amherststudent.amherst.edu/article/2018/04/03/college-admits-most -diverse-pool-ever-class-2022.html; Daniel Aloi, "Admitted Class of '21 Sets New Application, Diversity Records," *Cornell Chronicle*, March 30, 2017, https://news.cornell.edu/stories/2017 /03/admitted-class-21-sets-new-application-diversity-records.

2. Deirdre Fernandes, "The Majority of Harvard's Incoming Class Is Nonwhite," *Boston Globe*, August 2, 2017, https://www.bostonglobe.com/metro/2017/08/02/harvard-incoming -class-majority-nonwhite/5yOoqrsQ4SePRRNFemuQ2M/story.html.

3. W. Carson Byrd, *Behind the Diversity Numbers: Achieving Racial Equity on Campus* (Cambridge, MA: Harvard Education Press, 2021); Matthew Hartley and Christopher Morphew, "What's Being Sold and to What End? A Content Analysis of College Viewbooks," *Journal of Higher Education* 79, no. 6 (2008): 671–91; Natasha Kumar Warikoo, *The Diversity Bargain: And Other Dilemmas of Race, Admissions, and Meritocracy at Elite Universities* (Chicago: University of Chicago Press, 2016); Karly Sarita Ford and Ashley N. Patterson, "'Cosmetic Diversity': University Websites and the Transformation of Race Categories," *Journal of Diversity in Higher Education* 12, no. 2 (2019): 99; Megan M. Holland and Karly Sarita Ford, "Legitimating Prestige through Diversity: How Higher Education Institutions Represent Ethno-Racial Diversity across Levels of Selectivity," *Journal of Higher Education* 92, no. 1 (2021): 1–30.

4. Travis Andersen, "Goodbye Loans, Hello Grants: Smith College to Deliver Big Boost to Students Receiving Need-Based Aid," *Boston Globe*, October 22, 2021, https://www.bostonglobe

.com/2021/10/22/metro/goodbye-loans-hello-grants-smith-college-deliver-big-boost
-students-receiving-need-based-aid/; Nick Anderson, "Princeton to Cover All College Bills for
Families Making up to $100,000," *Washington Post*, September 8, 2022, https://www
.washingtonpost.com/education/2022/09/08/princeton-student-tuition-financial-aid/.

5. Lauren Rivera, *Pedigree: How Elite Students Get Elite Jobs* (Princeton, NJ: Princeton University Press, 2015); Amy J. Binder, Daniel B. Davis, and Nick Bloom, "Career Funneling: How Elite Students Learn to Define and Desire 'Prestigious' Jobs," *Sociology of Education* 89, no. 1 (October 15, 2015): 20–39, https://doi.org/10.1177/0038040715610883; Jennie E. Brand and Yu Xie, "Who Benefits Most from College? Evidence for Negative Selection in Heterogeneous Economic Returns to Higher Education," *American Sociological Review* 75, no. 2 (April 1, 2010): 273–302, https://doi.org/10.1177/0003122410363567; Raj Chetty et al., "Mobility Report Cards: The Role of Colleges in Intergenerational Mobility" (NBER, January 2017), http://www
.equality-of-opportunity.org/papers/coll_mrc_paper.pdf.

6. Rivera, *Pedigree*; Binder, Davis, and Bloom, "Career Funneling"; C. Wright Mills, *The Power Elite* (New York: Oxford University Press, 1956); Shamus Khan, "The Sociology of Elites," *Annual Review of Sociology* 38 (2012): 361–77; Chetty et al., "Mobility Report Cards." See also Allison L. Hurst et al., "The Graduate School Pipeline and First-Generation/Working-Class Inequalities," *Sociology of Education*, December 3, 2023, https://doi.org/10.1177
/00380407231215051.

7. Mitchell Stevens, Elizabeth Armstrong, and Richard Arum, "Sieve, Incubator, Temple, Hub: Empirical and Theoretical Advances in the Sociology of Higher Education," *Annual Review of Sociology* 34, no. 1 (2008): 127–51, https://doi.org/10.1146/annurev.soc.34.040507
.134737; Elizabeth Armstrong and Laura Hamilton, *Paying for the Party: How College Maintains Inequality* (Cambridge, MA: Harvard University Press, 2013); Jack, *The Privileged Poor*.

8. Armstrong and Hamilton, *Paying for the Party*; Stevens, Armstrong, and Arum, "Sieve, Incubator, Temple, Hub"; Jack, *The Privileged Poor*; Janel E. Benson and Elizabeth M. Lee, *Geographies of Campus Inequality: Mapping the Diverse Experiences of First-Generation Students* (New York: Oxford University Press, 2020).

9. Anthony Abraham Jack, "I Was a Low-Income College Student. Classes Weren't the Hard Part," *New York Times*, September 10, 2019, sec. Magazine, https://www.nytimes.com/interactive
/2019/09/10/magazine/college-inequality.html, https://www.nytimes.com/interactive/2019
/09/10/magazine/college-inequality.html.

10. Jack, *The Privileged Poor*; Jack, "I Was a Low-Income College Student."

11. I have pushed universities to update their policies regarding breaks. Amherst, Smith, Harvard, and scores of other universities have reversed their decisions to close eateries during spring break.

12. Jennifer M. Morton, *Moving up without Losing Your Way: The Ethical Costs of Upward Mobility* (Princeton, NJ: Princeton University Press, 2019).

13. Ahmad Khanijahani and Larisa Tomassoni, "Socioeconomic and Racial Segregation and COVID-19: Concentrated Disadvantage and Black Concentration in Association with COVID-19 Deaths in the USA," *Journal of Racial and Ethnic Health Disparities*, 9, no. 1 (2022): 367–75; Gerard Torrats-Espinosa, "Using Machine Learning to Estimate the Effect of Racial Segregation on COVID-19 Mortality in the United States," *Proceedings of the National Academy of Sciences*

118, no. 7 (2021): e2015577118; Randall Akee and Sarah Reber, "American Indians and Alaska Natives Are Dying of COVID-19 at Shocking Rates," *Brookings* (blog), February 18, 2021, https://www.brookings.edu/research/american-indians-and-alaska-natives-are-dying-of-covid -19-at-shocking-rates/.

14. Hannah Han, "Class of 2022 Set Since-Broken Records for Greatest Socioeconomic Diversity and Largest Applicant Pool," *Yale Daily News*, May 22, 2022, https://yaledailynews.com /blog/2022/05/22/class-of-2022-set-since-broken-records-for-greatest-socioeconomic -diversity-and-largest-applicant-pool/.

15. As sociologists Janel Benson and Elizabeth Lee put it, we must examine "with whom, in what contexts, and how—and at what cost" undergraduates, especially lower-income and first-generation college students, experience campus. Antonio Duran et al., "A Critical Quantitative Analysis of Students' Sense of Belonging: Perspectives on Race, Generation Status, and Collegiate Environments," *Journal of College Student Development* 61, no. 2 (2020): 133–53, https:// doi.org/10.1353/csd.2020.0014; Benson and Lee, *Geographies of Campus Inequality*, 20. See also Anthony M. Johnson, "Collaborating in Class: Social Class Context and Peer Help-Seeking and Help-Giving in an Elite Engineering School," *American Sociological Review*, October 29, 2022, https://doi.org/10.1177/00031224221130506; Elizabeth M. Lee and Jacob Harris, "Counterspaces, Counterstructures: Low-Income, First-Generation, and Working-Class Students' Peer Support at Selective Colleges," *Sociological Forum* 35, no. 4 (2020): 1135–56, https://doi.org/10 .1111/socf.12641. For a discussion of how college students perceive campus boundaries, see Shaolu Yu et al., "'Is There a Bubble to Burst?' College Students' Spatial Perception of Campus and the City, a Case Study of Rhodes College in Memphis, TN," *Urban Geography* 39, no. 10 (November 26, 2018): 1555–75, https://doi.org/10.1080/02723638.2018.1481602.

16. Jack, *The Privileged Poor*; Jasmine L. Whiteside, "Becoming Academically Eligible: University Enrollment among First-Generation, Rural College Goers," *Rural Sociology* 86, no. 2 (2021): 204–28; Elizabeth M. Lee, "Elite Colleges and Socioeconomic Status," *Sociology Compass* 7, no. 9 (September 1, 2013): 786–98. See also William A. Darity and A. Kirsten Mullen, *From Here to Equality: Reparations for Black Americans in the Twenty-First Century* (Chapel Hill: University of North Carolina Press, 2020); Douglas Massey et al., *The Source of the River: The Social Origins of Freshmen at America's Selective Colleges and Universities* (Princeton, NJ: Princeton University Press, 2003); David Brady et al., "The Inheritance of Race Revisited: Childhood Wealth and Income and Black–White Disadvantages in Adult Life Chances," *Sociological Science* 7 (2020): 599–627, https://doi.org/10.15195/v7.a25.

17. Nathan D. Martin, "The Privilege of Ease: Social Class and Campus Life at Highly Selective, Private Universities," *Research in Higher Education* 53, no. 4 (June 1, 2012): 426–52; Shamus Khan, *Privilege: The Making of an Adolescent Elite at St. Paul's School* (Princeton, NJ: Princeton University Press, 2011); Elena G. van Stee, "Privileged Dependence, Precarious Autonomy: Parent/Young Adult Relationships through the Lens of COVID-19," *Journal of Marriage and Family* 85, no. 1 (2023): 215–32, https://doi.org/10.1111/jomf.12895.

18. For a discussion of the bias toward Black/White comparison in poverty research, see Mario Luis Small and Katherine Newman, "Urban Poverty after the Truly Disadvantaged: The Rediscovery of the Family, the Neighborhood, and Culture," *Annual Review of Sociology* 27 (January 1, 2001): 23–45. For research on Latinos and growing anti-immigration resentment,

see Asad L. Asad, *Engage and Evade: How Latino Immigrant Families Manage Surveillance in Everyday Life* (Princeton, NJ: Princeton University Press, 2023). For a discussion of the lack of coverage of Native and Indigenous communities, see Bryan McKinley Jones Brayboy, Jessica Solyom, and Angelina Castagno, "Indigenous Peoples in Higher Education," *Journal of American Indian Education* 54, no. 1 (2015): 154–86; Amanda R. Tachine, Nolan L. Cabrera, and Eliza Yellow Bird, "Home Away from Home: Native American Students' Sense of Belonging during Their First Year in College," *Journal of Higher Education* 88, no. 5 (2017): 785–807; Jillian Fish and Moin Syed, "Native Americans in Higher Education: An Ecological Systems Perspective," *Journal of College Student Development* 59, no. 4 (2018): 387–403; Jennifer Lee and Min Zhou, *The Asian American Achievement Paradox* (New York: Russell Sage Foundation, 2015).

19. Massey et al., *The Source of the River*; Whiteside, "Becoming Academically Eligible"; Anthony Abraham Jack, "Culture Shock Revisited: The Social and Cultural Contingencies to Class Marginality," *Sociological Forum* 29, no. 2 (2014): 453–75, https://doi.org/10.1111/socf.12092.

20. W. E. B. Du Bois, *The Gift of Black Folk* (Boston: The Stratford Co., 1924); Monica Prasad, "Problem-Solving Sociology," *Contemporary Sociology* 47, no. 4 (2018): 393–98. For a discussion of proximity and positionality, see Reuben Jonathan Miller, *Halfway Home: Race, Punishment, and the Afterlife of Mass Incarceration* (New York: Little, Brown and Company, 2021).

21. While President Joseph Biden condemned the Supreme Court for ending affirmative action, he advocated for using first-generation college student status as an important factor that takes "into account the adversity a student has overcome when selecting among qualified applicants." See Brett Samuels, "Biden Urges 'New Path Forward' That Factors in Adversity after Affirmative Action Ruling," *The Hill* (blog), June 29, 2023, https://thehill.com/homenews/administration/4074024-biden-path-forward-supreme-court-affirmative-action/.

22. James Baldwin, *The Price of the Ticket: Collected Nonfiction, 1948–1985* (New York: St. Martin's/Marek, 1985).

Chapter One

1. Kevin Chen and Juliet Isselbacher, "Harvard College Adopts Universal Satisfactory-Unsatisfactory Grading for Spring 2020 due to Coronavirus," *Harvard Crimson*, March 28, 2020, https://www.thecrimson.com/article/2020/3/28/harvard-coronavirus-universal-satisfactory-unsatisfactory-grading/.

2. Vivian Louie, *Keeping the Immigrant Bargain: The Costs and Rewards of Success in America* (New York: Russell Sage Foundation, 2012); Leah Schmalzbauer, *Meanings of Mobility: Family, Education, and Immigration in the Lives of Latino Youth* (New York: Russell Sage Foundation, 2023).

3. Javier Auyero, *Patients of the State: The Politics of Waiting in Argentina* (Durham, NC: Duke University Press, 2012); Cameron Parsell and Andrew Clarke, "Charity and Shame: Towards Reciprocity," *Social Problems* 69, no. 2 (May 1, 2022): 436–52, https://doi.org/10.1093/socpro/spaa057.

4. So accustomed to such requests that lower-income students at Pitzer College in California created a template on how best to "sell your heartache" in their quest for support from the college.

5. Students from lower-income families face a similar issue when applying to college. They are coached to put trauma on display for admissions counselors who like "sob stories." See Jack, "I Was a Low-Income College Student"; Ben Gebre-Medhin et al., "Application Essays and the Ritual Production of Merit in US Selective Admissions," *Poetics* 94 (October 1, 2022): 101706, https://doi.org/10.1016/j.poetic.2022.101706.

6. Anemona Hartocollis, "'An Eviction Notice': Chaos after Colleges Tell Students to Stay Away," *New York Times*, March 11, 2020, sec. U.S., https://www.nytimes.com/2020/03/11/us/colleges-cancel-classes-coronavirus.html.

7. Anne Wen, "5 Students Share How They Spent Their COVID Gap Year," *Teen Vogue*, July 30, 2021, sec. Politics, https://www.teenvogue.com/story/covid-gap-years-what-to-do; Christian Rodriguez, "College Interrupted: Many Students Chose to Take Time off Instead of Remote Learning during the Coronavirus Pandemic," *CNBC*, June 9, 2021, sec. College Voices, https://www.cnbc.com/2021/06/09/many-college-students-chose-time-off-over-remote-learning-during-covid.html; James Bikales and Kevin Chen, "Over 20 Percent of Harvard Undergrads Do Not Intend to Enroll in Fall 2020," *Harvard Crimson*, August 7, 2020, sec. News, https://www.thecrimson.com/article/2020/8/7/harvard-coronavirus-fall-enrollment-numbers/.

8. van Stee, "Privileged Dependence, Precarious Autonomy."

9. David Oliver, "Airbnb, Vrbo More Popular than Hotels during COVID-19 Pandemic," *USA Today*, August 26, 2020, https://www.usatoday.com/story/travel/hotels/2020/08/26/airbnb-vrbo-more-popular-than-hotels-during-covid-19-pandemic/5607312002/.

10. Importantly, this travel was during a time where Native Hawaiians were struggling with the influx of tourism that went beyond long lines at the airport.

11. Alexandra Sternlicht, "As Wealthy Depart for Second Homes, Class Tensions Come to Surface in Coronavirus Crisis," *Forbes*, March 29, 2020, sec. Under 30, https://www.forbes.com/sites/alexandrasternlicht/2020/03/29/as-wealthy-depart-for-second-homes-class-tensions-come-to-surface-in-coronavirus-crisis/; Wednesday Martin, "The Rich Can Run (to Their Second Homes), but They Can't Hide from This Pandemic," *Washington Post*, April 1, 2020, https://www.washingtonpost.com/outlook/2020/04/01/covid-19-quarantine-new-york-rich/.

12. Schmalzbauer, *Meanings of Mobility*.

13. Eric Klinenberg, *Heat Wave: A Social Autopsy of Disaster in Chicago* (Chicago: University of Chicago Press, 2003); Eric Klinenberg, *Palaces for the People: How Social Infrastructure Can Help Fight Inequality, Polarization, and the Decline of Civic Life* (New York: Crown, 2018); Samantha Becker et al., "Opportunity for All: How the American Public Benefits from Internet Access at U.S. Libraries," *Institute of Museum and Library Services* (Institute of Museum and Library Services, March 2010), https://eric.ed.gov/?id=ED510740.

14. John Lai and Nicole O. Widmar, "Revisiting the Digital Divide in the COVID-19 Era," *Applied Economic Perspectives and Policy* 43, no. 1 (March 2021): 458–64, https://doi.org/10.1002/aepp.13104.

15. Amherst College and Pitzer College, for example, both offered students "stay at home stipends" in the semester immediately after closing to keep campus population density low. Colleges returned to this policy when overcrowding occurred when students returned from

voluntary leaves and gap years. Middlebury College offered students $10,000 to take a semester off, or at least stay off campus.

16. D'vera Cohn and Jeffrey S. Passel, "A Record 64 Million Americans Live in Multigenerational Households," *Pew Research Center* (blog), April 5, 2018, https://www.pewresearch.org /fact-tank/2018/04/05/a-record-64-million-americans-live-in-multigenerational-households/; Catherine A. Solheim et al., "Immigrant Family Financial and Relationship Stress from the COVID-19 Pandemic," *Journal of Family and Economic Issues* 43, no. 2 (June 1, 2022): 282–95, https://doi.org/10.1007/s10834-022-09819-2; Celeste Katz Marston, "Asian Americans Most Likely to Live in Multigenerational Homes. How Covid Has Taken a Toll," *NBC News*, September 28, 2020, https://www.nbcnews.com/news/asian-america/asian-americans-most-likely-live -multigenerational-homes-how-covid-has-n1241111.

17. Marjorie Faulstich Orellana, "Responsibilities of Children in Latino Immigrant Homes," *New Directions for Youth Development* 2003, no. 100 (2003): 25–39, https://doi.org/10.1002/yd .61; Marjorie Faulstich Orellana, "The Work Kids Do: Mexican and Central American Immigrant Children's Contributions to Households and Schools in California," *Harvard Educational Review* 71, no. 3 (December 31, 2009): 366–90, https://doi.org/10.17763/haer.71.3.52320g7n21 922hw4.

18. Chimamanda Ngozi Adichie, "The Danger of a Single Story," filmed 2009 in Oxford, UK, TED video, 18:33, https://www.ted.com/talks/chimamanda_ngozi_adichie_the_danger_of_a _single_story/transcript?language=en.

19. Kate Chopin, *The Awakening* (New York: Dover, 2012), 115.

20. van Stee, "Privileged Dependence, Precarious Autonomy."

Chapter Two

1. Daniel Lieberman, *Exercised: Why Something We Never Evolved to Do Is Healthy and Rewarding* (New York: Pantheon Books, 2020).

2. An email from a staff member stationed at Muir Woods confirmed that "Muir Woods was closed to the public completely due to COVID from Mar 17, 2020 to June 29th 2020. It has remained opened since, though with varying degrees of mitigation due to local, state, and federal health department orders, which we still have currently."

3. Dean Narciso, "Largest Human Trafficking Sting in Ohio History Nets 161, Including City Councilman," *USA Today*, October 5, 2021, sec. Nation, https://www.usatoday.com/story/news /nation/2021/10/05/ohio-sex-trafficking-sting-nets-161-arrests-elyria-councilman/60080 63001/; Jeremy Wilson and Erin Dalton, "Human Trafficking in the Heartland: Variation in Law Enforcement Awareness and Response," *Journal of Contemporary Criminal Justice* 24, no. 3 (August 2008): 296–313, https://doi.org/10.1177/1043986208318227.

4. Jack, "I Was a Low-Income College Student."

5. Camille Charles et al., *Taming the River: Negotiating the Academic, Financial, and Social Currents in Selective Colleges and Universities* (Princeton, NJ: Princeton University Press, 2009); Massey et al., *The Source of the River.*

6. Massey et al., *The Source of the River.*

7. Access to the outdoors during the COVID-19 pandemic was lifesaving. See Naomi Sachs, "Access to Nature Has Always Been Important; with COVID-19, It Is Essential," *HERD: Health Environments Research & Design Journal* 13, no. 4 (October 1, 2020): 242–44, https://doi.org/10 .1177/1937586720949792.

8. Reynolds Farley et al., "'Chocolate City, Vanilla Suburbs': Will the Trend toward Racially Separate Communities Continue?," *Social Science Research* 7, no. 4 (1978): 319–44; Douglas Massey and Nancy Denton, *American Apartheid: Segregation and the Making of the Underclass* (Cambridge, MA: Harvard University Press, 1993).

9. See *Running While Black: Finding Freedom in a Sport That Wasn't Built for Us* (New York: Portfolio/Penguin, 2022); Marya T. Mtshali, "The Great Outdoors Was Made for White People," *The Nation*, May 28, 2021, https://www.thenation.com/article/society/great-outdoors -race-camping/; see also Sarah Maslin Nir, "How 2 Lives Collided in Central Park, Rattling the Nation," *New York Times*, June 14, 2020, sec. New York, https://www.nytimes.com/2020/06/14 /nyregion/central-park-amy-cooper-christian-racism.html. See also Richard Fausset, "What We Know about the Shooting Death of Ahmaud Arbery," *New York Times*, August 8, 2022, sec. U.S., https://www.nytimes.com/article/ahmaud-arbery-shooting-georgia.html.

10. Lucy Tompkins, "Sierra Club Says It Must Confront the Racism of John Muir," *New York Times*, July 22, 2020, sec. U.S., https://www.nytimes.com/2020/07/22/us/sierra-club-john -muir.html.

11. Karyn Lacy, *Blue-Chip Black Race, Class, and Status in the New Black Middle Class* (Berkeley: University of California Press, 2007); Keeanga-Yamahtta Taylor, *Race for Profit: How Banks and the Real Estate Industry Undermined Black Homeownership* (Chapel Hill: University of North Carolina Press, 2019); see also Mary Pattillo-McCoy, *Black Picket Fences: Privilege and Peril among the Black Middle Class* (Chicago: University of Chicago Press, 1999).

12. Massey et al., *The Source of the River*.

13. Ned Blackhawk, *The Rediscovery of America: Native Peoples and the Unmaking of U.S. History* (New Haven, CT: Yale University Press, 2023); Michael J. Witgen, *Seeing Red: Indigenous Land, American Expansion, and the Political Economy of Plunder in North America* (Williamsburg, VA: University of North Carolina Press, 2022).

14. Kristi Ka'apu and Catherine E. Burnette, "A Culturally Informed Systematic Review of Mental Health Disparities among Adult Indigenous Men and Women of the USA: What Is Known?," *British Journal of Social Work* 49, no. 4 (June 1, 2019): 880–98, https://doi.org/10.1093 /bjsw/bcz009.

15. Robert Preidt and Ernie Mundell, "U.S. Murder Rate up 30% during Pandemic, Highest One-Year Rise Ever," *US News & World Report*, October 6, 2021, https://www.usnews.com/news /health-news/articles/2021-10-06/us-murder-rate-up-30-during-pandemic-highest-one-year -rise-ever; Neil MacFarquhar, "Murders Spiked in 2020 in Cities across the United States," *New York Times*, September 27, 2021, sec. U.S., https://www.nytimes.com/2021/09/27/us/fbi -murders-2020-cities.html.

16. Colleen M. Heflin and Mary Pattillo, "Poverty in the Family: Race, Siblings, and Socioeconomic Heterogeneity," *Social Science Research* 35, no. 4 (December 1, 2006): 804–22, https:// doi.org/10.1016/j.ssresearch.2004.09.002.

17. Joseph G. Allen and John D. Macomber, *Healthy Buildings: The Power of Indoor Spaces to Boost Performance and Wellbeing*, revised (Cambridge, MA: Harvard University Press, 2022).

18. Hallie Golden, "Native American Tribes Enforce Mask Mandates Regardless of State Bans," *The Guardian*, August 31, 2021, sec. US News, https://www.theguardian.com/us-news /2021/aug/31/native-american-tribes-mask-mandates-schools.

19. For a look at how tribes and nations adapted vaccine rollout, see Joanne Silberner, "Covid-19: How Native Americans Led the Way in the US Vaccination Effort," *BMJ* (Clinical Research Ed.) 374 (September 17, 2021): n2168, https://doi.org/10.1136/bmj.n2168; Alex Brown, "In Hard-Hit Indian Country, Tribes Rapidly Roll Out Vaccines," *Stateline* (blog), February 9, 2021, https://stateline.org/2021/02/09/in-hard-hit-indian-country-tribes-rapidly-roll -out-vaccines/. For a look at early disparities in contraction and death, see Randall Akee and Sarah Reber, "American Indians and Alaska Natives Are Dying of COVID-19 at Shocking Rates" (Brookings Institution, February 18, 2021), https://www.brookings.edu/research/american -indians-and-alaska-natives-are-dying-of-covid-19-at-shocking-rates/.

20. Native and Indigenous morticians familiar with traditional burial rites were few and overextended. Chris Serres, "'Where Is Our Humanity?' A Minnesota Man Is on a Mission to Keep Native Burial Customs Alive during the Pandemic," *Star Tribune*, January 30, 2021, sec. Coronavirus, https://www.startribune.com/where-is-our-humanity-a-minnesota-man-is-on-a -mission-to-keep-native-burial-customs-alive-during-the/600017108/.

21. Massey et al., *The Source of the River*; Nicole M. Stephens, Hazel Rose Markus, and L Taylor Phillips, "Social Class Culture Cycles: How Three Gateway Contexts Shape Selves and Fuel Inequality," *Annual Review of Psychology* 65 (September 25, 2013): 611–34.

22. Charles et al., *Taming the River*; Rebecca Covarrubias and Stephanie A. Fryberg, "Movin' on up (to College): First-Generation College Students' Experiences with Family Achievement Guilt," *Cultural Diversity and Ethnic Minority Psychology* 21, no. 3 (July 2015): 420–29, https://doi .org/10.1037/a0037844.

Chapter Three

1. Giulia McDonnell Nieto del Rio, "University of California Will No Longer Consider SAT and ACT Scores," *New York Times*, May 15, 2021, sec. U.S., https://www.nytimes.com/2021/05 /15/us/SAT-scores-uc-university-of-california.html; Maya Goldman, "Covid-19 Is Making SAT, ACT Harder to Take," *Wall Street Journal*, September 23, 2020, sec. US, https://www.wsj .com/articles/covid-19-is-making-sat-act-harder-to-take-11600862411.

2. Karl L. Alexander, Doris Entwisle, and Linda Olson, *The Long Shadow: Family Background, Disadvantaged Urban Youth, and the Transition to Adulthood* (New York: Russell Sage Foundation, 2014).

3. The Editorial Board, "Doing Schoolwork in the Parking Lot Is Not a Solution," *New York Times*, July 18, 2020, sec. Opinion, https://www.nytimes.com/2020/07/18/opinion/sunday /broadband-internet-access-civil-rights.html.

4. Daniel Eisenberg, Ezra Golberstein, and Justin B Hunt, "Mental Health and Academic Success in College," *B.E. Journal of Economic Analysis & Policy* 9, no. 1 (September 15, 2009), https://doi.org/10.2202/1935-1682.2191; Charles et al., *Taming the River*. For an examination

of this process in medical school, see Mytien Nguyen et al., "Demographic Factors and Academic Outcomes Associated with Taking a Leave of Absence from Medical School," *JAMA Network Open* 4, no. 1 (January 22, 2021): e2033570, https://doi.org/10.1001/jamanetworkopen.2020.33570.

5. Charles et al., *Taming the River*; Patrick Sharkey and Jacob W. Faber, "Where, When, Why, and for Whom Do Residential Contexts Matter? Moving away from the Dichotomous Understanding of Neighborhood Effects," *Annual Review of Sociology* 40, no. 1 (July 30, 2014): 559–79, https://doi.org/10.1146/annurev-soc-071913-043350. For an examination of this process in medical school, see Nguyen et al., "Demographic Factors and Academic Outcomes."

6. Lillian Mezey, "Navigating a Leave of Absence," in *College Psychiatry: Strategies to Improve Access to Mental Health*, ed. Michelle B. Riba and Meera Menon, vol. 1, Psychiatry Update (Cham, Switzerland: Springer, 2021), 113–22, https://doi.org/10.1007/978-3-030-69468-5_8.

7. In 2023 Yale University found itself embroiled in a scandal and lawsuit surrounding its leave policies. William Wan, "'What If Yale Finds Out?,'" *Washington Post*, November 11, 2022, sec. Social Issues, https://www.washingtonpost.com/dc-md-va/2022/11/11/yale-suicides-mental-health-withdrawals/.

8. William E. Hartmann et al., "American Indian Historical Trauma: Anticolonial Prescriptions for Healing, Resilience, and Survivance," *American Psychologist* 74, no. 1 (January 2019): 6–19, https://doi.org/10.1037/amp0000326; Alexander et al., *The Long Shadow*.

9. Joseph P. Gone et al., "The Impact of Historical Trauma on Health Outcomes for Indigenous Populations in the USA and Canada: A Systematic Review," *American Psychologist* 74, no. 1 (January 2019): 20–35, https://doi.org/10.1037/amp0000338; Hartmann et al., "American Indian Historical Trauma"; Dennis C. Wendt et al., "What Are the Best Practices for Psychotherapy with Indigenous Peoples in the United States and Canada? A Thorny Question," *Journal of Consulting and Clinical Psychology*, October 3, 2022, https://doi.org/10.1037/ccp0000757.

Chapter Four

1. Taylor Caldwell, *Dear and Glorious Physician* (San Francisco: Ignatius Press, 2008), 14. For a discussion of students' differential comfort engaging adults, and especially college professors, see Jessica McCrory Calarco, *Negotiating Opportunities: How the Middle Class Secures Advantages in School* (New York: Oxford University Press, 2018); Jack, *The Privileged Poor*.

2. A pedagogy fellow is a type of high-impact practice that promotes development and access to institutional resources. See Brian P. An and Chad N. Loes, "Participation in High-Impact Practices: Considering the Role of Institutional Context and a Person-Centered Approach," *Research in Higher Education*, August 25, 2022, https://doi.org/10.1007/s11162-022-09715-6.

3. Nicole Bateman and Martha Ross, "The Pandemic Hurt Low-Wage Workers the Most—and so Far, the Recovery Has Helped Them the Least," Brookings, July 28, 2021, https://www.brookings.edu/research/the-pandemic-hurt-low-wage-workers-the-most-and-so-far-the-recovery-has-helped-them-the-least/; Martha Ross and Nicole Bateman, "We Can't Recover from a Coronavirus Recession without Helping Young Workers," Brookings, May 7, 2020, https://www.brookings.edu/research/we-cant-recover-from-a-coronavirus-recession-without-helping-young-workers/.

4. Sarah Brown, "When Covid-19 Closed Colleges, Many Students Lost Jobs They Needed. Now Campuses Scramble to Support Them," *Chronicle of Higher Education*, March 25, 2020, sec. News, https://www.chronicle.com/article/when-covid-19-closed-colleges-many-students-lost-jobs-they-needed-now-campuses-scramble-to-support-them/.

5. According to the National Center for Education Statistics, approximately 40 percent of full-time college students work, and 25 percent work twenty or more hours a week. Patrick T. Terenzini and Patricia Yeager, *Work-Study Program Influences on College Students' Cognitive Development*, 1996, https://eric.ed.gov/?id=ED405781; Carol A Lundberg, "Working and Learning: The Role of Involvement for Employed Students," *NASPA Journal* 41, no. 2 (2004): 16; Anne-Marie Nuñez and Vanessa A. Sansone, "Earning and Learning: Exploring the Meaning of Work in the Experiences of First-Generation Latino College Students," *Review of Higher Education* 40, no. 1 (2016): 107. For the negative consequences of unstable work schedules, see Daniel Schneider and Kristen Harknett, "Consequences of Routine Work-Schedule Instability for Worker Health and Well-Being," *American Sociological Review* 84, no. 1 (February 2019): 82–114, https://doi.org/10.1177/0003122418823184.

6. Jessica McCrory Calarco, "The Inconsistent Curriculum: Cultural Tool Kits and Student Interpretations of Ambiguous Expectations," *Social Psychology Quarterly* 77, no. 2 (June 1, 2014): 185–209.

7. Martin, "The Privilege of Ease"; Sara Goldrick-Rab, *Paying the Price: College Costs, Financial Aid, and the Betrayal of the American Dream* (Chicago: University of Chicago Press, 2016).

8. For a discussion on-campus employment, see Nuñez and Sansone, "Earning and Learning"; An and Loes, "Participation in High-Impact Practices." See Sandra Susan Smith, *Lone Pursuit: Distrust and Defensive Individualism among the Black Poor* (New York: Russell Sage Foundation, 2007) for a discussion of rugged individualism among lower-income job seekers.

9. Ryan J. Golemme, "Harvard Is Sweeping Dorm Crew under the Rug," *Harvard Crimson*, September 24, 2021, sec. Opinion, https://www.thecrimson.com/article/2021/9/24/golemme-sweeping-dorm-crew-under-the-rug/. For a discussion of boundary work among college students, see Anthony Abraham Jack and Zennon Black, "Belonging and Boundaries at an Elite University," *Social Problems*, September 10, 2022, 18, https://doi.org/10.1093/socpro/spac051; Amy J. Binder and Andrea R. Abel, "Symbolically Maintained Inequality: How Harvard and Stanford Students Construct Boundaries among Elite Universities," *Sociology of Education* 92, no. 1 (January 1, 2019): 41–58, https://doi.org/10.1177/0038040718821073.

10. For a conversation on "survivor's guilt" among economically disadvantaged youth, see Covarrubias and Fryberg, "Movin' on up (to College)"; Geraldine K. Piorkowski, "Survivor Guilt in the University Setting," *Personnel & Guidance Journal* 61, no. 10 (June 1983): 620, https://doi.org/10.1111/j.2164-4918.1983.tb00010.x; Alfred Lubrano, *Limbo: Blue-Collar Roots, White-Collar Dreams* (Hoboken, NJ: John Wiley & Sons, 2004).

11. For an exploration of the social dynamics of entering mental health services, see Bernice A. Pescosolido, Carol Brooks Gardner, and Keri M. Lubell, "How People Get into Mental Health Services: Stories of Choice, Coercion and 'Muddling through' from 'First-Timers,'" *Social Science & Medicine (1982)* 46, no. 2 (January 1998): 275–86.

12. Wolfgang Lehmann, "Becoming Middle Class: How Working-Class University Students Draw and Transgress Moral Class Boundaries," *Sociology* 43, no. 4 (August 1, 2009): 631–47, https://doi.org/10.1177/0038038509105412.

13. Nuñez and Sansone, "Earning and Learning."

14. For an examination of persistence in STEM, see Maya A Beasley, *Opting Out: Losing the Potential of America's Young Black Elite* (Chicago: University of Chicago Press, 2011); Erin Cech et al., "Professional Role Confidence and Gendered Persistence in Engineering," *American Sociological Review* 76, no. 5 (October 1, 2011): 641–66, https://doi.org/10.1177/000312 2411420815; for a discussion of the privileged poor and their strategies for connecting with faculty, see Anthony Abraham Jack, "(No) Harm in Asking: Class, Acquired Cultural Capital, and Academic Engagement at an Elite University," *Sociology of Education* 89, no. 1 (2016): 1–19, https://doi.org/10.1177/0038040715614913.

15. Martin, "The Privilege of Ease," 445.

16. See Erin A. Cech, *The Trouble with Passion: How Searching for Fulfillment at Work Fosters Inequality* (Oakland: University of California Press, 2021). See also Jack, "(No) Harm in Asking"; Anthony Abraham Jack, "What the Privileged Poor Can Teach Us," *New York Times*, September 12, 2015, sec. Sunday Review.

17. Annette Lareau, "Cultural Knowledge and Social Inequality," *American Sociological Review* 80, no. 1 (February 1, 2015): 1–27, https://doi.org/10.1177/0003122414565814; April Yee, "The Unwritten Rules Of Engagement: Social Class Differences in Undergraduates' Academic Strategies," *Journal of Higher Education* 87, no. 6 (October 26, 2016): 831–58, https://doi.org/10 .1353/jhe.2016.0031; Becca Spindel Bassett, "Big Enough to Bother Them? When Low-Income, First-Generation Students Seek Help From Support Programs," *Journal of College Student Development* 62, no. 1 (2021): 19–36, https://doi.org/10.1353/csd.2021.0002; Peter J. Collier and David L. Morgan, "'Is That Paper Really Due Today?' Differences in First-Generation and Traditional College Students' Understandings of Faculty Expectations," *Higher Education* 55, no. 4 (April 1, 2008): 425–46.

18. Jack, *The Privileged Poor*; Jack, "(No) Harm in Asking."

19. Beasley, *Opting Out*; Maya A. Beasley and Mary J. Fischer, "Why They Leave: The Impact of Stereotype Threat on the Attrition of Women and Minorities from Science, Math and Engineering Majors," *Social Psychology of Education* 15, no. 4 (December 1, 2012): 427–48, https://doi .org/10.1007/s11218-012-9185-3; Cech et al., "Professional Role Confidence and Gendered Persistence in Engineering"; Dorian McCoy, Courtney Luedke, and Rachelle Winkle-Wagner, "Encouraged or Weeded Out: Perspectives of Students of Color in the STEM Disciplines on Faculty Interactions," *Journal of College Student Development* 58, no. 5 (July 2017).

20. Stephanie Saul, "At N.Y.U., Students Were Failing Organic Chemistry. Who Was to Blame?," *New York Times*, October 3, 2022, sec. U.S., https://www.nytimes.com/2022/10/03 /us/nyu-organic-chemistry-petition.html.

Chapter Five

1. Caitlyn Collins, *Making Motherhood Work: How Women Manage Careers and Caregiving* (Princeton, NJ: Princeton University Press, 2020); Caitlyn Collins et al., "The Gendered Consequences of a Weak Infrastructure of Care: School Reopening Plans and Parents' Employment during the COVID-19 Pandemic," *Gender & Society* 35, no. 2 (April 1, 2021): 180–93, https://doi.org/10.1177/08912432211001300; Liana Christin Landivar et al., "Research Note: School Reopenings during the COVID-19 Pandemic and Implications for Gender and

Racial Equity," *Demography* 59, no. 1 (February 1, 2022): 1–12, https://doi.org/10.1215/00703370-9613354.

2. Liann Herder, "Gap Year Youth Are Taking Advantage of a Temporarily Booming Job Market," *Diverse: Issues In Higher Education*, December 9, 2021, https://www.diverseeducation.com/students/article/15286161/gap-year-youth-are-taking-advantage-of-a-temporarily-booming-job-market; Wen, "5 Students Share How They Spent Their COVID Gap Year"; Rodriguez, "College Interrupted." For a larger discussion of unpaid internships, see Leslie Regan Shade and Jenna Jacobson, "Hungry for the Job: Gender, Unpaid Internships, and the Creative Industries," *The Sociological Review* 63, no. S1 (2015): 188–205, https://doi.org/10.1111/1467-954X.12249; Ross Perlin, *Intern Nation: How to Earn Nothing and Learn Little in the Brave New Economy* (New York: Verso Books, 2012).

3. Corey Moss-Pech, "The Career Conveyor Belt: How Internships Lead to Unequal Labor Market Outcomes among College Graduates," *Qualitative Sociology*, January 6, 2021, https://doi.org/10.1007/s11133-020-09471-y; Rivera, *Pedigree*; Perlin, *Intern Nation*.

4. For a discussion of parental support in college that leads to uneven advantages among already privileged students, see Laura T. Hamilton and Elizabeth A. Armstrong, "Parents, Partners, and Professions: Reproduction and Mobility in a Cohort of College Women," *American Journal of Sociology* 127, no. 1 (July 1, 2021): 102–51, https://doi.org/10.1086/714850; Laura T. Hamilton, *Parenting to a Degree: How Family Matters for College Women's Success* (Chicago: University of Chicago Press, 2016). For media coverage on the prevalence and rise of unpaid internships among today's undergraduates, see Michael Gaynor, "43 Percent of Internships at For-Profit Companies Don't Pay. This Man Is Helping to Change That," *Washington Post*, January 15, 2019, https://www.washingtonpost.com/lifestyle/magazine/his-quest-to-get-interns-paid-is-paying-off/2019/01/11/93df2b2a-ff2a-11e8-83c0-b06139e540e5_story.html; Phoebe Maltz Bovy, "Unpaid Internships Are a Rich-Girl Problem—and Also a Real Problem," *Atlantic*, February 13, 2013, sec. Sexes, http://www.theatlantic.com/sexes/archive/2013/02/unpaid-internships-are-a-rich-girl-problem-and-also-a-real-problem/273106/.

5. Creative industries are infamous for use of unpaid labor. See Shade and Jacobson, "Hungry for the Job." For a discussion of the funneling of elite students into finance, see Binder, Davis, and Bloom, "Career Funneling"; Rivera, *Pedigree*.

6. Jack and Black, "Belonging and Boundaries at an Elite University"; Binder and Abel, "Symbolically Maintained Inequality."

7. Rivera, *Pedigree*.

8. Shade and Jacobson, "Hungry for the Job"; Moss-Pech, "The Career Conveyor Belt."

9. Youth from marginalized racial and class groups feel an obligation to support their families across the life course, see Andrew J. Fuligni, Vivian Tseng, and May Lam, "Attitudes toward Family Obligations among American Adolescents with Asian, Latin American, and European Backgrounds," *Child Development* 70, no. 4 (1999): 1030–44, https://doi.org/10.1111/1467-8624.00075; Louie, *Keeping the Immigrant Bargain*; Yader R. Lanuza, "Giving (Money) Back To Parents: Racial/Ethnic and Immigrant–Native Variation in Monetary Exchanges During the Transition to Adulthood," *Sociological Forum* 35, no. 4 (2020): 1157–82, https://doi.org/10.1111/socf.12642; Ranita Ray, *The Making of a Teenage Service Class: Poverty and Mobility in an American City* (Oakland: University of California Press, 2018). For a discussion of the various "capitals" that should be acknowledged and valued, see Tara Yosso, "Whose Culture Has Capital? A

Critical Race Theory Discussion of Community Cultural Wealth," *Race Ethnicity and Education* 8, no. 1 (March 1, 2005): 69–91, https://doi.org/10.1080/1361332052000341006.

10. Abel Valenzuela, "Gender Roles and Settlement Activities among Children and Their Immigrant Families," *American Behavioral Scientist* 42, no. 4 (January 1, 1999): 720–42, https:// doi.org/10.1177/0002764299042004009; Vanessa Delgado, "Children of Immigrants as 'Brokers' in an Era of Exclusion," *Sociology Compass* 14, no. 10 (2020): e12832, https://doi.org/10.1111 /soc4.12832; Marjorie Faulstich Orellana, Lisa Dorner, and Lucila Pulido, "Accessing Assets: Immigrant Youth's Work as Family Translators or 'Para-Phrasers,'" *Social Problems* 50, no. 4 (November 1, 2003): 505–24, https://doi.org/10.1525/sp.2003.50.4.505.

11. Schmalzbauer, *Meanings of Mobility*.

12. Stefanie DeLuca, Susan Clampet-Lundquist, and Kathryn Edin, *Coming of Age in the Other America* (New York: Russell Sage Foundation, 2016), 126; Jennifer M. Silva, "High Hopes and Hidden Inequalities: How Social Class Shapes Pathways to Adulthood," *Emerging Adulthood* 4, no. 4 (August 2016): 239–41, https://doi.org/10.1177/2167696815620965; Laura Napolitano, "'I'm Not Going to Leave Her High and Dry': Young Adult Support to Parents during the Transition to Adulthood," *Sociological Quarterly* 56, no. 2 (2015): 329–54, https://doi.org/10 .1111/tsq.12088.

13. Yosso, "Whose Culture Has Capital?," March 1, 2005.

Chapter Six

1. Marisa Iati, "A Small College Is Eliminating Loans from Its Financial Aid Packages," *Washington Post*, April 21, 2022, https://www.washingtonpost.com/education/2022/04/20/williams -college-loans-financial-aid/. On the reality of working in college, see Anthony P. Carnevale et al., "Learning While Earning: The New Normal," *Georgetown University Center on Education and the Workforce*, 2015, https://cew.georgetown.edu/cew-reports/workinglearners/; Ernest T. Pascarella et al., "Does Work Inhibit Cognitive Development during College?," *Educational Evaluation and Policy Analysis* 20, no. 2 (June 1, 1998): 75–93, https://doi.org/10.3102 /01623737020002075; Goldrick-Rab, *Paying the Price*. For a push to understand the social processes undergirding job seeking strategies, see Smith, *Lone Pursuit*.

2. Making explicit the hidden curriculum surrounding access to institutional resources is incredibility important for disrupting the reproduction of inequality. See Calarco, "The Inconsistent Curriculum"; Jessica McCrory Calarco, *A Field Guide to Grad School: Uncovering the Hidden Curriculum* (Princeton, NJ: Princeton University Press, 2020); Rachel Gable, *The Hidden Curriculum: First Generation Students at Legacy Universities* (Princeton, NJ: Princeton University Press, 2021); Jack, *The Privileged Poor*. For a discussion of these processes outside of academic contexts, see Matthew K. Clair, *Privilege and Punishment: How Race and Class Matter in Criminal Court* (Princeton, NJ: Princeton University Press, 2020).

3. Jack and Black, "Belonging and Boundaries at an Elite University"; Lehmann, "Becoming Middle Class"; see also Michèle Lamont, *Money, Morals, and Manners: The Culture of the French and American Upper-Middle Class* (Chicago: University of Chicago Press, 1992).

4. Ricardo D. Stanton-Salazar, "A Social Capital Framework for the Study of Institutional Agents and Their Role in the Empowerment of Low-Status Students and Youth," *Youth & Society* 43, no. 3 (2011): 1066–109.

5. Binder, Davis, and Bloom, "Career Funneling."

6. Binder, Davis, and Bloom, "Career Funneling"; Rivera, *Pedigree*; Lolade Fadulu, "Why Aren't College Students Using Career Services?," *The Atlantic*, January 20, 2018, https://www.theatlantic.com/education/archive/2018/01/why-arent-college-students-using-career-services/551051/.

7. Bassett, "Big Enough to Bother Them?"; Bassett, "'Do You Know How to Ask for an Incomplete?' Reconceptualizing Low-Income, First-Generation Student Success through a Resource Acquisition Lens," *Harvard Educational Review* 93, no. 3 (September 22, 2023): 366–90, https://doi.org/10.17763/1943-5045-93.3.366. See also Binder, Davis, and Bloom, "Career Funneling"; Lauren Rivera, "Ivies, Extracurriculars, and Exclusion: Elite Employers' Use of Educational Credentials," *Research in Social Stratification and Mobility* 29, no. 1 (January 1, 2011): 71–90, https://doi.org/10.1016/j.rssm.2010.12.001; Rivera, *Pedigree*; Moss-Pech, "The Career Conveyor Belt."

8. Nuñez and Sansone, "Earning and Learning," 109; Jenny Stuber, "Class, Culture, and Participation in the Collegiate Extra-Curriculum," *Sociological Forum* 24, no. 4 (2009): 877–900; Brian Kisida, Jay P. Greene, and Daniel H. Bowen, "Creating Cultural Consumers: The Dynamics of Cultural Capital Acquisition," *Sociology of Education* 87, no. 4 (August 30, 2014): 281–95, https://doi.org/10.1177/0038040714549076.

9. Nuñez and Sansone, "Earning and Learning."

10. Danielle Li, Lindsey R. Raymond, and Peter Bergman, "Hiring as Exploration," Working Paper 27736 (National Bureau of Economic Research, August 2020), https://doi.org/10.3386/w27736; Lauren Rivera, "Hiring as Cultural Matching: The Case of Elite Professional Service Firms," *American Sociological Review* 77, no. 6 (December 1, 2012): 999–1022, https://doi.org/10.1177/0003122412463213.

11. In October 2019, Common Application updated their Activities Section to provide additional information to students: "Family responsibilities come in many forms and can be permanent or temporary. They are different from chores in that you are meeting an important need for your family as opposed to simply lending a hand. Examples might include engaging in the following several hours every week: Caring for your children, Supervising a younger sibling, Regularly assisting a grandparent or older adult relative, Routinely taking care of household tasks like cooking, cleaning, and running errands, Working to provide family income." For recent work exploring differences in familial obligations and extracurricular involvement, see Julie J. Park et al., "Inequality beyond Standardized Tests: Trends in Extracurricular Activity Reporting in College Applications across Race and Class," *EdWorkingPapers.Com* (Annenberg Institute at Brown University, April 12, 2023), https://www.edworkingpapers.com/index.php/ai23-749.

12. Tara Yosso, "Whose Culture Has Capital? A Critical Race Theory Discussion of Community Cultural Wealth," *Race Ethnicity and Education* 8, no. 1 (March 1, 2005): 69–91, https://doi.org/10.1080/1361332052000341006.

13. Rakshitha Arni Ravishankar, "It's Time to Officially End Unpaid Internships," *Harvard Business Review*, May 26, 2021, https://hbr.org/2021/05/its-time-to-officially-end-unpaid-internships.

14. Naomi Harris and Jocelyn Gecker, "Unpaid Internships Face New Scrutiny as Barriers to Careers," *Washington Post*, September 30, 2022, https://www.washingtonpost.com/business

/unpaid-internships-face-new-scrutiny-as-barriers-to-careers/2022/09/30/1087f5a2-40af
-11ed-8c6e-9386bd7cd826_story.html; Bovy, "Unpaid Internships Are a Rich-Girl Problem";
Darren Walker, "Internships Are Not a Privilege," *New York Times*, July 5, 2016, sec. Opinion,
https://www.nytimes.com/2016/07/05/opinion/breaking-a-cycle-that-allows-privilege-to-go
-to-privileged.html.

15. Ravishankar, "It's Time to Officially End Unpaid Internships"; Harris and Gecker, "Unpaid Internships Face New Scrutiny as Barriers to Careers"; Gaynor, "43 Percent of Internships
at For-Profit Companies Don't Pay"; Amy Wang, "White House to Pay Its Interns, Biden Administration Announces," *Washington Post*, June 2, 2022, https://www.washingtonpost.com
/politics/2022/06/02/biden-white-house-paid-internship/.

Chapter Seven

1. Jancee Dunn, "Day 2: The Secret Power of the 8-Minute Phone Call," *New York Times*,
January 3, 2023, sec. Well, https://www.nytimes.com/2023/01/02/well/phone-call-happiness
-challenge.html.

2. David A. Graham, "How a Single Campus Cop Undermined Cincinnati's Police Reforms,"
The Atlantic, July 30, 2015, sec. Politics, https://www.theatlantic.com/politics/archive/2015/07
/samuel-dubose-local-police/399977/.

3. Habiba Braimah et al., "Can We Just Talk? Exploring Discourses on Race and Racism
among U.S. Undergraduates during the COVID-19 Pandemic," *Educational Review* 74, no. 3
(May 18, 2022): 576–90, https://doi.org/10.1080/00131911.2022.2054956.

4. Daniel Solorzano, Miguel Ceja, and Tara Yosso, "Critical Race Theory, Racial Microaggressions, and Campus Racial Climate: The Experiences of African American College Students,"
Journal of Negro Education 69, no. 1/2 (2000): 60–73; Jeremy Franklin, "Racial Microaggressions,
Racial Battle Fatigue, and Racism-Related Stress in Higher Education," *Journal of Student Affairs
at New York University* 12, no. 44 (2016): 44–55.

5. Solorzano, Ceja, and Yosso, "Critical Race Theory"; Tara Yosso et al., "Critical Race Theory,
Racial Microaggressions, and Campus Racial Climate for Latina/o Undergraduates," *Harvard
Educational Review* 79, no. 4 (December 1, 2009): 659–91; Derald Wing Sue, *Microaggressions in
Everyday Life: Race, Gender, and Sexual Orientation* (Hoboken, NJ: Wiley, 2010); Julie Minikel-
Lacocque, "Racism, College, and the Power of Words Racial Microaggressions Reconsidered,"
American Educational Research Journal 50, no. 3 (June 1, 2013): 432–65, https://doi.org/10.3102
/0002831212468048.

6. James Baldwin, "A Report from Occupied Territory," *Nation*, July 11, 1966, https://www
.thenation.com/article/culture/report-occupied-territory/.

7. Ishara Casellas Connors and Henrika McCoy, "Performing Anti-Racism: Universities
Respond to Anti-Black Violence," *Race and Justice* 12, no. 3 (July 1, 2022): 588–613, https://doi
.org/10.1177/21533687221101787; Eddie R. Cole and Shaun R. Harper, "Race and Rhetoric:
An Analysis of College Presidents' Statements on Campus Racial Incidents," *Journal of Diversity
in Higher Education* 10 (2017): 318–33, https://doi.org/10.1037/dhe0000044.

8. W. Carson Byrd, *Poison in the Ivy: Race Relations and the Reproduction of Inequality on Elite
College Campuses*, The American Campus (New Brunswick, NJ: Rutgers University Press,

2017); Camille Zubrinsky Charles et al., *Young, Gifted and Diverse: Origins of the New Black Elite* (Princeton, NJ: Princeton University Press, 2022); Eddie Rice Cole, *The Campus Color Line: College Presidents and the 1960s Struggle for Black Freedom* (Princeton, NJ: Princeton University Press, 2020); Joe Feagin, Hernan Vera, and Nikitah Imani, *The Agony of Education: Black Students at White Colleges and Universities* (New York: Routledge, 1996).

9. Charles et al., *Taming the River*; Benson and Lee, *Geographies of Campus Inequality*.

10. Natasha K. Warikoo and Sherry L. Deckman, "Beyond the Numbers: Institutional Influences on Experiences with Diversity on Elite College Campuses," *Sociological Forum* 29, no. 4 (December 2014): 959–81; Beverly Daniel Tatum, *"Why Are All the Black Kids Sitting Together in the Cafeteria?" And Other Conversations about Race*, 3rd trade paperback ed. (New York: Basic Books, 2017).

11. Nolan L. Cabrera, *White Guys on Campus: Racism, White Immunity, and the Myth of "Post-Racial" Higher Education* (New Brunswick, NJ: Rutgers University Press, 2019); Eduardo Bonilla-Silva and Tyrone A. Forman, "'I Am Not a Racist But . . .': Mapping White College Students' Racial Ideology in the USA," *Discourse & Society* 11, no. 1 (January 1, 2000): 50–85, https://doi.org/10.1177/0957926500011001003. See also Yung-Yi Diana Pan and Daisy Verduzco Reyes, "The Norm among the Exceptional? Experiences of Latino Students in Elite Institutions," *Sociological Inquiry* 91, no. 1 (2021): 207–30, https://doi.org/10.1111/soin.12354.

12. Victor Ray, "A Theory of Racialized Organizations," *American Sociological Review* 84, no. 1 (February 1, 2019): 26–53, https://doi.org/10.1177/0003122418822335; Byrd, *Behind the Diversity Numbers*.

13. Braimah et al., "Can We Just Talk?"; Tatum, *"Why Are All the Black Kids?"*

14. Outside of campus contexts, we also see this in how White homeowners and renters police their neighborhoods, especially in times of demographic change. See Sarah Mayorga-Gallo, *Behind the White Picket Fence: Power and Privilege in a Multiethnic Neighborhood* (Chapel Hill: University of North Carolina Press, 2014).

15. Kerry A. Bailey, "Racism within the Canadian University: Indigenous Students' Experiences," *Ethnic and Racial Studies* 39, no. 7 (May 27, 2016): 1261–79, https://doi.org/10.1080/01419870.2015.1081961; see also Sylvia Hurtado, "The Campus Racial Climate: Contexts of Conflict," *Journal of Higher Education* 63, no. 5 (September 1, 1992): 539–69; Brayboy, Solyom, and Castagno, "Indigenous Peoples in Higher Education."

16. Bailey, "Racism within the Canadian University"; Brayboy, Solyom, and Castagno, "Indigenous Peoples in Higher Education." For a discussion of how affirmative action means admitting unqualified students of color, see Warikoo, *The Diversity Bargain*; Byrd, *Behind the Diversity Numbers*.

17. David R. Williams, Jourdyn A. Lawrence, and Brigette A. Davis, "Racism and Health: Evidence and Needed Research," *Annual Review of Public Health* 40, no. 1 (2019): 105–25, https://doi.org/10.1146/annurev-publhealth-040218-043750; Linda Villarosa, *Under the Skin: Racism, Inequality, and the Health of a Nation*, (New York: Doubleday, 2022).

18. Ryan Doan-Nguyen, J Sellers Hill, and Nia Orakwue, "Four Harvard Students Held at Gunpoint by Campus Police in 'Swatting' Attack," *Harvard Crimson*, April 4, 2023, sec. News, https://www.thecrimson.com/article/2023/4/4/lev-swatting-attack/.

19. Cabrera, *White Guys on Campus*; Minikel-Lacocque, "Racism, College, and the Power of Words Racial Microaggressions Reconsidered"; see also Sue, *Microaggressions in Everyday Life*.

20. Stephen John Quaye, Shaun R. Harper, and Sumun L. Pendakur, *Student Engagement in Higher Education: Theoretical Perspectives and Practical Approaches for Diverse Populations* (Philadelphia: Routledge, 2019). For a discussion of the wealth and whiteness of sports teams at elite colleges, see Jeffrey J. Selingo, *Who Gets in and Why: A Year inside College Admissions* (New York: Scribner, 2020).

21. Paige L. Sweet, "The Sociology of Gaslighting," *American Sociological Review* 84, no. 5 (2019): 851–75.

22. Benson and Lee, *Geographies of Campus Inequality*; Casellas Connors and McCoy, "Performing Anti-Racism."

23. Casellas Connors and McCoy, "Performing Anti-Racism"; Cole and Harper, "Race and Rhetoric."

24. For a discussion of cultural taxation, see Amado M. Padilla, "Research News and Comment: Ethnic Minority Scholars; Research, and Mentoring; Current and Future Issues," *Educational Researcher* 23, no. 4 (May 1, 1994): 24–27, https://doi.org/10.3102/0013189X023004024; Laura E. Hirshfield and Tiffany D. Joseph, "'We Need a Woman, We Need a Black Woman': Gender, Race, and Identity Taxation in the Academy," *Gender and Education* 24, no. 2 (2012): 213–27.

25. Padilla, "Research News and Comment: Ethnic Minority Scholars; Research, and Mentoring: Current and Future Issues. For a discussion of Harvard departures, see Graciela Mochkofsky, "Why Lorgia García Peña Was Denied Tenure at Harvard," *New Yorker*, July 27, 2021, https://www.newyorker.com/news/annals-of-education/why-lorgia-garcia-pena-was-denied-tenure-at-harvard; Timothy Bella and Susan Svrluga, "Cornel West Says in Resignation Letter over Tenure Dispute That Harvard Is in 'Decline and Decay,'" *Washington Post*, July 13, 2021, https://www.washingtonpost.com/education/2021/07/13/cornel-west-harvard-tenure-resignation/.

26. Lee and Harris, "Counterspaces, Counterstructures"; Sherry L. Deckman, *Black Space: Negotiating Race, Diversity, and Belonging in the Ivory Tower* (New Brunswick, NJ: Rutgers University Press, 2022).

27. See Lee and Harris, "Counterspaces, Counterstructures"; Andrew D. Case and Carla D. Hunter, "Counterspaces: A Unit of Analysis for Understanding the Role of Settings in Marginalized Individuals' Adaptive Responses to Oppression," *American Journal of Community Psychology* 50, no. 1 (September 1, 2012): 257–70, https://doi.org/10.1007/s10464-012-9497-7.

28. Deckman, *Black Space*; Tabitha L. Grier-Reed, "The African American Student Network: Creating Sanctuaries and Counterspaces for Coping with Racial Microaggressions in Higher Education Settings," *Journal of Humanistic Counseling, Education and Development* 49, no. 2 (2010): 181–88; Tara Yosso and C. Benavides Lopez, "Counterspaces in a Hostile Place," *Culture Centers in Higher Education: Perspectives on Identity, Theory, and Practice*, 2010, 83–104; Lee and Harris, "Counterspaces, Counterstructures"; Micere Keels, *Campus Counterspaces: Black and Latinx Students' Search for Community at Historically White Universities* (Ithaca, NY: Cornell University Press, 2020).

29. Rivera, "Ivies, Extracurriculars, and Exclusion."

30. Elijah Anderson, *Black in White Space: The Enduring Impact of Color in Everyday Life* (Chicago: University of Chicago Press, 2021); see also Ray, "A Theory of Racialized Organizations."

31. Prudence Carter, *Stubborn Roots: Race, Culture, and Inequality in U.S. and South African Schools* (New York: Oxford University Press, 2012); Bonilla-Silva and Forman, "'I Am Not a Racist But . . .'"

Chapter Eight

1. Nat Jacobwith, "Man Caught Defacing George Floyd Memorial Once a UMN Medical Student," *Minnesota Daily*, August 21, 2020, sec. News, https://mndaily.com/261958/news/admemorial/.

2. Mia Bay, *Traveling Black: A Story of Race and Resistance* (Cambridge, MA: Harvard University Press, 2023); Richard J. Lundman and Robert L. Kaufman, "Driving While Black: Effects of Race, Ethnicity, and Gender on Citizen Self-Reports of Traffic Stops and Police Actions," *Criminology* 41, no. 1 (2003): 195–220, https://doi.org/10.1111/j.1745-9125.2003.tb00986.x; Sharon Lafraniere and Andrew W. Lehren, "The Disproportionate Risks of Driving While Black," *New York Times*, October 24, 2015, http://www.nytimes.com/2015/10/25/us/racial-disparity-traffic-stops-driving-black.html; Ranae Jabri, "Algorithmic Policing," SSRN Scholarly Paper (Rochester, NY, November 1, 2021), https://papers.ssrn.com/abstract=4275083.

3. Richard Fausset, Nicholas Bogel-Burroughs, and Marie Fazio, "8 Dead in Atlanta Spa Shootings, with Fears of Anti-Asian Bias," *New York Times*, March 17, 2021, sec. U.S., https://www.nytimes.com/live/2021/03/17/us/shooting-atlanta-acworth; Yan Zhang, Lening Zhang, and Francis Benton, "Hate Crimes against Asian Americans," *American Journal of Criminal Justice* 47, no. 3 (2021): 1–21; Hannah Tessler, Meera Choi, and Grace Kao, "The Anxiety of Being Asian American: Hate Crimes and Negative Biases during the COVID-19 Pandemic," *American Journal of Criminal Justice* 45 (2020): 636–46.

4. Justin T. Huang et al., "The Cost of Anti-Asian Racism during the COVID-19 Pandemic," *Nature Human Behaviour*, January 19, 2023, 1–14, https://doi.org/10.1038/s41562-022-01493-6.

5. Richard Mosholder and Christopher Goslin, "Native American College Student Persistence," *Journal of College Student Retention: Research, Theory & Practice* 15, no. 3 (2013): 305–27; Aaron P. Jackson, Steven A. Smith, and Curtis L. Hill, "Academic Persistence among Native American College Students," *Journal of College Student Development* 44, no. 4 (2003): 548–65.

6. Annita Lucchesi and Abigail Echo-Hawk, "Missing and Murdered Indigenous Women & Girls: A Snapshot of Data from 71 Urban Cities in the United States," Urban Indian Health Institute, August 23, 2018, https://www.uihi.org/resources/missing-and-murdered-indigenous-women-girls/.

7. Blythe George, Jessica Elm, and Nan Benally, "To' Kee Skuy 'Soo Ney-Wo-Chek': Missing and Murdered Indigenous Women, Girls, and Two Spirit People of Northern California," Yurok Tribal Court, July 2022, https://yuroktribalcourt.org/wp-content/uploads/2022/07/Yurok-Tribe-Year-Three-Report-Toolkit-FINAL-DRAFT.pdf?fbclid=IwAR0g0hSFvUR4OUHofwO z5q0t4b9CVW-no0qP7o_sz0OA4lq61caUwirdAT8.

8. Thadeus Greenson, "The Yurok Tribe Offers 'Blueprint' to End the MMIP Crisis," *North Coast Journal*, August 4, 2022, https://www.northcoastjournal.com/humboldt/the-yurok-tribe -offers-blueprint-to-end-the-mmip-crisis/Content?oid=24263857; George, Elm, and Benally, "To' Kee Skuy 'Soo Ney-Wo-Chek'"; Cheryl Redhorse Bennett, *Our Fight Has Just Begun: Hate Crimes and Justice in Native America* (Tucson: University of Arizona Press, 2022).

9. Bennett, *Our Fight Has Just Begun.*

10. Fear of bias in autopsies is pervasive and not without merit; see Itiel Dror et al., "Cognitive Bias in Forensic Pathology Decisions," *Journal of Forensic Sciences* 66, no. 5 (2021): 1751–57, https://doi.org/10.1111/1556-4029.14697. In 2023 Colin Kaepernick, former quarterback of the San Francisco 49ers and Civil Rights activist, launched an initiative to fund second autopsies in police-related deaths. See Scott Ostler, "How Colin Kaepernick's Autopsy Initiative Led to $100M Lawsuit over a Police Shooting," *San Francisco Chronicle*, January 12, 2023, sec. 49ers, https://www.sfchronicle.com/sports/49ers/article/Colin-Kaepernick-Autopsy-Initiative -17690356.php.

11. Roudabeh Kishi Jones Sam, "Demonstrations and Political Violence in America: New Data for Summer 2020," *ACLED* (blog), September 3, 2020, https://acleddata.com/2020/09 /03/demonstrations-political-violence-in-america-new-data-for-summer-2020/.

12. Addisu Dabi Wake and Usha Rani Kandula, "The Global Prevalence and Its Associated Factors toward Domestic Violence against Women and Children during COVID-19 Pandemic— 'The Shadow Pandemic': A Review of Cross-Sectional Studies," *Women's Health* 18 (January 1, 2022): 17455057221095536, https://doi.org/10.1177/17455057221095536; Saravana Ravindran and Manisha Shah, "Unintended Consequences of Lockdowns: COVID-19 and the Shadow Pandemic" (Cambridge, MA: National Bureau of Economic Research, July 2020), https://doi .org/10.3386/w27562; Odette R. Sánchez et al., "Violence against Women during the COVID-19 Pandemic: An Integrative Review," *International Journal of Gynecology & Obstetrics* 151, no. 2 (November 2020): 180–87, https://doi.org/10.1002/ijgo.13365.

13. Gabrielle was not alone. COVID-19 brought increases in not only domestic partner violence but also sexual assault among teenage girls. Ramya Emandi et al., "Measuring the Shadow Pandemic: Violence against Women during Covid-19" (United Nations, 2021), https://data .unwomen.org/sites/default/files/documents/Publications/Measuring-shadow-pandemic .pdf; Centers for Disease Control and Prevention, *Youth Risk Behavior Survey Data Summary & Trends Report: 2011–2021* (Centers for Disease Control and Prevention, 2023), https://www.cdc .gov/healthyyouth/data/yrbs/yrbs_data_summary_and_trends.htm.

Chapter Nine

1. Sara Weissman, "A Subtle Subterfuge, an Outrage or Both?," *Inside Higher Ed*, February 3, 2023, https://www.insidehighered.com/news/2023/02/03/outrage-follows-florida-college -presidents-statement-crt; Anthony Izaguirre, "Florida Gov. DeSantis Pushes Ban on Diversity Programs in State Colleges," *PBS NewsHour*, January 31, 2023, sec. Education, https://www.pbs .org/newshour/education/florida-gov-desantis-pushes-ban-on-diversity-programs-in-state -colleges.

2. Franklin, "Racial Microaggressions, Racial Battle Fatigue"; William A. Smith, *Racial Battle Fatigue in Higher Education: Exposing the Myth of Post-Racial America* (Lanham, MD: Rowman & Littlefield, 2014); Yosso et al., "Critical Race Theory, Racial Microaggressions, and Campus Racial Climate for Latina/o Undergraduates"; Solorzano, Ceja, and Yosso, "Critical Race Theory, Racial Microaggressions, and Campus Racial Climate"; Sue, *Microaggressions in Everyday Life*; Derald Wing Sue et al., "Racial Microaggressions and the Asian American Experience," *Cultural Diversity and Ethnic Minority Psychology*, 2007, http://psycnet.apa.org/journals/aap/S /1/88/.

3. Cole, *The Campus Color Line*.

4. Michèle Lamont, *Seeing Others: How Recognition Works—and How It Can Heal a Divided World* (New York: One Signal Publishers/Atria, 2023).

5. Kate Hidalgo Bellows, "A University's New Approach to Student Mental Health: Put Therapists in the Dorms," *Chronicle of Higher Education*, April 21, 2023, sec. News, https://www .chronicle.com/article/a-universitys-new-approach-to-student-mental-health-put-therapists -in-the-dorms.

6. Colleen Walsh, "Renaming Committee Seeks Input from Harvard Community," *Harvard Gazette*, February 25, 2021, sec. Campus & Community, https://news.harvard.edu/gazette/story /2021/02/renaming-committee-seeks-input-from-harvard-community/.

7. Casellas Connors and McCoy, "Performing Anti-Racism."

8. Tanzina Vega, "Students See Many Slights as Racial 'Microaggressions,'" *New York Times*, March 21, 2014, http://www.nytimes.com/2014/03/22/us/as-diversity-increases-slights-get -subtler-but-still-sting.html.

9. Lamont, *Seeing Others*. For a discussion of "I, too, am Harvard," see Catherine Okafor, "I, Too, Am Harvard," *Huffington Post*, March 4, 2014, http://www.huffingtonpost.com/catherine -okafor/i-too-am-harvard_b_4885878.html; Vega, "Students See Many Slights as Racial 'Microaggressions.'"

10. For research on college presidents' direct actions on civil rights issues, see Davarian L. Baldwin, *In the Shadow of the Ivory Tower: How Universities Are Plundering Our Cities* (New York: Bold Type Books, 2021); Cole, *The Campus Color Line*; Adam Harris, *The State Must Provide: Why America's Colleges Have Always Been Unequal—and How to Set Them Right* (New York: Harper-Collins, 2021); Matthew Johnson, *Undermining Racial Justice: How One University Embraced Inclusion and Inequality*, Histories of American Education (Ithaca, NY: Cornell University Press, 2020); Craig Steven Wilder, *Ebony & Ivy: Race, Slavery, and the Troubled History of America's Universities* (New York: Bloomsbury, 2013). For an understanding of the limitation of statements, see Tom Bartlett, "The Antiracist College," *Chronicle of Higher Education*, February 15, 2021, sec. Racial Reckoning, https://www.chronicle.com/article/the-antiracist-college; Braimah et al., "Can We Just Talk?"

11. Casellas Connors and McCoy, "Performing Anti-Racism."

12. See Wilder, *Ebony & Ivy*.

13. Lee and Harris, "Counterspaces, Counterstructures"; Keels, *Campus Counterspaces*; Deckman, *Black Space*; Yosso and Lopez, "Counterspaces in a Hostile Place." See also Veronica Jones, "Challenging Race Neutral Rhetoric: Black Student Leaders' Counternarratives of Racial Salience in PWI Student Organizations," *Journal of Diversity in Higher Education* 13, no. 1 (2020): 23.

14. For a discussion of initiatives created to understand the legacy of slavery on college campuses, see The Presidential Committee on the Legacy of Slavery, ed., *The Legacy of Slavery at Harvard: Report and Recommendations of the Presidential Committee* (Cambridge, MA: Harvard University Press, 2022). See Johnson, *Undermining Racial Justice,* for a cautionary tale of coopting student voice.

15. Shametrice Davis and Jessica C. Harris, "But We Didn't Mean It Like That: A Critical Race Analysis of Campus Responses to Racial Incidents," *Journal of Critical Scholarship on Higher Education and Student Affairs* 2, no. 1 (2016): 62–78.

16. Sara Ahmed, *On Being Included: Racism and Diversity in Institutional Life* (Durham, NC: Duke University Press, 2012); Ibram X. Kendi, *How to Be an Antiracist* (New York: One World, 2019).

Conclusion

Epigraph: James Baldwin, *Nobody Knows My Name: More Notes of a Native Son* (London: Penguin, 1991).

1. Yu et al., "Is There a Bubble to Burst?"
2. Baldwin, *Nobody Knows My Name.*
3. Ladson-Billings, "I'm Here for the Hard Re-Set."
4. Whiteside, "Becoming Academically Eligible."
5. Darity and Mullen, *From Here to Equality*; Witgen, *Seeing Red.*
6. Stevens, Armstrong, and Arum, "Sieve, Incubator, Temple, Hub."

Appendix

1. See William Julius Wilson and Anmol Chaddha, "The Role of Theory in Ethnographic Research," *Ethnography* 10, no. 4 (2009): 549–64; David Willer, *Scientific Sociology: Theory and Method* (Englewood Cliffs, NJ: Prentice-Hall, 1967).

2. The Learning Network, "For Most Latinos, Latinx Does Not Mark the Spot," *New York Times,* June 15, 2021, sec. The Learning Network, https://www.nytimes.com/2021/06/15/learning/for-most-latinos-latinx-does-not-mark-the-spot.html; Ruth Hailu and Olivia Scott, "Harvard Undergrads Form First Campus Group for All Mixed-Race Students," *Harvard Crimson,* November 20, 2018, https://www.thecrimson.com/article/2018/11/20/union-of-mixed-students/.

3. Maria K. E. Lahman et al., "A Rose by Any Other Name Is Still a Rose? Problematizing Pseudonyms in Research," *Qualitative Inquiry* 21, no. 5 (2015): 445–53.

4. Annette Lareau, *Listening to People: A Practical Guide to Interviewing, Participant Observation, Data Analysis, and Writing It All Up,* Chicago Guides to Writing, Editing, and Publishing (Chicago: University of Chicago Press, 2021).

5. Lareau; Kathleen Gerson and Sarah Damaske, *The Science and Art of Interviewing* (New York: Oxford University Press, 2020); Robert Stuart Weiss, *Learning from Strangers: The Art and Method of Qualitative Interview Studies* (New York: Free Press, 1994).

6. Nicole Arlette Hirsch and Anthony Abraham Jack, "What We Face: Framing Problems in the Black Community," *Du Bois Review: Social Science Research on Race* 9, no. 1 (2012): 133–48, https://doi.org/10.10170S1742058X12000185.

7. Nicole M. Deterding and Mary C. Waters, "Flexible Coding of In-Depth Interviews: A Twenty-First-Century Approach," *Sociological Methods & Research* 50, no. 2 (2021): 708–39, https://doi.org/10.1177/0049124118799377; Kathy Charmaz, *Constructing Grounded Theory: A Practical Guide through Qualitative Analysis* (Thousand Oaks, CA: Sage, 2006).

8. Catherine H. Stein and Eric S. Mankowski, "Asking, Witnessing, Interpreting, Knowing: Conducting Qualitative Research in Community Psychology," *American Journal of Community Psychology* 33 (2004): 21–35. For research on sexual assault on college campuses, see Jennifer S. Hirsch and Shamus Khan, *Sexual Citizens: A Landmark Study of Sex, Power, and Assault on Campus* (New York: W. W. Norton, 2020).

9. Asad, *Engage and Evade*; Karina Santellano, "Fieldwork during a Pandemic: Navigating Personal Grief and Practicing Researcher Flexibility," *Latino Studies* 20, no. 3 (September 1, 2022): 408–14, https://doi.org/10.1057/s41276-022-00350-x.

INDEX

Jamie (LI,W), 45–51, 168, 251–53
Jane (LI,A), 199
Jerome (LI,A), 7–11, 14, 183–84, 251
Jessie (LI,N), 137, 170, 204–8, 210, 215, 219, 243
Jo (UI,A), 29–30
Johannes (UI,A), 26, 113, 118, 134
Julian (UI,B), 170
Julian (UI,W), 121
Julie (UI,W), 62
June (UI,A), 72, 74, 79

Kaepernick, Colin, 283n10
Kane, David, 190
Kelile (LI,B), 175, 189, 195–96
Kevin (LI,W), 33, 102–3, 113, 228

Lacy, Karyn, 62
Lahman, Maria, 245
Lamont, Michele, 220
Lareau, Annette, 245
Latinos and Latino students: campus
    closures and, 10; COVID-19 and, 72, 74;
    discrimination toward, 13; disrupted
    tenures, 80, 84; faculty losses and, 190;
    first-generation, 5; focus on, 13; home
    disorder and violence, 84; neighborhood
    fear, 84; recognition gaps, 220; terminol-
    ogy used, 241; violence and, 197; White
    students' reactions to, 168–69
Laura (LI,A), 104–5
LBJ (LI,A), 182, 245
Lee, Elizabeth, 222, 267
Leland (W), 178–80
Long, Robert Aaron, 200
lower-income neighborhoods: COVID-19
    community impact, 74–75; COVID-19 and
    economic impact, 75–76; COVID-19
    exposure, 76–77; dangers of, 60, 63–65,
    67–70; drug use comparisons, 182–83
lower-income students: academic leaves of
    absence, 84–88; adult responsibilities,
    137–40, 144, 146, 151; on-campus jobs
    and, 98–101, 105, 123; community cultural

wealth, 158; COVID-19 effect, 16,
    33; COVID-19 escape from home,
    39–40; COVID-19 exposure, 75–76, 109;
    COVID-19 response, 80; culture shock,
    104, 107; destabilizing events, 89;
    disrupted tenures, 83; double discount-
    ing of skills, 127, 152; expectations, 7;
    family business and, 125–26, 135–37, 140,
    142–43, 147, 149–50; financial situation,
    41, 101, 105–6, 113, 145, 153; home and
    family, 31, 51, 63, 109–10; mental health
    trainings, 90; neighborhood safety, 56,
    63–64, 68–69, 71; networking with
    faculty, 111–12, 154–55; off-campus jobs,
    105, 108–9, 112; self-
    confidence and, 102–4, 111; unpaid labor
    and, 127, 147, 151–52, 156–57. See also
    privileged poor

Manuel (UI,L), 115
Maria (LI,M), 33–34, 45, 76, 111–12, 124
Marianne (LI,L), 30–31, 45, 76–77, 88
Mariel (UI,M), 120
Mark (UI,W), 120–21
Martin, Nathan, 114
Mary (UI,B), 61–62, 115
McCoy, Henrika, 189
McDade, Tony, 164
Melissa (LI,L), 100
mental health and mental health services:
    addiction and, 138; asking for help,
    214; barriers to school reentry, 85;
    campus availability, 218; counselors,
    89–90; diversity and, 230; stresses
    and, 100, 218–19; students' homes and,
    66, 88
Meredith (UI,N), 116–17, 121, 170
methodology: interview questions, 246–48;
    interviews, 12, 242–46; previous re-
    search, 235; pseudonyms, 245; research
    team, 249–50; study subjects, 13, 238–41,
    242t
Mia (LI,M), 32, 100–101, 203–4

A NOTE ON THE TYPE

This book has been composed in Arno, an Old-style serif typeface in the
classic Venetian tradition, designed by Robert Slimbach at Adobe.